Law and Life in Common

Law and Life in Common

Timothy Macklem

OXFORD
UNIVERSITY PRESS

UNIVERSITY PRESS

Great Clarendon Street, Oxford, OX2 6DP,
United Kingdom

Oxford University Press is a department of the University of Oxford.
It furthers the University's objective of excellence in research, scholarship,
and education by publishing worldwide. Oxford is a registered trade mark of
Oxford University Press in the UK and in certain other countries

© T Macklem 2015

The moral rights of the author have been asserted

First published 2015
First published in paperback 2017

All rights reserved. No part of this publication may be reproduced, stored in
a retrieval system, or transmitted, in any form or by any means, without the
prior permission in writing of Oxford University Press, or as expressly permitted
by law, by licence or under terms agreed with the appropriate reprographics
rights organization. Enquiries concerning reproduction outside the scope of the
above should be sent to the Rights Department, Oxford University Press, at the
address above

You must not circulate this work in any other form
and you must impose this same condition on any acquirer

Published in the United States of America by Oxford University Press
198 Madison Avenue, New York, NY 10016, United States of America

British Library Cataloguing in Publication Data
Data available

Library of Congress Cataloging in Publication Data
Data available

ISBN 978–0–19–873581–6 (Hbk.)
ISBN 978–0–19–881241–8 (Pbk.)

Cover photo © Gail Thorson

Links to third party websites are provided by Oxford in good faith and
for information only. Oxford disclaims any responsibility for the materials
contained in any third party website referenced in this work.

For John Gardner
Fellow student and friend,
with whom I took my first steps in the philosophy of law
and a great many of those that followed

Preface

Any moderately ambitious, stage-setting preface (or introduction, or foreword) that hopes to ease access to a complicated argument has a pretty challenging task before it. It must sketch the contours of what is to follow and yet be alive to the fact that it will take a book to capture those contours adequately. It must offer a sense of the problem that the book seeks to resolve and what might possibly be interesting about it, together with an outline of what the suggested resolution looks like, each attractive to even the sceptical reader. It must be couched in terms that are at least a little more accessible than the balance of the book (otherwise why not move straight into the opening pages?), and yet do not make matters seem simpler than they are. It must offer a kind of guide to what follows, helping dedicated readers maintain a sense of direction that is stronger than the structure of the book can provide on its own, while at the same time enabling more opportunistic readers to focus on the passages that are likely to prove the most fruitful to them. It must be brief and to the point, and yet establish a sense of the style and approach of the work as a whole.

Inevitably, this preface will not do all of those things, or at least will not do all of them well, if for no other reason than that success in terms of some of them is at odds with success in terms of others. What it will do, I hope, is to set the scene: first by pointing to certain dissonances in recent writing on the philosophy of law that suggest, if not a need for, at least the potential disciplinary reward of an inquiry of this kind, to be looked for in moving beyond what have by now become all too familiar oppositions; second by drawing attention to certain recurring disappointments in the contemporary experience of governors and the governed, of those who make the law and those who look to be guided by it, in terms of the life in common they seek to build in co-operation with one another and the better world they hope to realize, which seem to stem from misguided expectations of law and what it is capable of doing for us; and finally, by explaining the nature of the present inquiry and its possible value, both to those who habitually reflect upon law and to those whose engagement with law for the most part precludes such reflection (I will leave aside those who are simply uninterested in reflection).

i. Let me begin with a suggestion, prompted by reflection on the overly partisan character of much of contemporary jurisprudence. It is a notable and rather unhappy feature of the divisions that have marked, and indeed dominated, the philosophy of law in the past 30 years or so that they have been attended by a startling lack of sympathy, respect, or even common courtesy on the part of many of those involved. Rival views have been treated with incredulity, dismay, and something close to contempt, most notoriously in a relatively recent, dyspeptic pair of papers by Ronald Dworkin and Brian Leiter.[1] How such disputes have arisen, and how their tenor has become debased, is no part of my concern. Their genealogy is unlikely to be in any way edifying. What is worth noticing, however, is their cost. There is an all too human tendency, perhaps born of self-protection, perhaps born of lack of empathy, perhaps born of an insufficiently complex understanding of the moral universe—a tendency that is most prominently displayed in religious and political affairs but that occurs nearly everywhere—to treat one's intellectual opponents as either fools or villains, to put it only somewhat crudely. In the grip of that tendency one acts as if the views that one's opponents hold are not ones that any upright, rational, self-respecting person could possibly hold. The real shame about this attitude is not simply the intolerance that it gives rise to, for while intolerance matters very much, it matters derivatively. It is that such an attitude prevents one from grasping aspects of understanding that would enrich and assist both one's own point of view and the project of human understanding more generally. It is an attitude born of an adversarial approach to ideas, one that raises the

---

[1] Ronald Dworkin, 'Thirty Years On' 115 *Harvard LJ* 1655 (2002); Brian Leiter, 'The End of Empire: Dworkin and Jurisprudence in the 21st Century' 36 *Rutgers LJ* 165 (2005). To be fair to Leiter, it was Dworkin who threw the first punch, in print at least, as the publication dates show.

question of whether (or to what extent) a non-adversarial approach is available, and if so what it might look like.

ii. I do not wish to be in the position of denying the obvious here. As we all know to our cost, and sometimes and painfully to our embarrassment as well, there is folly and villainy aplenty in the world. On the whole, however, one's intellectual opponents tend to be on to something that one has neglected oneself, or, to put it another way, they are in a position to perceive something that one's own awareness of has been obscured, or suppressed, by one's entirely proper attention to, and consequent immersion in, the views that one has committed oneself to. What is true of oneself is as true of those with whom one is in broad agreement. Congenial as their company may be, one has little to learn from one's fellow travellers. They can help to deepen one's understanding but they are unlikely to extend it into unfamiliar and unexpected domains, let alone to challenge it fundamentally. One usually has a great deal to learn, however, from the holders of views that one disagrees with fundamentally, perhaps even despises. To grasp the truth that lies behind their errors, and to make it one's own, is to approach the beginnings of wisdom.

iii. The possibility that this line of thought suggests is that the fault lines in contemporary jurisprudence obscure the extent to which the insights that exist on either side of those lines are capable of contributing to the richness and depth of the ideas to which they are opposed. Philosophers on both sides of those lines are as exercised as they are because they believe, and very often rightly so, that the core of what they have committed themselves to, the fundamental insight into human social practices that animates them, ought not to be denied by any rational person who has given the matter serious consideration. True as that may be, it does not, however, support the conclusion that is too often reached—that the core of what such philosophers have rejected ought to be similarly rejected by any rational person who has given the matter in question serious consideration. On the contrary, there are a great many forms of rationally viable accommodation between ideas that are opposed to one another. Both ideas may be true, despite their opposition, for there is a difference between opposition and contradiction, bearing in mind that contradiction is only one of the reasons that certain ideas cannot be endorsed and pursued simultaneously. More frequently, the ideas in question may well be complex and multifaceted, so as to be unsound in some respects yet sound in others. Good ideas, like other good things, are often inextricably embedded in bad ones. Rather more interestingly, perhaps, such ideas may depend on the unsoundness of certain of their aspects for access to the soundness that is to be discovered in their other aspects. Falsehood is very often the gatekeeper to certain features of genuine understanding. Bad ideas, once again like other bad things, are often the progenitors of good ideas, and more disturbingly, given all the bad things that by definition follow (good luck and bad judgement aside) from the pursuit of bad things and all the bad things that are likely to follow from looking to bad ideas for guidance, may even be the necessary progenitors of those good ideas. Sometimes, that is, one can reach good ideas only by going through bad ideas to get to them.

iv. In more specific terms, part of what this book seeks to explore is the extent to which, for example, Austin's understanding of the law remains attractive to many, despite its devastating (albeit graceful) criticism by Hart, not simply because straight-forward ideas continue to attract those with straight-forward minds, and not simply because Austin's picture (like that of the many others who think of law in terms of force) resonates with a familiar working understanding held profitably by many of the subjects of law, but because Austin's focus on the will, over-emphasized as it may be, captures what those who are concerned to explain the rationality of the law may neglect: namely that, in a moral universe in which there are very often good reasons to do other than the law requires, the will has an essential role to play, both in the construction of law and in compliance with the law. Similarly, it is possible that Ronald Dworkin's ideas remain attractive to many lawyers in training—whose professional idealism is at something close to its zenith—despite the somewhat baroque consequences of taking them fully seriously, just because they capture something that legal positivism often tends to diminish: namely that in a moral universe of the kind just described, in which the achievement of a life in common depends upon arational as well as rational forms of persuasion,[2] the role that imagination,

---

[2] I use the word arational, here and elsewhere, as a way of referring to those forms of persuasion, those calls upon our attention, that are wholly consistent with reason (and so not in any way irrational) but are not determined by reason. For example, where more than one course of action is rationally permissible, yet neither is rationally defeated by the other, it may be possible, through various devices of presentation to one's mind (by oneself or by another), to highlight the rational contours of one of those courses of action in such a way as to make that course appear to be, all things considered, rationally superior to its rival, although in fact it is not. To prefer the course of action that has been

individual and cultural, has to play in the construction of a life in common is as telling as the roles played by reason and by will. This, it need hardly be said, is not how either Austin or Dworkin would have understood what they had to say, yet it may well be the way in which their work is to be most fruitfully understood—the way in which modern legal positivists, for example, who otherwise reject those views may nevertheless be in a position to learn something important from them.

v. Set that thought to one side, so as to consider another that might offer a further, admittedly anecdotal, indication of the possibilities for a fuller grasp of law as a social practice to be discovered in the line of inquiry that informs this project. Just as notable and as unhappy as the divisions that have marked the philosophy of law in the past 30 years is the parallel decline in belief in the possibility of politics, and consequent disappointment in the democratic project (at least in Western societies, those most experienced in and so familiar with that project). This decline and disappointment has been chronicled most fully from the point of view of the governed, and that chronicle has made all too familiar the cynicism that the governed feel toward the practice of politics and the character of politicians. Yet partiality in the telling of the tale should not be allowed to obscure the fact that it has been no less the tale of a decline in faith in the possibilities of politics on the part of those who govern. The drive by governments over the past 30 years and more to privatize many public institutions and public services, for example, has been sparked as much by despair on the part of politicians as by any ideology of the market. Let someone else take the blame for what can only fail, or the responsibility for what cannot be happily managed or resolved, is all too often the politician's thought. Yet in a democracy the fact of the matter is that by and large all these people are us: we are both the governors and the governed. How then has it come to this? What has led us to fall prey to self-doubt, has led us to lose belief in our capacity to govern ourselves (given that scepticism about the possibility of good government now largely transcends party lines) and to be governed by ourselves, and so has led us to succumb to what

---

so highlighted, on the basis that it is rationally superior to its rival just because of the way it has been presented as such, is to take account of what I am calling an arational form of persuasion, because it is to commit oneself to an entirely rational but not rationally superior course of action on the basis of its rational superiority. For a fuller account see paras xxiv and xxvii of this preface, and para 116 and note 9 in the main text.

amounts to something close to self-loathing, in our several capacities as the authors and addressees of law?

vi. One possibility, and again it is offered as no more than a suggestion—one that some might recognize, but on the accuracy of which nothing that follows depends—is that in seeking to govern ourselves we have expected too much of our political selves, of the project of self-governance, and, uniting and informing those, of the possibilities that law has to offer; that we have told ourselves that with all power in our hands and all the resources of reason at our disposal we could do nearly anything, or, to be more modest about it, could do everything that was required to achieve justice. The soundness of such a belief depends on the idea that it is possible to achieve justice through perfect rationality and an uncorrupted will alone, the idea that if the force of law stems from the weight it gives to the reasons it embodies, a clear-thinking democracy that is fearful of nothing other than fear itself has everything to achieve in the articulation and regulation of its destiny. If we have relied upon any such idea we have been quite mistaken to do so.

vii. If it is the case, as the argument of this book seeks to show it is, that the project of securing a life in common through the enactment and operation of law, democratically or otherwise, depends for its success upon a collaboration between what one might loosely call rational and arational claims upon the addressees of law, any neglect of that partnership—or, more particularly, any failure to apprehend its true contours—is bound, in most settings at least, to render the ambitions of law ineffective, so engendering existential disappointment in governors and in all those who support, or are expected to support, their brand of government. Laws fail in part because we take their rational pull to be all the warrant they need for their effectiveness, and because we then further and consequently believe that failure of that rational pull is something that can be experienced only by those of us who are less than fully rational (the criminally minded being the usual example), and that is consequently capable of being fully addressed either by the attachment to the laws in question of an appropriate sanction, so as to buttress their entirely rational claims with claims of an allied yet different, prudential character, or by the packaging of those laws as something that they are not, so that medicine tastes more like candy.

viii. This overly rationalized view of human action leads governors to cynicism about, and hence a generally covert reliance upon, arational methods of securing co-operation and compliance with what their laws seek to achieve, while leading the governed to a corresponding suspicion of and disdain for their governors, as and when they recognize and thus see through the manipulative strategies in which their governors seek to engage them. As citizens, we speak contemptuously and disdainfully of what we think of as spin and deceit on the part of governments, as if it were possible, even in principle, to govern successfully without such practices; as if it were possible, that is, to build the kinds of communities that we all aspire to without a significant degree of beguilement of the addressees of law, or at least of some of them, on the part of those who are its authors. Conversely, from the perspective of those who are engaged in government, recognition of certain aspects of the partnership between rationality and arationality at the expense of others—most notably, an attention to the significance of the will that follows from the recognition of arationality, together with an accompanying failure to have due and consequent regard for the proper role of reason as the will's partner, or an attention to the corresponding significance of imagination and beguilement, together with a failure to have due regard to the rational responsibility that must accompany the exercise of imagination and the practice of beguilement—leads governments into the very sorts of corruptions of which they currently stand accused by much of their citizenry, the corruptions of force and deceit.

ix. Part of what this book seeks to explore, then, is the scope of an appropriately modest set of expectations about law and what it is capable of achieving, both in general and in particular domains of legislative and judicial ambition. Modesty, it should be emphasized, is not in any way to be equated with lack of significance. Small things can matter greatly, as we know from our experience of the significance that small lives possess—not only to those whom they touch most immediately, on whom their imprint can be deep and indelible, but to the worlds in the functioning of which those lives are but cogs, yet in the absence of which lives the machinery of collective existence would not run in the way that it does, could not secure the values (and disvalues) that it secures. From a proper modesty about law might come a proper expectation of what law can achieve, and from such an expectation might come a (modest) recovery of political hope—hope in democracy in particular.

x. Let me turn now to the earnest (and rather more extended) part: the part that explains the kind of philosophy on offer here, and that describes the place that this philosophy seeks to occupy between even more abstract forms of reflection, such as those that characterize much of contemporary jurisprudence, and ordinary forms of understanding, on which we rely in the bulk of our lives, including lives in the law. (Those with no more than a passing interest in method may skip to paragraph xxii.) Just what is distinctive about this way of looking at the world, and what value might it have to offer us? What kinds of questions does it raise, and why might the answers be interesting ones? The suggestion I want to put forward in outline form here, and develop over the course of the book, couples modesty and ambition. It is the at once entirely recognizable and yet neglected thought that certain basic understandings of the world we live in, in this case certain central aspects of our comprehension of the social practice of law (the kind of comprehension sought by those who are properly ambitious about the possibilities of jurisprudence), are discoverable only by thinking about law from a perspective that is relatively modest, local, and immediate, pursuing seams that have long been worked by practitioners, though not with the same tools in hand or goals in mind. This is not an imperialistic manoeuvre, an attempt to maintain, in something like the Dworkinian manner, that philosophy knows best about everything, including the everyday. On the contrary, it is a suggestion born of distance, sympathy, and a sense of mutual respect. Abstraction and engagement are different ways of approaching the world, but they range over the same terrain and often depend on one another for their distinctive richness and success. Close engagement has much to bring to philosophy, just as philosophy has to bring to close engagement, although in both cases something is also lost, something philosophical as well as something practical. The question that such a claim gives rise to is just what it means for philosophy to become closely engaged with law, and what might we learn therefrom.

xi. The point being pursued here can be seen as an inversion of, as well as a companion to, the familiar idea that describes the project of applied philosophy: namely, that a philosophical outlook has a valuable contribution to make to ordinary practical reasoning. Here the further thought, albeit to the opposite effect, is that the detailed institutions, forms, and practices of ordinary practical reasoning have much to teach philosophy, in that a sound understanding of those phenomena is capable of yielding philosophical insights that would otherwise be inaccessible. Put in terms of roles, it is the suggestion that there are insights in the philosophy of law that are more readily available to lawyers, and more particularly to those lawyers who have not only academic training in law but also a sound grasp of legal practice, than to those who have training and an interest in the philosophy of law but who have little or no experience of legal practice. It is the thought that engagement and abstraction are as apt to be fruitful companions as to be rivals, that the fabric of law is a special source of philosophical insight, and that lawyers and philosophers can be one another's best collaborators in the quest for understanding. It is a point about what law has to teach philosophy, yet it will begin here with reflection on what philosophy has to teach law.

xii. Many lawyers, academic as well as practising, may well raise an eyebrow at this point. Law is among the most fundamental of organized social practices, and, what is more, self-consciously so. Its outlook is, for that reason, both characteristically and naturally practical to the core, so as to focus habitually on the details of its workings in practical domains such as lawyering, legislation, policing, adjudication, and others of that ilk. 'It's a bit like learning plumbing' is what my law school's tutor for admissions told me, when I asked him what learning the law might be like and just where it might lead me.[3] I was puzzled but thought perhaps I could see what he meant: just what sort of fittings connect what sort of pipes? Could be tricky; might be interesting. I was a machine operator at the time, and the sense of recognition felt reassuring. For many lawyers it seems somewhat odd, and perhaps inappropriate, to think of law in any other way. Deep reflections on law, on just what it is and what it might perhaps be good for, have not only to overcome self-understandings of that kind, and the various species of inhibition and distaste that those understandings give rise to, but also, and more broadly, to warrant their place and claim on ordinary attention in an increasingly practical world. 'What practical use are such reflections?', not only lawyers but others want to know. What is more, given that there has been a very great deal written in the philosophy of law since HLA Hart published *The Concept of Law* 50 years or more ago, and in doing so brought the field to life after decades of relative neglect and decline, has not nearly all of what might usefully be said on the subject already been said, as demonstrated by what

---

[3] Acidly embracing, although I was not in a position to recognize it then, the journeyman's approach to university legal education that had been disparaged by William Twining in 'Pericles and the Plumber', 83 *LQR* 396 (1967).

even certain legal philosophers regard as the somewhat tired state of jurisprudential enquiry today?

xiii. The question being pressed here is only partly sceptical. It is not simply the overly apologetic question of why one should do philosophy—a question that philosophers, on the whole, might be best off overlooking. It is also a question that is driven by a sense of uncertainty as to the particular *kind* of usefulness that deep reflection might give rise to, and so a question that is liable to be pressed by philosophers as well as by lawyers. If the usefulness of such reflection is both real and something more than self-referential, in just what domain does that usefulness lie? How is it to be properly pursued? Unless and until we know that, we are liable to seek usefulness in the wrong place, looking for it where it is not and failing to see it where it might be. Those who claim attention for what legal philosophy has to tell us need to be clear just whose attention they are claiming, if and to the extent that it goes beyond that of philosophers of law themselves.

xiv. Lawyers and others who raise such questions are sometimes blinkered, sometimes self-serving, sometimes parochial, yet they have a point—though it is one that is easy to misapprehend. *Pace* Dworkin, deep reflections on law are not useful in the ordinary, everyday understanding of practical usefulness that most lawyers have in mind, and such lawyers and their friends are accordingly quite right to be sceptical of the value of philosophy in that particular practical setting. It does not follow, however, that deep reflections on law are not in any way useful, so as to warrant a broader scepticism on the part of practical reasoners generally. On the contrary, everything that human beings are capable of registering is registered with usefulness in mind, but usefulness is an idea that is much richer than many (including utilitarians) take it to be. Usefulness is nothing other than the value (and disvalue), in all its variety and complexity, that engagement with the world (theoretical and practical, though it is practical engagement I will primarily have in mind here) is capable of giving rise to. The scope of the value (and disvalue) that law and reflections on law can give rise to, and the range of understanding that is required in order to perceive the elements of what that scope embraces, is infinitely greater than that which would make any analogy between legal rules and the elements of plumbing an apt one.

xv. Still, to say only this much and no more might reasonably be thought to be avoiding the question, a question that proceeded from doubt as to the usefulness, in any recognizably practical sense, however extended, of deep reflections on law. Either such reflections are useful on the standard notion of usefulness, it might be said (as followers of Dworkin would contend they are, but which others are understandably doubtful about), or to describe them as useful is simply something akin to a magician's trick, a case of persuasive definition. Perhaps one can call them useful without betraying the meaning of that word, but they are not useful in the sense that people normally have in mind when they speak of usefulness. Or so the argument might run.

xvi. The more nuanced answer to the question, then, is that the idea of usefulness at work here runs deeper than the standard view recognizes as a matter of everyday usage, but not so deep as to betray what the standard view has in mind. One way to see this is to notice that the standard view of usefulness is itself rather more accommodating than is sometimes recognized—sufficiently accommodating, for example, to embrace the realm of aesthetics. Aesthetic value is not a domain that one reaches only by departing from the idea of usefulness in the ordinary sense: there is beauty to be found in well-executed pipework and in the fabric of the law, and part of that beauty stems from the niceties of practical execution, so that pipework and laws are the more beautiful the more that all their many and detailed elements tend to the success of their practical function. One does not need to venture into some different, let alone higher realm in order to participate in aesthetic value. To notice this much is to notice simply that the standard view of usefulness is not as narrow or as single-minded as some practical reasoners would have it. However there is also usefulness beyond the standard view of the term yet true to what it has in mind. Certain forms of usefulness, philosophical usefulness in particular, are instances of what I might call deep usefulness—the kind of usefulness that is analogous to what we are thinking of when, in speaking of human psychology, we say of a person that he or she is very grounded, has a very sure sense of himself or herself. Philosophical enquiry, and the understanding that it seeks, bears the same sort of relationship to understanding in general (or to the general understanding of a domain such as law, or of some particular domain within law) that such a person has to the grasp of his or her character and capacities, and its usefulness is of a similar order.

xvii. Plainly there is real value (and disvalue) to be found in the grounding that philosophy can provide, and the question, to which the analogy to human psychology suggests an intuitive answer, is what sort of value that is and in what realms of human activity it is to be found. A conventional picture associates that value with the general and the abstract, seeks to gain access to it through a process of reflection and detachment, thinks of it as informing and sustaining, and contrasts it with the particular, the immediate, the engaged, and the dependent. There are two ways in which that picture might be disturbed without being denied. The first is to diminish the contrast, and so suggest that there is rather less distance between the domains of the philosopher and the everyday actor than is commonly assumed, thereby and to that extent miniaturizing the concerns of philosophy (and enlarging the import of ordinary action). The second is to suggest that the contrast in question is to be looked for not between domains in relation to which one picture or the other offers the superior explanation, but between modes of understanding and action, of explanation and operation, both of which are available in a wide range of domains. What is more, the value of each of these modes is not merely different from that of the other, but typically conflicting, giving reason to prefer one to the other in particular contexts, themselves not susceptible to broad categorization, including the contexts of particular actions in particular lives, as driven by particular values, disvalues, or some combination thereof, be they the actions and lives of individuals or of communities.

xviii. Put shortly, the approach that I have sought to pursue in the work that follows is based on the conviction that deep thinking, in this case deep thinking about law and what it is capable of, can be profitably pursued in relatively fine-grained settings—or, to use a different metaphor, in relation to thick understandings of law—but that the perspective that such thinking provides is neither exclusive nor superior, and indeed is often purchased at the price of no less valuable understandings of law, most obviously those understandings that are deeper than it on the one hand (and so thinner and more coarse-grained) and those that are less deep on the other (and so thicker and more fine-grained). Philosophical reflection is just one more way of apprehending the world, with its attendant benefits and burdens, and the interest to be had in pursuing it here is the interest in discovering what it has to offer when pursued in more concrete settings than it is conventionally pursued in, in thinking less about law as a whole and more about laws of different kinds:[4] in other

---

[4] The kinds that I have in mind here are distinguished from one another by the extent to which they characteristically rely for their success, in terms of their capacity to build

words, in exploring what is to be discovered by taking as one's starting point not a general, broadly abstracted picture of law but a suite (in the present case a triptych) of particular pictures of law, themselves subordinate, interdependent, mutually informing, and fundamentally deferential to one another and to their rational rivals.

xix. One might stop there, but there is something more that can be said, briefly and by way of illustration, so as to capture the relative simplicity of the distinction and the relative complexity of its potential articulation in thought and practice. Begin by establishing what deep thinking is not; in other words, what it can helpfully be contrasted to. In much, perhaps the bulk, of our everyday lives we learn by doing, not by thinking about what doing means and what that meaning might be good for. When we engage in an everyday practical task, like that of driving a nail; or when we seek to express our thoughts and feelings, whether in words, or music, or dance, or some other language; or when we enter into exchanges with others, and so build relationships, be they transient or long-lasting, we put practice to the fore, to the exclusion of other modes of understanding and engagement, and so become successful practitioners by a set of incremental, cumulative practical steps, without any need for the intervention of deep thought. There is a way of holding a nail, of starting to drive it, of picking up the swing of the hammer, of following through on the final blow so that the wood is not bruised; there are ways of becoming one with words, or music, or dance, there are ways of establishing rapport and exchange with humans and other animals, none of which bear much thought. Indeed, in a great many cases it is a damaging error to think very much at all. One can all too easily know less by understanding more. Some of these kinds of doing involve deliberation, some involve preparation, some involve education, but none of them are any the less cases of bare doing for all that. These aspects of our lives flow through us, as Leo Kottke once put it of music, from one generation of practitioners to the next, as we inherit, become versed in, and then bequeath the many arts of living, sometimes well and for the good, sometimes not.[5]

---

a life in common, on the strength of the reasons they refer and give rise to alone, or further on the strength they derive from various supporting strategies of will and of imagination—sometimes rational, but more commonly, and more interestingly perhaps, sometimes arational.

[5] Interviewed for an anthology of the first 15 years of his career, and asked to reflect on the shape of his achievement, from newcomer to mature artist, Kottke observed:

xx. If life is, or at least has the potential to be, so rich without the intervention of what I have been calling, as a kind of placeholder for an explanation, deep thought, what can deep thought bring to the table? When can it help us and when is it liable to damage the value of our pursuits, by misdirecting the patterns of practical reasoning that govern our actions and engagements? There is, of course, no categorical answer to such questions, just because philosophy is a way of thinking rather than a mode of being or a way of doing, a way of thinking about nearly anything and not about anything in particular. Yet that fact suggests that the domains in which philosophy may be rewarding are potentially rather more varied, rather more local, rather more specialized, than is commonly taken to be the case. Put simply, to be philosophical is to place one's commitment to reason ahead of one's commitment to whatever it is that reason is a reason for, in any of the domains that are capable of giving rise to reasons. One checks the crude flow of practical life, so that it does not only flow through one, and seeks to assess the manner of its operation, the nature of its meaning, and the significance of its value (or disvalue). Because philosophy steps back from everyday life in this way, it is often thought of or described, and not entirely wrongly so, as detached, dispassionate, uncommitted, and other similar terms that function as gestures at an explanation of its distinctive stance. Philosophy is characteristically rigorous, because a failure of rigour undermines, to the extent of that failure, everything that philosophy might possibly have to offer. Finally, and unlike much of everyday action, philosophy is self-conscious and self-aware. Yet just how far need it be any one or all of these things?

xxi. Unsurprisingly perhaps, there is something of a temptation to identify philosophy with what might appear to be its purest case, and so to regard the most detached forms of reflection and understanding as the most philosophical. Yet in fact philosophy offers an alternative understanding to that inherent in bare doing, and is capable of being

---

I've joined the soundstream. I'm part of that thing that was going through me before I could play, and now I'm swimming in it. . . . All I know is that I fit in somewhere, but it's like fitting into a river. . . . I may have dreamed up some of this, but I dreamed it up working through other players. . . . Robbie [Basho] was at one of my first gigs and I said, 'I'm going to go up and play tonight, and I'm afraid I'm going to sound an awful lot like you.' He said, 'That's OK. We all go through somebody.' Robbie was the first guy I went through, and people go through me, but they're on their way to somewhere else.

Liner notes to *The Leo Kottke Anthology*, Rhino 1997.

brought to bear upon and so to operate in a wide range of settings. When philosophy gets it right our engagement with those settings is distinctively grounded, for better and for worse, although not in the psychological sense of being sure of oneself, which is accessible to any actor sufficiently in tune with his or her being and existence, sufficiently versed in its articulation. It is a grounding in reason, or to put it more precisely in what is taken to be an understanding of reason, which is liable to alter the quality of one's engagement without necessarily enhancing its value as a result. One does not become a better person by becoming a successful moral philosopher, any more than one becomes a better musician by understanding musical theory. On the contrary, in certain settings at least, one is liable to become a less good person, just as a musical savant may lose something of his or her musicality as the result of a formal musical education.

xxii. Thinking philosophically about the law involves a departure, in varying degree, from the fact of engagement with law, in any respect, general or specific, in which that engagement takes place. The lessons that philosophical reflection on law is capable of providing are not simply lessons about law, as a general social practice; they are, or can be, lessons about particular kinds of laws, about particular ways of couching laws, and of attending to laws, in the absence of which we would not understand law, as a general practice, in the same way. All this is familiar enough, both to those who philosophize about law in general and to those who philosophize about particular domains of law, such as criminal law, or torts, or human rights. Yet it contains a twist, for the familiar domains of law, such as criminal law and so on, are not simply specific settings for the operation of the general practice—though they are that too—but also settings in which special implications of the general practice, implications that are not readily discoverable by thinking about the practice generally, are given effect to. To reflect on law as a general phenomenon is to put oneself in a position to discover such general lessons about law as are discoverable by thinking generally about law, but it is by the same token to disable oneself from discovering general lessons about law that are discoverable only by ceasing to think generally about law, in order to focus on certain species of law in particular.

xxiii. It is my sense, and the project of this book to explain and defend, that different laws, and different domains of law, work in different ways, by making appeals to those to whom they are addressed that are based on various admixtures of reason, will, and imagination—sometimes through the operation of law alone, and sometimes in collaboration with other social practices, other modes of authority—and that one can understand this only by reflecting first on the roles that reason, will, and imagination are necessarily called upon to play in the operation of law, and second on the different ways that those roles may be played out in different domains of the law. That is my starting point, the first step on the route into the detailed narrative that follows: the idea that one cannot understand law solely in terms of its appeal to reason, or to imagination, or to respect for the exercise of will. An account of law that begins in any one of those ways, however illuminating it may be, will by that token inevitably be incomplete, albeit that its incompleteness in that respect may well be one of the bases of its capacity to illuminate as it does. In nearly all settings, law is only capable of doing what it exists to do (both for good and for ill) when it invokes the assistance of some combination of reason, will, and imagination, and a true account of law is one that explores the significance of any one of those phenomena, or of their combination, and that is careful in doing so not to suppress any, or to conflate any one with another.

xxiv. Yet why should that be so? To put it in the way that I have put it is simply to offer a conclusion without explaining its basis, or even outlining the general character of the kind of account that might be thought to show the conclusion to be sound. A proper answer must await the balance of the book (though its initial outline is sketched in the second chapter, 'Decision, For One and For the Many', at paras 10–23), but what can be said at this stage is that the claim being made here is not one that flows from the concept of law, however that might be understood, or from the institutional realities that such a concept might imply. Rather it flows from the very nature of a rational life—from the challenge of living well, as experienced by every one of us, individually and collectively: or, more precisely, as experienced in and through the various capacities and activities that we have in common with, and indeed in collaboration with, the creatures that surround us, most notably those people whose lives are intertwined with ours, with whom we interact, and with whose existences and practices we are as a consequence deeply engaged, in all or virtually all that we do. The reasons for action that confront us, individually and collectively, are typically manifold and incommensurable, so that the exercise of reason alone typically cannot tell us which reason to prefer above all others. Yet we must act, and in order to do so we must decide (including those cases where we slide into decision without deliberation), and in a world in which reason is incapable of providing all the resources of decision we are bound to decide by calling upon the exercise of not only reason, but also imagination and will. The consequence is that our lives as rational beings depend for their success upon the interplay of both rational and arational forces, and upon our ability to navigate and manipulate those forces in the right way or, once again more precisely, in a way that is no less good than any other way, and that hence remains rationally undefeated.

xxv. We do this no less when we seek to act in common, as we do through the social practice of law, than when we seek to act on our own. Indeed, we cannot hope to build a life in common solely on the strength of the reasons embodied in law, such as they may be. On the contrary, it is only possible to build a life in common through law by further calling upon collective ways of engaging imagination and will. The predicament that we face, and that we must overcome, is one that stems from our condition as rational creatures, and the distinctive social practice of law, together with its social and political companions in the exercise of authority, constitutes an enterprise that enables us, at its best, to navigate that predicament successfully and in common.

xxvi. So much for the impetus and ambitions of this project. For more opportunistic readers, as well as those who prefer to have a clear sense of the direction they are taking before they take it, a brief outline of the course of the narrative that follows. The book begins with a statement of the puzzle of law as I see it (paras 1–9), together with an account of the moral worldview that gives rise to that puzzle (10–23). The balance of the book has three main movements, of which the third is by far the most extended and complex. It looks first at accounts of law that focus on the will, the extent to which they fall short of completeness, and yet what they have to teach us about the role that will is bound to play in the formation and functioning of the law (24–39). It looks second at an account of law, that offered by Ronald Dworkin, that I take to be best explained in terms of the understanding it proposes of the role played in the reasons that law offers by the operation of imagination, and suggests the extent to which that account distorts the roles played by reason and by imagination and yet has much to teach us about the significance of imagination (40–64): in fact almost uniquely so, given the lack of attention paid to imagination in most writing on the philosophy of law. It looks finally, and at length, at the service that law may offer to a life in common (65–215). In particular, it examines the different ways in which different types of law may embody or may be sustained by claims upon our reason, imagination, and will, and explores the limits to what law can do for us.

xxvii. The claims of some laws upon us can be sustained entirely by the claims of the reasons that they embody (80–4). Any other course of action is made rationally inferior by virtue of the very existence of such laws. In that setting, the fact that the law tells us to do something is determinative of what we ought to do there, either because the law is echoing, for expressive reasons perhaps, a conclusion that of its own force has a stronger claim upon us than any other, or because the very fact that the law requires it gives the claim in question a rational priority that it would otherwise lack. In such cases the balance of reasons favours what the law requires, so that the prospect of a life in common in those settings is just as great as people are rational. These, however, are the easy cases for the realization of a life in common through the operation of law. One should not assume that they are the most common cases, let alone the most typical. The claims of other laws, even when well founded, offer us reasons that have no greater rational pull upon us than do other reasons that apply to us in the same settings. If such laws are to have any hope of establishing a life in common in respect of what they lay down, they need to be buttressed by the pull of something more than reason alone, something that is compatible with reason but not determined by it. In the absence of such buttressing their addressees are liable to attend to other reasons that have no less strong a claim upon them, to the peril of a life in common. The most familiar instance of that kind of buttressing is the exercise of the will of the law-maker and the various species of coercion that embody that will (85–92). A less familiar yet possibly rather more pervasive instance of buttressing is that provided by political appeals to public imagination, of a kind with which we today are all too familiar, made in ways that are sometimes extrinsic to the law (108–12), yet sometimes intrinsic to it (113–23). These claims may be made as part of the legislative process or as part of the adjudicative process, and in their character and mode of operation tell us much that is helpful about the separation of powers and the politics of the judiciary (124–33), as well as of the price of allowing oneself to be guided by the call of imagination (134–50), even when that guidance is consistent with reason.

xxviii. The book concludes with an examination of certain matters that are on the face of it ancillary to the challenge of establishing a life in common through the operation of law, yet have a direct bearing on the significance of that project: the limits to the guidance that legal authority can offer (158–80); the criteria by which the legitimacy of authority is to be assessed (181–215); the relationship between a law and its justification (216–50); and the degree to which a life in common is (259–87) and is not (251–8) dependent upon the presence of law. Further detail of the scheme of the book is set out in its table of contents, while specific topics (from arationality to the separation of powers) are identified in the index.

xxix. A word on approach. At one extreme, a work of philosophy can seek to address a problem entirely afresh, paying little or no attention to what has been written on the subject before. Many of the finest works in philosophy, from Aristotle on down, have proceeded from that point of view. At another extreme, a work of philosophy can seek to address a problem by means of response to what has been written (or said) on the subject before. Many just as fine works in philosophy, from Plato on down, have proceeded from that point of view. This book seeks to occupy a position somewhere between those extremes. At heart it is a work in the first tradition, seeking to address a problem afresh by stepping outside the familiar parameters of scholarly exchange on the subject. At the same time, as I suggested at the beginning of this preface, it is a work that seeks to emphasize how much we have to learn from those who have gone before us, and in particular how much we have to learn from those with whom we disagree. Yet by the same token it would clearly be a mistake to conclude from the latter, second-order, largely compensatory commitment to a proper degree of deference to an intellectual tradition that one should expect this book to offer something in the nature of a definitive assessment of the works of scholarship that it takes account of. In particular, it would be a mistake to look for a fully developed defence of my disagreement with certain scholars in the setting of an analysis of which, on my part, the underlying goal is to learn something valuable from that which I otherwise disagree with. Ultimately if not immediately, my interest is in what I have in common with the scholars I disagree with, not on what divides us, and in ways that they can be proved right rather than wrong. I have paid attention to the work of others for what I could learn from it, and for ways in which I might develop a fuller understanding of law on the basis of its achievements; I have then sought to offer some modest further moves of my own, and to set out, as clearly as I can, what all that looks like.

xxx. Finally, a comment on the text. I began this project as a set of notes, in the thought that I might interest John Gardner in our writing something further together. I'm not sure why I thought it necessary to write my ideas down, or why the notes soon escaped point form to become properly written, yet still numbered, paragraphs. As things turned out, John didn't pick up on the prospect immediately, and at the same time I began to feel that this was something I really ought to do on my own. The project turned into a book, but somehow the numbered paragraphs survived. I found that I liked the compression that they called for; the commitment that they implied, that each numbered paragraph should be based on a new idea (a commitment that I can't promise to have honoured in every case); the consequent discipline that arose from the inability to allow a train of thought to run on as long as there was any mileage to be had out of it; and not least, in the setting of a life dominated by other commitments, the capacity of such a modular structure to lend itself to intense focus on detailed topics, considered often in isolation and over a period of nearly five years. Having finished the book I can set my natural attachment to its structure against my awareness of the limitations, as well as the possibilities, that such a structure gives rise to. Whether the same or similar ideas could be better expressed by other means I leave to those who will, I hope, be prompted to take my suggestions, or some form of reaction to them, to places that I have as yet not even begun to think of. In the meantime, at least I can say that this is one book it should be easy to retrieve one's place in even more precisely than by turning down the page or using a bookmark.

Acknowledgements

There are too many people to whom I owe too much to be able to thank properly, but I would like to single out Alex Flach, who raised the possibility of a book with me; selected the idea for this one as the more promising of the two proposals that I was able to sketch over lunch—although at the time this one did not extend to much more than three words (reason, beguilement, force) and a little something about what I thought might be their roles in law; told me that he would be happy to publish a project whatever its length, be it as few as 50 pages; and then left me entirely free to get on with it. Without that initial encouragement, and the confidence that came of knowing that I was not committing myself to an extended endeavour at a time when I had little opportunity for proper research (I was then head of my law school), this book would not have been written. I am extremely grateful that I had the opportunity to write it, and so would like to thank Alex profoundly, while at the same time suggesting that there are many projects out there that rely for their realization not only on that kind of support but on the prospect of a publication that falls somewhere between an article and a book. This is not simply a story about marketing and what we have to learn from the example of Harry Frankfurt. Beautifully written, masterful, and piquant as it is, Frankfurt's 'On Bullshit' had a well-secured life in print without a need for independent presentation, astute though its publisher was in perceiving the possibilities of its publication in free-standing form, for placement immediately next to the cash register. Rather, it is a story about medium and message. Different problems require different degrees of consideration, and there are many problems in the world that are too knotty to be dealt with adequately in an article, yet not so knotty as to warrant a book. Between the long article and the short book lies a terrain in which there are few vehicles for publication, and with it a range of topics that fail to attract academic attention. As not only I but also others have noted before, our thoughts are necessarily shaped and constrained by the vehicles in which they are able to find expression, and it seems to me that whether it be through the flexibility of digital publication or through the more imaginative editing and marketing of printed matter there is a great deal to be said, in terms of the human understanding that might be achieved there, for the development of fresh vehicles for the publication of academic research, and in particular for recourse to brief and pointed essays, broadsides, or pamphlets, in the manner proposed and encouraged by Alex Flach—even though this particular project did not, as it happens, turn out to be one of them.

I would of course also like to thank the careful and thoughtful readers for Oxford University Press, from whom I learned much, though perhaps not as much as I should have, and whose rich and suggestive comments are reflected in a great many significant adaptations and accommodations throughout the book. I'm afraid, however, that it needs to be said in their defence that in at least a few cases I have been stubborn enough to stay true to myself and to my initial perspective, when it might well have been rather wiser to have taken on the somewhat different colours that they diplomatically drew my attention to.

Finally, beyond the very broad debt described in the dedication, I would once again like to thank John Gardner for his last-stage, extremely careful and detailed reading of the manuscript, undertaken in snatched moments on various train journeys, and for the many fine-grained, deeply informed, sympathetically sceptical yet consistently helpful queries, challenges, and shrewd proposals for improvement that he offered as a result. It's like having a musical instrument subtly retuned by a friendly listener with acute pitch, or a camera lens similarly refocused: whatever the merits of their composition and execution, the sounds and images that one has fastened upon suddenly lock much more surely into place.

A somewhat abridged version of Chapter 8 appeared as 'Ideas of Easy Virtue' in *Reason, Morality, and Law: The Philosophy of John Finnis*, ed John Keown and Robert P George (2012).

Contents

1. The Problem of Law — 1
2. Decision, For One and For the Many — 11
3. The Exaltation of the Will — 21
4. The Genius of the Place — 33
5. The Service Law May Offer to Life in Common — 51
   A. Concepts of Law — 52
   B. Different Laws as Different Catalysts for a Life in Common — 56
      1. Authority as Perfecting Reason — 57
      2. Authority, Reason, and Will — 60
      3. Authority, Reason, and Imagination — 66
         a) Force and Imagination — 67
         b) Reason and Imagination — 69
         c) Extrinsic Imaginative Appeals — 76
         d) Intrinsic Imaginative Appeals — 79
         e) The Separation of Powers — 85
         f) The Price of Imagination — 91
   C. Different Kinds of Life in Common — 103
6. Appreciating the Limits of the Service Conception of Authority — 109
   A. Limits to Guidance — 113
   B. The Criteria of Legitimacy and Their Value — 124
   C. Alternative Authorities, Alternative Regulation — 134
7. Ideas of Easy Virtue: Descriptions and Evaluation — 149
8. Law and Life in Common — 175
   A. Life Without Law — 175
   B. Law, Social Change, and Modernity — 179
   C. Law, Regulatory Sophistication, and Ambition — 185
   D. Law and Community, Past, Present, and Future — 187

Index — 205

1

The Problem of Law

1. One of the acknowledged goals of law is to describe and shape a life in common. Could we possibly imagine a legal system that did not have this ambition, whether for good or ill? Law is paradigmatically the instrument of government, in the broadest sense of government (though not the only such instrument), and the point of government is to regulate the conduct of agents within its domain by shaping their actions in one way or another, in the case of law through rules and standards of more or less general application. The claim being made here is a conceptual one, albeit with functional implications—a claim about any government, not simply about good government. The project of law can be selective; it can be circumspect, and so broadly permissive; it can even be deliberately destabilizing in certain settings, as part of a wider strategy of shaping conduct; it can be all these things, but it cannot be fundamentally either anarchic or indifferent.[1]

---

[1] I have put the point in the practical frame of a life in common in reliance on the practical fact that legal systems govern communities, and further that nearly all laws are addressed, in general terms, to that class of agents whose actions, present or prospective, fall within their scope. That being the case, the connection between law and a life in common, and whatever difficulties it may give rise to, is, as a practical matter, both inescapable and central. Yet is the connection either inescapable or central in principle? That seems less obvious. One is bound to notice that it is entirely possible for a law to be addressed to only one person, as when it confers a status upon that person—a title perhaps, or legitimacy of birth—and so makes no overt attempt to establish a life in common. Of course, a ready response to that fact would be to point out that there are inevitably general implications to such laws, because particular declarations of status entail general requirements that those declarations be appropriately acknowledged and observed. That much having been granted, however, there remains a question of whether the difficulties involved in connecting law and a life in common are indeed at heart a

2. Let me approach the point from a slightly different direction, because I think it is important to be as clear as possible right from the outset about precisely what is and what is not at stake in the claim I am seeking to make, lest its conceptual reach be misunderstood. The idea of a life in common can mean many different things, ranging from mere consonance of behaviour to thick conceptions of community, the bulk of which the project of law need not be in any sense dedicated to. Most obviously, and as already indicated, a life in common can be a good thing or a bad thing, as well as a mixture of the two. Yet beyond the latter particular and perhaps overly discussed dimension of possibility, a life in common may or may not amount to a community, may or may not be tied to a territory, may or may not allow for dissent in key respects, may or may not be tied to notions of membership. These variations can be multiplied in a host of further ways, for both the idea and the practice of a life in common are open to a range of renderings that is no less rich and manifold than the full palette of social forms and practices that human beings are constitutionally capable of inventing and drawing upon. Many such lives in common do not require law, many would not be helped by law, and most importantly, the bulk of them are ventures that law need not be in any way committed to.[2]

---

function of the project of commonality, as I am claiming, for it is clear that, whomever law addresses, the connection between law and action is, in the first instance, a problem for each and every addressee of law, and only by extension a problem for addressees collectively. That being the case, it might reasonably be thought that the problem of connecting law and action is a function of the claims made by and through law, whether to one or many, and thus a function, as many have claimed, of authority rather than of a life in common. Entirely reasonable as that thought clearly is, one should be careful not to view the choice between the frame of authority and that of a life in common as a choice between sound and unsound perspectives on the nature of law. It is undoubtedly true that the difficulties of connecting law and action can be understood and expressed successfully in terms of authority, as Raz has shown so powerfully, and that there is a great deal to be learned by looking at them in that way. Yet that is true because those difficulties are even more fundamentally the practical difficulties of negotiating the rational landscape, alone or in concert—difficulties that stem directly from the challenge presented by the underdetermination of reasons for action, and which as a consequence can be expressed fruitfully either in terms of authority or in terms of a life in common. I have chosen to express them in terms of a life in common in order to bring out what a focus on authority tends to downplay, namely the quandary faced by addressees of law and the consequent challenge for a community shaped by law, in the lack of rational pre-eminence in what the law calls for and the impact of that fact on law-making and law-abiding, even in cases where the law's claim to authority is rationally justified, whether it be in terms of Raz's normal justification thesis or something similar.

[2] For further consideration of law and life in common, see Chapter 5C, Different Kinds of Life in Common and Chapter 8, Law and Life in Common.

3. The claim that I am making, about the necessary connection between law and a life in common, is based on something much more modest and elemental. As the instrument of governance (and, most commonly, of government), law is committed to playing an active role in maintaining and developing the social forms and practices that its addressees can be expected to draw upon in the course of contemplating and pursuing the various projects of their lives. Sometimes, perhaps most familiarly in relatively modern, progressive settings, the role of law is an explicitly creative one, as when law-makers seek to forge new and better social practices for what they take to be a new and better world. Sometimes, however—perhaps in more defensive, self-protective settings—the role is a destructive one, as when law-makers seek to censure or dismantle social practices that they regard either as objectionable in themselves, or as standing in the way of the better worlds they are attempting to build. It is the minimal sense of a life in common at stake in these settings, namely a social form or practice that a person may call upon, in whatever form or degree, in the articulation of his or her particular life, which law is necessarily committed to the formation (or destruction) of. Law cannot but attempt to shape the range of social forms and practices that are available in the world it speaks to. Law may seek to do rather more than this, of course, but it cannot do less.

4. The point could be put even more simply yet. Whenever law lays down a standard of behaviour, a guide to belief and action, that is intended to apply to more than one person, as the generality of its form nearly always implies, it necessarily faces the challenge of constructing a life in common—that is, a life that is in that particular respect shared by the people whom law addresses and seeks to govern, in the face of whatever reasons may exist to do other than law would have it. Yet, simple though it is, that is enough but not quite all. To that essential, elemental degree of commonality must be added the fact that law is often called upon to do rather more than the bare minimum that it is necessarily committed to, and when that is the case the life in common that law is necessarily committed to is correspondingly extended. This means that a proper consideration and analysis of the connection between law and life in common has to be capable of embracing, at a minimum, the full range of commonalities, from minimal to maximal, that law characteristically seeks to secure in the legal orders that we are sufficiently familiar with to hope to understand. The discussion that follows tries to take proper account of that range, and so will make reference to a number

of different renderings of a life in common and what each entails for the project of law. Put shortly, law has different ways of serving different forms of life in common, and an account of the service that it is capable of rendering to our lives must register not only what is necessary to that service, but also the most prominent instances of what is possible within it.

5. The real difficulty, and the question that animates this project, comes in the next step. What is the connection between law and action, in one life or in many?[3] The answer to that question is only in part to be discovered in a resolution to the familiar problem of the identification of law. Whatever is identified as law must be capable of describing and shaping a life in common if it is to function as law at all, for that is the necessary ambition of any legal system and the project of governance to which all legal systems are by their nature committed. Yet law cannot describe or shape a life in common solely in terms of its content, however that content may be identified. The content of law can offer us reasons for action (or can claim to do so) but it cannot normally offer us reasons that defeat all others. To put it from the opposite perspective, there is normally no game-theoretical rational answer to the question of what the content of law should be, or, more broadly, to the question of what the addressees of law should do; rather, there are normally many reasonable answers to both questions. It follows that the content of law, however it may be identified, cannot completely explain the connection between law and the life in common that it is the purpose of law to sustain. As long as there is the possibility of undefeated reasons to do other than what the law requires—which would seem to be a great deal, perhaps even most of the time—there is the possibility that what is identified as law will be incapable of performing law's inescapable function of establishing a life in common.[4] The claims of

---

[3] Law may also seek to offer us reasons for belief, whether as an intermediate step in the generation of reasons for action or as an end in itself. In both cases the challenges that law faces in attempting to describe and shape a life in common through the generation of reasons for belief, and the methods that law calls upon in order to meet those challenges, are as described in what follows, *mutatis mutandis*, though the discussion will speak largely of action. However, see Chapter 5, section B3: Authority, Reason, and Imagination.

[4] Value monists who believe in the value of authority (utilitarians, for example) would reject the claim that there are very often undefeated reasons to do other than what the law calls for (cases of equality being rare). For them the problem of connecting law and action becomes a problem of competing *candidates* for reasons for action, an issue taken up in Chapter 4, The Genius of the Place. Granted, for the sake of argument, that there is a single right answer to the question of what the law requires, it remains an issue

competing reasons may be altered by the enactment of law, but they are rarely silenced by it. On the contrary, they survive, to press their claims anew upon the addressees of law, now in competition with the claims of whatever action the law has identified as legally required.

6. Joseph Raz has offered an account of law as a system of (alleged) reasons for action the value of which derives from the service conception of authority. Law is an aid to our rational life when it offers us a better way, through submission to its authority, of doing what we otherwise have reason to do. The normal justification of any authority, according to Raz, is that we do better by acceding to its demands than we would by consulting our own judgement, both assessed according to the same standard. When a claim of authority is justified in this way we have reason to do as it requires[5]—unless, Raz adds puzzlingly, there is reason to decide for ourselves.[6] Does this not return us to the problem with which we began? Does it not explain the hold that a good law has over us only to disavow the exclusivity of that hold? On the face of it, Raz's argument shows only that submission to law's authority may be reasonable; in doing so it consciously leaves the problem of reasonable conformity to law only partly resolved, because it does not pretend to suggest that conformity is necessarily any more reasonable than non-conformity, even in the case of a law that meets the normal justification of authority.

whether that answer has been identified correctly from among the competing candidates for correctness by those, such as courts and legislatures, who have taken themselves to be in a position to identify what the law requires with at least some degree of accuracy and consequent authority. Of course, this issue is, in modified form, as much a problem for value pluralists as it is for value monists, since pluralists must also identify defeated reasons correctly, but at least for those pluralists who are legal positivists the problem does not stand in the way of identifying the law. The same would be true, of course, of a monist positivist.

[5] Given that there are liable to be a number of relevant standards applicable to any claim to authority, it may well be that the authority's claim is justified according to one standard but not according to another. It follows that the reason to dissent from what even a justified authority requires may but need not be based on autonomy, for there are apt to be other undefeated reasons available.

[6] Raz's most recent treatment of the service conception of authority is to be found in his 'The Problem of Authority: Revisiting the Service Conception', in *Between Authority and Interpretation: On the Theory of Law and Practical Reason* (2009) 126; on the particular issue of conflict between the wisdom of letting the law decide for one (the normal justification thesis) and deciding for oneself (the independence condition) see 136–42. Earlier treatments of the service conception are to be found in *The Authority of Law* (1979) and *The Morality of Freedom* (1986), while the underlying picture of exclusionary reasons is persuasively set out in *Practical Reason and Norms* (1975).

7. It follows from Raz's account that one cannot seek to identify the content of law by reference to the very values that it exists to reconcile. If we had to ask ourselves what it would be right to do in a given situation in order to know what the law called upon us to do in that situation, the law would be incapable of justifying its own authority—indeed, its very existence. But to many observers, of whom Ronald Dworkin is the most notable, this is a puzzling notion of authority.[7] They point out that in many settings we invoke notions of authority that are on the face of it very different. We speak of a person as a moral authority, or a literary authority, if and to the extent that what he or she has to say embodies moral or literary wisdom. Such people are regarded as authorities because they are expert in the identification of certain facts, moral or literary. It follows that if there is a correct moral resolution to each of the many practical issues that face us as a community, as Dworkin believes there is, and if law is best understood as embodying that resolution, then law's authority is best regarded as moral authority, the rational import of its goodness. It further follows that the authority of those bodies that identify the law, such as appellate courts, is the derivative authority of those whose talent and expertise enables them to identify moral facts successfully. From this point of view Raz's account seems conclusory, or at least can be portrayed as being so, because it defends the positivist view that law is decisive by insisting that there is something for law to decide.[8] This defence is persuasive only to those who are otherwise inclined to believe that in nearly every case there is more than one correct moral resolution to the practical issues that law addresses, so that decision becomes inescapable and a potential role for law in helping us reach a decision becomes undeniable. The blunt ontological parry to Raz's account is to deny the validity of both its branches. Law's authority cannot be a matter of decision because there is nothing to decide.

8. Many of Dworkin's critics have challenged his ontological premise. Value pluralists are unpersuaded by the parry because

---

[7] For an explicit identification and analysis of the alleged puzzle see Dworkin, 'Thirty Years On', 115 *Harvard LR* 1655 (2002).

[8] It is not in fact conclusory, of course; if it were, the Dworkinian point of view would be no less conclusory in defending the anti-positivist view that law is not decisive by insisting that there is nothing for law to decide. In fact each account is derivative of and consistent with a different moral world view. Raz's account is underpinned by his extensive consideration of value pluralism and incommensurability.

they are unpersuaded by the claim that there is nothing to decide. Moral life, individual or collective, is not so straightforward, reason not so determinative. But this leaves both defenders and critics of the Razian account with nothing much to offer one another. Their explanations of law develop the implications of their respective moral world views without doing anything to sustain those views. By the same token, but from the opposite perspective, the question of the soundness of their respective accounts of law is diverted into the question of the soundness of their moral world views, leaving fundamental aspects of their accounts of law unexamined, other than as embodiments of particular moral world views. Yet can the escape be as straightforward as Dworkin suggests, and as his critics tacitly assume, even granted its ontological premise? Does Dworkin's account not simply shift the focus of concern from the ontological to the epistemological, while leaving the place of decision intact?

9. Certain radical critics of Dworkin have emphasized the role played by the will in the functioning of legal authority.[9] In many cases their emphasis is inspired by a moral world view that is to a greater or lesser degree sceptical of moral objectivity. To that extent defenders and critics of Dworkin's account are, like the defenders and critics of the Razian account, simply speaking from different moral world views, apparently with nothing to offer one another. Yet in the critical case something more is revealed by the distinctive emphasis that radical critics place on the role played by the will, because the denial of the ontological premise of their accounts, even if sound, cannot altogether deny the role played by the will in the exercise of authority in any moral world view. What their emphasis on the will has to teach us is that Raz's account of decision is incomplete, indeed self-consciously so, as its explicit returning of the problem of authority to the original puzzle of its hold over us emphasizes. This revelation does not establish that his account is mistaken, of course, because in itself it fails to establish that the will can do as much to generate decision as these proponents of its significance suppose. That being the case, Raz's account of law and authority can be tentatively regarded as circumspect but sound. The

---

[9] A representative if unusually sophisticated version of this position is set out, both critically and constructively, in Roberto Mangabeira Unger, *The Critical Legal Studies Movement* (1986). A more dramatic version, drawn from a different tradition, can be found in Jacques Derrida, 'Force of Law: The "Mystical Foundation of Authority"', 11 *Cardozo LR* 919, at 935ff (1990).

revelation is ultimately fatal, however, to the Dworkinian account,[10] which offers no room to the will in the formation of a life in common through law (though obviously it recognizes the role of the will in securing compliance with the law, both through enforcement by officials and through decisions by the addressees of law to be guided by its terms).[11] As significantly, the circumspection that it identifies in

[10] I chose my words here (and elsewhere in the book) at a time when Ronald Dworkin was still alive, and thus with a certain trepidation. Were he to notice what I had said (as he of course might not have), his formidable powers made a possible reply a fearsome prospect. Now that he is sadly dead, I have nothing to be afraid of in terms of reply, and that, ironically, is also a sad thing. I find myself somewhat ill at ease with my choice of words, not because it is wrong to speak ill of the dead—whose number, after all, includes almost everyone it is worth one's while to speak ill of—but because the respect that one owes to their legacy is different in kind from the respect that one owes to the living, with whom one is in dialogue, and with the consideration of whose ideas one can be properly robust. All in all, I would prefer to let my words stand rather than attempt to retrospectively revise them, but in doing so I would like to pay full tribute to the vibrant, complex, brilliant, and hugely creative scholarly enterprise that inspired them. I may think that certain of the claims that Dworkin chose to make in the course of that enterprise are ultimately mistaken, but I would not be having that thought (and so would not be benefiting from any of its productive consequences) but for their existence, and for that—and for the exhilaration that was almost always to be felt in his presence and in the company of his ideas—I am and will remain profoundly grateful.

[11] This is a fairly strong claim, and on the face of it perhaps a surprising one to some. Is it overstated? There are at least two reasons why one might think so. First, it is perfectly clear that Dworkin, like everybody else, believes that in exercising his or her function a judge necessarily decides something, namely the basic disposition of the case, for plaintiff or defendant, for appellant or respondent, and it follows that in doing so the judge must exercise his or her will, for decision by its very nature involves an act of will. Second, Dworkin further makes clear that part of the intellectual armoury upon which a judge is to draw when pursuing Dworkin's scheme of law as integrity is the repertoire of past political decisions in the jurisdiction in question, all of which decisions, by that same token, involve acts of will. So how can it be true to say that Dworkin offers no role to the will in the formation of a life in common through law? Put shortly, my sense of the answer to both questions, as I hope will be clear in the course of the more detailed consideration in the text below (see Chapter 4, The Genius of the Place, in particular), is that Dworkin offers no role to the will in the formation of law, and hence offers no role to the will in the formation of a life in common through law. In deciding a case as Dworkin sees it, a judge does not necessarily identify the law (for, despite best efforts, the judge may be mistaken), and past political decisions do not necessarily constitute what Dworkin would regard as the grounds of law (they too may be mistaken, most obviously by reason of a majoritarian cast), so that the presence of will in the identification of law is contingent upon the consonance of the act of will with the law's necessary moral remit— making the role of will in the formation of law a matter of identifying the content of a legal actor's beliefs about what morality requires, which may or may not be sound and so may or may not be law. Were it otherwise, Dworkin would be a legal positivist.

Raz's account suggests that there is a good deal more to law and the role it plays in facilitating a life in common than the rational claim that it is capable of making upon us as a scheme of exclusionary reasons that live up to the requirements of the service conception of authority. The question is just what that good deal more is.

2

Decision, For One and For the Many

10. The landscape of decision can be most readily depicted by setting aside, temporarily, its collective complexities and focusing on the individual case. A rational being confronted with reasons for action is motivated to act in accordance with those reasons but not, as Bernard Williams emphasized, conclusively so.[1] To put it in everyday terms, it is often the case that one does not feel like doing something that one can readily recognize one has reason to do, or, in a modest variation of the same experience, does not feel sufficiently like doing the something in question. These are the cases that Williams had in mind, and that he sought to explain in terms of the problem of motivation: the problem born of what he took to be a gap between the presence of a reason and the impetus to act in accordance with that reason. Just as familiarly, however, one often feels profoundly indecisive in the face of alternative courses of action, both of which one feels like doing. It is a fine late Saturday afternoon, let us suppose, and there is good reason to go for a walk, yet one dallies over the newspaper, or the computer, often to the point of missing the opportunity for a walk that one would very much have liked to take. The afternoon wanes, let us further suppose, evening begins to draw down, and one's attention shifts to the question of how best to spend the remains of the day: one may think of dinner at a well-regarded local restaurant, or of a favourably reviewed film currently playing at the local cinema, and yet find oneself not merely undecided but

---

[1] See in particular Williams, 'Internal and External Reasons' in *Moral Luck* (1981).

uncertain as to just how one ought to go about deciding. In such situations one often asks one's partner what best to do, so seeking to pass the problem on to him or her, only to have the question returned ('whatever you want'), and if one asks again ('I asked you first') tends to find the question batted back once again, this time usually rather less sympathetically. The predicament is a familiar one, but the explanations of it are various, and none are conclusive.

11. Sometimes the explanation is to be found in irrationality, in the fact that a decision-maker suffers from intellectual confusion, or from weakness of will, or from chronic indecisiveness. Yet one can bracket such cases and still be left with no less strong a sense of the problem. Sometimes the explanation seems to be traceable to lack of motivation, of the kind that concerned Williams. Yet even if one accepts Williams' view—that motivation is a real and distinct problem, born of the limited claims upon us of certain kinds of reason—one can once again bracket such cases and still believe in the existence of the predicament. There are situations, like that of the dinner and the film, in which there is too much motivation rather than too little, so giving rise to a conflict not merely between external reasons but between what Williams sought to distinguish and label as internal reasons, those in which motivation is embedded. Sometimes the explanation seems to be connected to an absence of relevant information, to the fact (say) that one does not know enough about the dinner or the movie to be able to determine which of the two is the most rationally compelling as a way of spending the present evening well. Undoubtedly that too may sometimes be the case, but is it the end of the story? For many, doubt remains. It seems that one can know all that one needs to know about alternative courses of action and yet remain undecided in the face of them, without committing any rational error in the handling of one's knowledge. That quandary remains intact even if one returns to the question of motivation, for one can know all one needs to know about alternative courses of action, be motivated to engage in each, and still feel that one has good reason to be undecided in the face of them.

12. For some, the explanation of such a predicament is that the alternatives before one are equal or roughly equal. The dilemma in question is then revealed as a trivial one. Either option will do, and while one is bound to decide between the two, one ought to recognize that the decision is not a significant one, precisely because the equality of the options makes each a perfect substitute for the

other. Yet the classification of such dilemmas as trivial seems at once to be conclusory and to beg the question. Are such decisions always trivial? That is certainly not the way in which we typically experience them, and while experiences can often be misleading, and while they are no less often misinterpreted, one would hope for some surer sense than a bare assertion of triviality can provide of the basis on which one is so often apt to be misled, so often liable to misinterpret (if our experiences are as deceiving as the explanation assumes). And if and to the extent that such decisions are indeed trivial, what makes them so? Is equality the only rationally sound explanation of the superficiality and arbitrariness of such decisions, such that informed rational creatures will find themselves properly indecisive only in circumstances of equality? (Such decisions are rightly described as superficial not in their import, for that would be conclusory, but in the sense that their resolution is not to be discovered through an examination of the reasons for either course of action.)

13. The by now familiar suggestion, of course, is that the claims of reasons upon us differ not only in degree but also, and perhaps more frequently, in kind. We find ourselves undecided (and not merely undecided, but grappling with the resources of decision) not so much because the options before us are equal or roughly equal (few of us experience any difficulty in making a selection among like items on a supermarket shelf), but because the options are in some sense fundamentally incomparable, the sense in which they are more technically described as incommensurable, meaning that in one or more relevant respects they simply cannot be evaluated in terms of the same standard. Most of the things that are good, or that can reasonably be expected to be good, about dinner at a well-regarded local restaurant are very different from the things that can reasonably be expected to be good about the favourably reviewed film currently playing at the local cinema. For example, the former will include the good of conversation while the latter will preclude it.[2]

---

[2] For a more extended consideration of value pluralism and incommensurability, and comparison of that meta-ethical outlook to a monistic view of value, see Macklem 'Choice and Value', 7 *Legal Theory* 1 (2001). For a rival view of incomparability and incommensurability see Ruth Chang's 'Introduction' to her edited collection, *Incommensurability, Incomparability, and Practical Reason* (1997), to which my subsequent article 'Choice and Value' responds, as well as her *Making Comparisons Count* (2002).

14. Very often an assessment of the options before us, even at its most penetrating and detailed, enables us to determine the value or disvalue of each option, or more precisely the various values and disvalues present in each option, without thereby enabling us to prefer one option to the other. The reasons that tell in favour of either option do not defeat, or at least do not defeat completely, the reasons that tell in favour of the other. In such cases there remain undefeated reasons to endorse whichever option we choose to neglect, or find ourselves neglecting if the case is one of spontaneity, drift, or compulsion—reasons that continue to assert their claims upon us thereafter, so giving rise to rational practices of second-guessing and regret. It is true that such practices can all too easily threaten our commitment to the decision and thereby undermine the value that would otherwise be derivable from it, but it is only when they do so that they become irrational. Old saws need careful reading: there is very good reason to regret the spilling of milk, albeit that there is seldom good reason to cry over it.

15. In happy moments, both of the incommensurable options before us are attractive, so that the quandary we experience in deciding between them is on the whole a pleasant one, marred only by any angst we may feel in establishing which valuable course to neglect. In such moments we are beset by the richness of value in the world, as an actor might be beset by admirers. We may get too much of this, of course, but if so it is too much of a good thing. In unhappy moments, however, both options before us are unattractive, and we find ourselves as if in a runaway car, racked by the prospect of just what kind of crash we are about to experience, and by the role we might have to play in a failure to prevent that particular crash, and the responsibility we might have to bear for it. That is the stuff of tragedy, large and small.

16. The suggestion that the claims of reason differ in kind as well as in degree is one that many reject on principle. There is a long line of thought to the effect that it is in the nature of reason and evaluation to provide us with an answer to the question of what we ought to do in any particular situation, or at least to be in principle capable of providing us with such an answer. That, the thought goes, is what morality is for. The answer to the question of what to do may be difficult to discern in a particular case—and what is more, many of us are not as morally discerning as we ought to be—but it is in the very nature of morality that there be a decisive answer to every

moral predicament, for otherwise morality would lack the capacity to guide us fully on moral issues, something that cannot (for some) be reconciled with the very idea of morality. There is as long a line of connected although not entailed thought that moral responsibility turns on the quality of the decision that one makes in such a situation. One either lives up to the demands of morality or one does not, and it is in the choosing of the course that morality calls upon us to choose, and in the choosing alone that moral achievement lies. We do good and so live well if and to the extent that we consciously commit ourselves to the course that morality calls upon us to pursue.

17. And yet this analysis is counter-intuitive to the extent that it treats choice as significant only because and to the extent that it is liable to be less than fully rational. The thought to the opposite effect is that choice is all the more significant when it is fully in accordance with reason, yet not fully determined by reason. When we consider how to spend our light, as so many of us (at least in the contemporary Western world) spend so much time considering—particularly in the early stages of our adult lives—the various options that we consider, the outlines of which we seek to trace and develop in our mind's eye, are in most cases all more or less rationally sound. Should one become a musician or a gardener, a builder or a mechanic? Should one use one's leisure time in appreciation of aesthetic value, in the arts and elsewhere (reading novels, visiting galleries, going to the local cinema), in immersion in sybaritic pleasures (an autumn walk in the park; dinner at a local restaurant, perhaps), or in physical challenge (distance running or walking, rock-climbing)? All these are good ways to spend a life, but the goodness that they offer is goodness that on the face of it varies greatly in kind, and that if realized will yield lives the quality of whose goodness, and the significance of whose narratives, will similarly differ. Surely that is at least an important aspect, if not the only aspect, of what can make the choice among them so difficult? Can it be the case that these apparently intractable differences of value are but a mask for a common value that underpins them and to which they can all ultimately be reduced, a value that we are so often unable to perceive? Are our difficulties in seeing through this alleged mask any more consistent with the plausible notion that morality is guiding than with the idea that the differences in question are in fact real rather than a mask?

18. As I have already suggested, there is no conclusive answer to the question of how the predicament of decision should be

explained, whether as characterized by the challenge of quantifying the value of the options before one, or as characterized by the existential burden of a decision on which a great deal may turn but on which moral guidance is incomplete. One's views on the issue seem to be connected to deep-seated features of one's moral outlook, so deep-seated that it is difficult to establish the sort of distance from them that would enable one to conclude with confidence that they represent moral reality or moral error. The question is made the more difficult by the fact that our grasp of the nature and content of morality might be expected to be relatively sure at the level of application in daily living (*pace* grand theory), but is nothing that one can be confident of at the levels of abstraction at which this debate takes place, where there is little testing of convictions against the deeply considered experience of moral life, in the Aristotelian manner.

19. For those who believe that all values can in the end be reduced to one (whatever that might be), the problem of decision is ultimately one of perception, analysis, or calculation. Whether we are deciding as individual people or as groupings of people, one course of action is always to be preferred to another, other than in cases when both are equal. Any inclination to act otherwise must be predicated on moral error, and is to be remedied by education, or by enforcement, or by some mixture of the two. There can be no good reason to dissent from what one ought to do. However, for those who believe that values differ in kind as well as in degree, there is very often reason to dissent from what one ought to do, namely—the reason to pursue a value of a different kind, or, more precisely, the reason to pursue a course of action that embodies or is likely to yield values and disvalues that are in key respects values of a different kind from those that are embodied in the alternative course of action. It can be the case that one ought to do more than one thing in any given setting. If and to the extent that that is so, there is a problem of action, of how to arrive at a decision when reason runs out—a problem for individuals and a problem for communities, or, more precisely, a problem for both, just because it is a problem stemming from the nature of value. The present project is predicated on this latter view. The problems it seeks to explore arise only if one believes that there can be good reason to do two things and no good reason to prefer one to the other overall. If one does not believe in the existence of that problem, or is not interested in its possibility, or in some ramifications of that

possibility, there is perhaps no very compelling reason to pursue the line of argument here.

20. Suppose, however, that one accepts the value pluralist premise, or at least is piqued by it. To return to the landscape of decision and the absence from it of the resources necessary for complete determination, something more is needed to enable one to proceed. Assume for the moment that the moral universe is such that we are confronted by reasons for several different actions, each of which is no less rationally compelling than the others. In order to proceed, by one action rather than another, or by action rather than inaction or vice versa, we must call upon not only reason but imagination and will. We must call upon imagination, in conjunction with reason, to envision the possibilities for rational action—some known, some yet to be invented—in the circumstances that confront us. We must call upon imagination further, again in conjunction with reason, in order to contemplate the ways in which each of those possibilities might be played out, the narrative power of our imagination lending greater rational weight to one possibility than to another as the course of the possibility is articulated—or, more precisely, appearing to lend such weight, even as that power informs and gives life to the possibility, whether before the decision or (as Finnis has emphasized) after it. We show too little imagination in our actions and inactions when our decisions are no more than conformist, or when we fail even to see the possibility of decision and so continue in what we are doing for lack of the capacity, the quality of vision, to contemplate any alternative.[3] We show too much imagination in our actions and inactions (or, more precisely, too little discipline of our imagination) when we allow ourselves to be continually assailed by all the implications of the possibilities we have neglected, continually second-guess ourselves as a result, and so find it difficult to let any of our decisions stand in the face of our acute awareness of their all-too-sound alternatives.[4]

---

[3] Thanks to Gail Thorson for the latter point.

[4] I say 'in our actions and inactions' in order to recognize and make room for the presence or absence of imagination in domains other than that of practical reasoning. These remarks further assume that the exercise of imagination is rationally sound. In practice, of course, like the exercise of will described in the following paragraph, the exercise of imagination is all too often rationally flawed, as when, for example, we allow ourselves to be beguiled by its visionary power and so neglect certain of the rational tensions, contradictions, and qualifications that actually confront us, in favour of the compelling attractions of unity, clarity, and coherence that narrative vision typically has

21. Yet even when we get imagination right we do no more than develop possibilities for action and their implications, only some of which are discountable upon rational reflection. Once again something more is needed if we are to proceed in any way at all, the most obvious being the exercise of will. We must call upon will (and the attendant virtue of courage) in order to legislate a path of action, both in awareness of the price of that path (in terms of the possibilities that it forecloses) and in awareness of its lack of rational pre-eminence, be the path the one sketched out by imagination or some other, be it one that is rationally required or rationally forbidden. We show too little will when we vacillate, either in the face of incommensurable reasons or in the face of a host of imaginative possibilities. We show too much will when we value decision over reason and so decide merely for the sake of deciding, act merely for the sake of acting.

22. Certain aspects of the record of these exercises of reason, imagination, and will come to be formally inscribed upon our rational personalities in the shape of conscience. In effect, we codify in our conscience certain of the commitments that we have made (or commit ourselves to making in the future) by reference to reason, imagination, and will, sometimes so as to archive conclusions in order to save the effort of arriving at them many times over, sometimes as a way of developing a rational personality that can offer us distinctive personal guidance in the face of the many, often troubling, alternatives for action that confront us.[5] But conscience is a special implication of reason, imagination and will. It is self-conscious, self-defining, usually self-idealizing (hence its connection to vanity), and relatively stable over time. Ordinary cases of action, by contrast, may involve all of these things but require none of them. Ordinary action can be unconscious, unreflective, non-idealizing, and restless. What is more, there is no algorithm governing the respective roles of reason, imagination, and will in the articulation and undertaking of any action in particular. Even when we act in accordance with reason (as malfunctions of reason, imagination, and will may sometimes

---

to offer, just because and to the extent that it is less than fully answerable to the demands of reality. That possibility is what makes narrative vision a potential source of both value and confusion, what makes it both good and not good to imagine and to dream. For further consideration of the rational and arational aspects of imagination, see Chapter 4, paras 60–4; on arationality see Chapter 5 para 116 and note 9.

[5] See further 'Conscience and Commitment', in my *Independence of Mind* (2006).

prevent us from doing), the extent to which we are committed to action by imagination and by will respectively varies from decision to decision.

23. The role played by imagination and will—being a function of the rational landscape, and so applicable to all reasoning creatures—remains present yet gains new form in the setting of a life in common, a setting such as the law seeks to describe,[6] in adapting to the distinctive demands and possibilities of collective activity. The role played in that setting by imagination and will has been noticed in a number of accounts of law, but the noticing has been indirect and its significance not fully developed as a result. The reason for this stems from two vulnerabilities and one possibility faced by accounts of collective action that focus primarily or exclusively upon any one of the elements of decision, namely, reason, imagination, or will. The possibility, of course, is that the account in question is accurate albeit incomplete, in the manner of Raz's reconciliation of law and rationality. There is nothing objectionable about such incompleteness in an account; on the contrary, it can be the product of focus in the development and articulation of the account and the source of consequent insight. The vulnerabilities that I referred to are objectionable, therefore, not by reason of incompleteness in the accounts that exhibit them, but by the conflation in those accounts of the separate phenomena of reason, imagination, and will, or by a misdescription of the significance of any one of those phenomena, such as will, in an account that otherwise respects their separateness. It is vulnerabilities of these kinds to which the leading accounts of collective action in terms of will or imagination have (as it happens and as I will seek to explain) succumbed.

---

[6] Describe as in describing a circle, not as in depicting.

3

The Exaltation of the Will

24. Certain accounts of law, most prominently those that label themselves critical, draw attention to what they take to be the crucial role played by the will in law's construction of a life in common. The point made here may find its contemporary home in critical theory but it is not by its nature critical, for the legacy it draws upon reaches back to Austin, who intended no criticism of what he took to be the place of force in the law. Some accounts present the point in terms of will, as I have, others in terms of force, or compulsion, or coercion, but the basic insight is the same.[1] Many have condemned such accounts as fundamental misunderstandings of law. The condemnations are sound, as I have said, when they draw attention to

---

[1] On the face of it, this seems rather too quick an assimilation, for it is surely perfectly plain that will and coercion cannot be straight-forwardly identified with one another. Critical legal scholars are not necessarily Austinians, nor Austinians critical legal scholars. Given that fact, if I am to maintain that as far as my purposes are concerned the basic insight underlying the two perspectives is the same, I need to offer some degree of explanation and qualification. After all, recourse to force, compulsion, or coercion is something that is (or at least can be) called for by reason and responded to for reason. What is more, not only are those three phenomena not animated by will alone; they cannot be responded to by will alone. In conflating them in the present setting, therefore, what I am seeking to clarify and draw attention to is the fact that the reasons that inspire recourse to coercion at least include (and may be confined to) the fact that the reasons embodied in the balance of the law in question (its substance) are not (or cannot be counted on to be) fully rationally determinative of the beliefs and actions of the law's addressees, and that as a consequence the reasons appealed to in and through the use of coercion are correspondingly prudential rather than moral. It is in this sense that the basic insight can be said to be the same: recourse to will is necessary, and is typically (here meaning rationally) had, because response to the law in question *qua* act of will, rather than or in addition to response to the substance of what it calls for, is in those settings necessary to the achievement of a life in common.

tendencies to conflate reason, imagination, and will and present the result as will, or, when that error is avoided, to misdescribe the significance of will (or force, or compulsion, or coercion). But the condemnations are wide of the mark when they dismiss accounts of will altogether, as having to do with the efficaciousness of law rather than its practical rationality, for example. Will plays as vital a role in collective action as it does in individual action, but with one crucial difference—namely, that there is no such thing as a collective will. It follows that the operation of will in the setting of life in common has no straight-forward parallel in the setting of the life of any one person. It follows further that the operation of will in such a setting is often indirect, obscure, and so apt to be labelled covert, particularly so when that operation is ignored or denied, as it has been in many accounts of law.

25. Broadly speaking, there are two stages to the role of the will in the articulation of a life in common. The first stage, temporally and analytically, is the act of will needed to determine the contours of a possible collective course of action. The second stage is the act of will needed to endorse that course of action by conforming to its requirements. In the setting of the law, the first act of will is that of the legislator, be that one person or many. If and to the extent that legislation is enacted by a body of people, such as a parliament or other legislature, and so is itself an instance of collective action, then the problems sketched below and the resolutions offered there will be mirrored in the legislative setting and indeed in any case of collective action that lies behind that setting and the collective action that takes place there. Assume for the moment, so as to preserve a focus on the operation of the law in describing and shaping a life in common, either that the legislator is one person or that the problem of collective action has been resolved in the legislative setting by reference to the principles identified below; further, postpone, for later consideration, the question of the role played by the legislator's will in establishing the content of law. In the setting of the application of law, the second stage of will, if left entirely to the exercise of reason, will, and imagination on the part of each person to whom the law in question is applicable, would in virtually every case fail to yield a life in common, even if there were no failure in the exercise of reason, will, and imagination by any person subject to the law. While there may be good reason to conform to the law's requirements there is typically no less good reason not to do so, as Raz has allowed,

even when the normal justification of authority has been met. The reasons not to conform to the law include not only those reasons to engage in other, incompatible forms of action, but also reasons of autonomy (the reasons to think for oneself rather than let the law do one's thinking for one) and indeed of non-conformity (the reasons to think in a way that differs from the thinking of the crowd). That being the case, the content of the law typically requires enforcement (subject to what I will say about imagination further on) if and to the extent that the law hopes to establish a life in common.

26. Of course, not all laws seek to describe and shape a life in common, and so not all laws require enforcement. Particularly in a liberal society, law may not only tolerate but actually encourage a diversity of responses to its provisions. As Hart emphasized, a great many laws (such as those governing contracts or wills) are designed precisely so that those who are subject to them may opt into their provisions or not as they please. Commonality (with respect to form or process, perhaps) is only a subsidiary part of the purpose of laws like these. In relation to that subsidiary part, enforcement may well be required (as contemporary defenders of Austin's account have pointed out); otherwise it is not. It follows that enforcement is far from a necessary condition of the existence of a law, though it is something close to a necessary feature of a legal system.

27. What is more striking, perhaps, is that enforcement is not a sufficient condition for the establishment of a life in common through law, because—unlike law itself—force can only supplement our reasons for action. Force is not in itself a pre-emptive reason, although it is frequently thought of as such. That thought is persuasive only because and to the extent that there is a human psychological tendency to treat the prudential as prior to the moral. In practice, the psychological tendency is far from universal, and its rational basis is deeply contested. There seem to be far better explanations available of our reasons to particularize responsibility and attachment than the divide between the prudential and the moral. That being the case, the impact of enforcement upon conformity to the law is patchy even among those who are properly rationally attentive both to the content of the law and to the significance of coercion. What is more, a law that is complied with merely in order to avoid the coercion that would follow from non-compliance is complied with for instrumental reasons: conformity to the requirements of the law in such cases is no more than a means to the end of avoiding the

penalty for non-conformity. Put another way, coercion can secure personal compliance but it cannot secure personal commitment (as Locke emphasized in the context of religion). This matters if and when it is commitment rather than compliance that is necessary to the achievement of a life in common, as is often the case. It follows that the role played by force is only a necessary condition for the establishment of a life in common if and when force operates hand in hand with something more—that something more, I would suggest, being the role played by imagination, as described further on. Indeed, in many cases imagination will do all that is required to secure commitment, so rendering force superfluous.

28. There are at least two well-recognized objections to claims that force is in any degree a necessary feature of a legal system. The first objection is that force is a matter of a legal system's efficaciousness, not of its existence. The objection is sound, but misses the point. It assumes that efficaciousness is a function of irrationality, as indeed it is, and in doing so overlooks the fact that efficaciousness is also a function of rationality where a life in common falls to be constructed in circumstances of moral diversity. Something about the law must lend rational priority, or the appearance of that priority, to the course of action it describes. Otherwise the reasons for conforming to the law will have no greater claim upon the addressees of law than the many no less good reasons for not conforming, and the prospects for a life in common (that is, the chances of its arising) will be no greater than the prospects for lives apart. Indeed, in such a case the reasons for conforming to the law may have a rather weaker claim than their rivals upon the addressees of law, perhaps no claim at all, for whenever law seeks to construct a life in common its content, to the extent that it is driven by the goal of creating a life in common, is a practical reason for one person just to the extent that it is a practical reason for others, which is only the case when it is capable of functioning effectively as such.[2]

29. The second objection to claims that force is in any sense a necessary feature of a legal system is that force is rendered superfluous by the rationality of the particular resolution of the problems of moral diversity and lack of specificity that is determined by and declared in law. It will be clear that this objection merges with the

---

[2] For a much more detailed and nuanced explanation of this problem, see the discussion in Chapter 5 entitled 'Different Laws as Different Catalysts for a Life in Common'.

first. Underlying both is the assumption that reason is determinative of action, individual or collective. In fact, as I have emphasized, there are typically good reasons to do other than what the law requires, among them the reason to do other just because it is not what the law requires (though of course how widespread they are varies). That being the case, the rational appeal of the law is not enough to secure a life in common. Under certain circumstances and to a limited degree, force can augment the rational appeal of what the law calls for (or can appear to do so) and so can augment the prospects for the establishment of a life in common through the operation of law. A failure to acknowledge this on the part of those with legal authority would either lead to a withering of life in common (for failure to sustain the law's requirements with appropriate enforcement) or render its achievement through the operation of force, incomplete though that would almost certainly be, fortuitous or covert.

30. On the other hand, accounts of law that emphasize the place of force in a legal system all too often fall prey to one or another of the vulnerabilities described above. To conflate reason, will, and imagination in an account of force, or to exalt the role played by will at the expense of its companions in action, is to betray the crucial roles played by reason and imagination in shaping a life in common, and so to regard force as a warrant of goodness, as a sufficient condition of a life in common, or both. In the hands of those in authority the error converts wise leadership into the worst tyranny; in the hands of commentators it converts the analysis of reason, its proper force and limits, into the analysis of unreason (often by treating prudential reasons as pre-emptive).

31. The analytic aspect of this point can be illustrated by considering the practice of tyranny. Tyrannies are paradigmatic instances of government by the operation of will, both in securing the contours of a possible collective course of action (in the form of the tyrant's demand, about which more later) and in securing a high degree of conformity to that demand (by a draconian approach to enforcement). Yet it would be a mistake to think that exposure of those facts tells us nearly enough about tyranny or its proper replacement. In its details at least, tyrannical rule may well be consistent with reason, for what it calls for may in that detailed respect be good and, what is more, tyranny may be crucial to the realization of that good, though in both cases the good is unlikely to be worth the price of tyranny. Sometimes the tyrant reasons as well as wills (and so is a

benevolent despot); sometimes the tyrant's will alone is sufficient, even necessary to the securing of a good. More interestingly perhaps, tyranny very often calls upon imagination in the securing of its ends, simply because there is very often good reason to be imprudent in the face of force, even tyrannical force, given that force is not a pre-emptive reason. This helps to explain why tyrannies are often endorsed by their subjects and depend on that endorsement for their survival. To notice only the place of the will (and force) in tyranny (and other forms of governance), whether it be to praise or condemn that fact, is to neglect all these things, and so to misunderstand much of the workings of tyranny and much of the underpinnings of a life in common.

32. Many contemporary accounts of law, however, particularly those that label themselves critical, are less interested in the second stage of the will (that of conformity to law) than in the first (that of determining the contours of a possible collective course of action). Such accounts are concerned to expose (as they might put it) the role played by the will of the judiciary in establishing the law, by exposing the degree to which legal judgments are not logically derivable from the premises that judges officially take notice of. As I see it, there is ultimately a good deal to be learned from projects of this kind, not least because and to the extent that they succeed in illuminating the importance of the will in rational decision-making, and in consequence the markedly incomplete character of a number of accounts of law put forward in the 50 and more years since Hart, in *The Concept of Law*, so effectively demolished the long-standing picture offered by Austin. Too little may have been said about the place of the will in establishing the content of law, and the self-conscious radicalism of these critiques has helped to expose that neglect and so to lay the foundations for a fuller, more rounded understanding of law.

33. There is a real difficulty, however, in extracting sound insights about the will and its place in the law from these radical critiques of certain conventional analyses of judicial action. First, critics of this radical kind are not concerned with the problem of a life in common as such, and hence do not pursue the question of the relative roles of reason, will, and imagination in its construction. Rather, they are concerned to expose the role played by the will in judicial decision-making in response to analyses that are allegedly silent about that role, whether out of neglect or deliberate

concealment. That being the case, their consideration of the significance of the will is incomplete at best, distorted at worst, simply because it makes little or no attempt to identify or allow for a legitimate role for the will (as distinct from reason and imagination) in the shaping of a life in common. Second, their primary concern is with exposure and criticism of the political vision that is said to inform the exercises of the will that they identify. That means that their insights into the role of the will are very often entangled with their politics, to the confusion of both. Retrieval of genuine insight here consequently requires a careful unpicking of the elements of the tangle, through appreciation of the aims of the radical critique, appraisal of the extent to which it is successful in finding its targets, and assessment of the extent to which its by-products are sound and unsound.

34. The radical critique raises an immediate puzzle, having to do with the views of law that it sets out to challenge: just what are those views, who exactly holds them, and to what extent are they in fact vulnerable to critique of this kind? How plausible is it to propose that the dominant accounts of law in the years since the publication of *The Concept of Law* are as blinkered as much of the radical project makes them out to be? How could as important an element in the understanding of law as the role of the will have come to be overlooked by so many able scholars? And if that neglect has indeed been real, is it profound? One possible explanation might be this. For certain readers of Hart, rightly persuaded by him that law could not be understood as the command of a sovereign backed by the threat of a sanction, it may have been easy to overlook the extent to which Austin was right and Hart agreed that he was. In particular, Austin was right to believe that the will, in its various manifestations, plays a vital role in constituting law (and thus a life in common where that is dependent on law), most obviously in helping to secure compliance with the requirements of law (as is explicit in his reference to the threat of a sanction)—something that Hart himself readily accepted in his analysis of duty-imposing rules and their enforcement[3]—but also in helping to determine the content of law (as might be said to be implicit, at least in part, in his idea of a command), something that Hart just as readily accepted in all those cases, involving vehicles

---

[3] Hart was of course careful to distinguish between the existence of a legal duty and the need for its enforcement.

in a park perhaps, where a judge is bound to make new law or, as Hart somewhat unfortunately put it, to legislate.

35. The common ground between Austin and Hart having been overlooked in this way, it might have been natural for those who immediately followed Hart to focus on the vulnerabilities of Hart's own contributions to the analysis of law (or to endorse their strengths) and in doing so to neglect the role of the will that he had inherited from Austin.[4] Yet that neglect (or so the explanation might run) came to be the legitimate focus of radical critique. For those who noticed with distaste the extent to which law is called upon to buttress, extend, and even invent schemes of privilege, and who further noticed that the role played by the will of the privileged in establishing the law, and thereby in establishing schemes of privilege, was ignored by certain accounts of law, there was good reason to attack that omission, and further to suspect that there was something more than neglect involved in an omission that was not only glaring but in many ways self-serving. Yet even on that analysis, the radical critique—understandable, even admirable as it may have been in these respects—itself fell into a comparable omission, by failing to take proper notice of the extent to which rather more than will is at stake in the constitution of law, and what is more, the extent to which the accounts that it criticized in fact (and quite rightly) accommodated the will, either explicitly or implicitly.

36. It is not easy to trace the genealogy of a confusion accurately without succumbing to confusion oneself. It may in fact be that critical scholars simply failed to see past their immediate target, most obviously the account offered by Dworkin, and so failed to see that the critique they deployed had little purchase against those who merely downplayed rather than denied the role of the will in constituting law (not including Hart himself, of course).[5] If that less charitable explanation is correct, then the radical critique is itself blinkered, and the scale of its challenge to conventional understandings of law much exaggerated. Yet however the radical view may have been arrived at, whatever intellectual and political currents may have brought it into being, what matters to the understanding

---

[4] Apart, of course, from those scholars who sought to defend Austin's account against Hart's objections, and those, like Dworkin, who recognized the place of the will in Hart's account and challenged the account on that ground.

[5] This might perhaps be said of the critical aspect of the argument offered by Roberto Mangabeira Unger in *The Critical Legal Studies Movement* (1986).

of law rather than the history of ideas is that a positivist account of law, namely one that treats decision rather than merit as essential to the existence of law, is not touched by a critique that is concerned to expose the role of the will in the constitution of law. Positivists may have neglected to say so, in some cases at least, but they are committed by their very positivism to the idea that the law, as an artefact of decision, is necessarily willed, by reason of the plurality of the good and the possibility of the bad. As much is true of the work of a scholar such as Finnis, who would disavow the label 'positivist' yet is at pains to identify the significance of human determination, through law, in helping to mitigate the moral challenges that pluralism and abstraction pose for the conduct of a practically reasonable life, even in a community of saints. Nor, it must be said, does the emphasis on decision and the will, in and of itself, obtain much purchase against even the account offered by Dworkin, other than as an assertion of value pluralism. Yet there is surely a good deal more to worry about in Dworkin's account than its denial of value pluralism, and a good deal more to understand about law than the role played in it by the will; the radical critique neglects both that worry and those dimensions of understanding, and so fails to commend itself not only to all those who are unconvinced by value pluralism but also to those pluralists who have reason to doubt the Dworkinian account on more than pluralist grounds.

37. What the radical critique does successfully, however, and what is much to be welcomed, is to emphasize the role played by the will in connecting reasons to action, whether the action be that of deciding upon a rule, so as to determine one of the contours of a possible life in common, or that of deciding to conform to what a rule requires, so as to play one's part in the description of a particular instance of a life in common. The problem with the critique, therefore, lies merely in the limits of its ambitions, for to make this much clear and no more is at best to fall short of what a full understanding of the law requires, at worst to betray that understanding by suppressing the roles played in action by reason and by imagination. To show that the will is present in judicial action is not to show that only will is present there: that would be true only if nothing but the will could possibly be present there. Yet to believe that the will is all that could be present there is to embrace deep scepticism about the possibility of rational action, a position that as quintessentially radical a critic as Unger is careful to reject.

In fact we know full well that reason and imagination are typically exercised in judicial decision-making, as the radical critique itself accepts in criticizing bad reasons and class-bound imagination. Of course, it is entirely possible for any given judicial decision to be based on will alone, when neither deliberation nor imagination are present there—as is undoubtedly sometimes, perhaps often, the case. The question then arises whether such a decision can be objected to on that ground.

38. In truth, to show that nothing other than will is responsible for a decision is not in itself to show that the decision is objectionable. Decisions that are based on will alone are not necessarily bad. On the contrary, some outcomes are preferable to their alternative just because and to the extent that they have been willed. It is important to recognize this, because many valuable outcomes are dependent for their determination on the exercise of will alone. We stop at red lights and go on green ones, rather than the opposite, simply because that particular scheme of signalling has been willed, and it is the willing and the willing alone that makes that scheme preferable to its most straight-forward alternative, that of stopping at green and going on red. Other outcomes that are preferable to their alternative for reasons other than their willed character may be stumbled upon by will alone and may be the better for having been arrived at by that means, spontaneously, without reflection, as Bernard Williams' famous example of choice in rescue shows.[6] This is true in all cases where a critical portion of the value of a rule is established by a practice that grows up in response to the rule, without having been in the contemplation of the rule-maker, simply because the practice did not yet exist to be contemplated in advance of the formulation of the rule that the practice arose in response to. Nor, finally, to address the common critical political point, is even a conjunction between a willed decision and self-interest in itself objectionable, for self-interest and goodness may well coincide: sometimes the rich are right to think that taxes ought to be lowered, even when they are led to that conclusion by their self-interest; sometimes the recipients of government benefits that are dependent upon strong tax revenues are right to think that taxes ought to be raised. It is only when a decision or an action has multiple moral meanings that the goodness or

---

[6] Bernard Williams, 'Persons, Character and Morality' in *Moral Luck* (1981), 1 at 17–18.

badness of its motivation is potentially determinative of its goodness or badness overall.[7]

39. It is in the end a fatal ambiguity in analysis and ambition that lends many critical accounts the paradoxical character of insisting that the law as we know it is as decisive as Austin took it to be and yet ought to be as self-determining as Dworkin maintains that it is (when the critique is animated by an ideal of justice) or as Unger suggests (when animated by an ideal of instability). But why should justice or instability be regarded as prior to other values, and why, that possibility granted, should the assumption of that priority not itself be vulnerable to the radical critique?

---

[7] The motivation for a decision may of course be relevant to an evaluation of the moral character of the decision-maker.

4

The Genius of the Place

40. The account of law that comes closest to capturing the role played by imagination in the establishment of a life in common for a particular set of people is that offered by Dworkin. The account is complex and its rendering has shifted over time, but what is crucial to all its variants is the view that law is to be identified (paradigmatically by the courts) by asking, first, which one or more of the possible principles that would provide a resolution to an issue of law could be said to fit the legal and political culture of the jurisdiction, and second, which of the principles that satisfies the foregoing test of fit makes the legal and political culture of that jurisdiction the best that it can be.[1] Among the many issues raised by this account is that of the significance of judicial decision and its output. Clearly a decision has no immediate role to play in the creation of law: it is no more than the court's report of the court's assessment of the present state of legal principle in its jurisdiction. It is not law in and of itself. That being the case, one is bound to ask what significance ought to be attached to the content of that decision, that is to say, to the report of the court's beliefs.

41. The most obvious and perhaps most tempting answer is that the court's judgment merely constitutes an element of the pre-interpretive data that will be drawn upon by subsequent courts in asking themselves the two questions Dworkin identifies: data

---

[1] Dworkin's picture of law was initially set out in *Taking Rights Seriously* (1978), particularly in 'The Model of Rules I' and 'Hard Cases'; received its fullest treatment in *Law's Empire* (1986); and has been most recently revisited in 'Thirty Years On' 115 *Harvard LR* 1655 (2002).

that will enable those subsequent courts to report their beliefs on the then current state of legal principle in that jurisdiction, reports that will in turn constitute the pre-interpretive data upon which yet subsequent courts will draw, and so on. The obvious worry with this answer is that at no point in the process would we have reason to believe that we had discovered the law, and so at no point would we be in a position to be guided by that reason. A Dworkinian response to that worry would presumably be two-fold. The internal, exegetical response would be that the content of legal judgments is neither a necessary nor a sufficient condition for the identification of the pre-interpretive data upon which subsequent courts are to draw. On the one hand, according to Dworkin's account, in arriving at a judgment courts are entitled to treat as pre-interpretive data many different aspects of a social and political culture, and so are not in any sense expected to regard themselves as confined to the consideration of legal judgments. On the other hand, many legal judgments are not entitled to be treated as aspects of the pre-interpretive data because, as in the case of *Plessy v Ferguson*, they have singularly failed to report the state of the law correctly. More interestingly and more tellingly perhaps, it could be said on behalf of the Dworkinian account that all moral judgment is as provisional as that described by Dworkin. In seeking to act morally a person can do no more than exercise his or her moral judgment and then act on the conclusions of that judgment, in full awareness of the frailties to which it is subject and the consequent revision of it that may be called for in light of further experience and reflection. There is no other option. It is not possible to apprehend morality directly without the intercession of one's own judgment and belief (conscious or unconscious). In this regard Dworkin's account does no more than track well-recognized features of the landscape of reason and action, simply extending the features of one life to that of many. Judgments are no less significant, no less available to be relied upon, simply because they are provisional and so subject to revision.

42. Yet there is a flaw in this line of thinking (whether the thinking is Dworkin's or not) that stems from its equation of the judgment of one person with that of many, or more precisely with that made in the name of many. Personal moral judgment, at least when consciously arrived at, presents no difficulties of identification. Simply to make the judgment is to establish its content.

(Unconscious judgments, of course, are another matter, for they, as distinct from their consequences, may be identifiable only with the aid of psychoanalysis.) Not so with a moral judgment that is made in the name of a community, for a community no more has a mind capable of judgment (conscious or unconscious) than it has a will. If the conclusion reached by a court (assumed here, as before, to be either one person or a group of people in regard to whom the problems of collective judgment have been resolved) is to have a status any different from the conclusion reached by any other person considering the same issues, as it must if it is to establish any aspect of a life in common, the addressees of law must be entitled to regard the decision as an accurate report of the present state of the law, law being understood as Dworkin would have it. In that lies the authority of the decision. Were it otherwise, the decision would have no particular status, no claim upon the community it is expected to govern. The problem here is not one of moral diversity (for that is denied by the Dworkinian account and bracketed for the purposes of this analysis) but of moral error. Judicial decision must stand for something or we would have no reason to pay any attention to it. If that something is the embodiment of the moral wisdom and analytic talent that Dworkin attributes to the judge whom he calls Hercules, then the judgment's claim upon us is that of superior moral, legal, and socio-cultural intelligence.

43. To accord legal judgments a status of this kind, however, is to accord a significance to decision that brings the Dworkinian account very close to that offered by legal positivists. Ontological uncertainty having been ruled out, there is only epistemological uncertainty between a body of people, such as the inhabitants of a legal jurisdiction, and their individual apprehension of the content of law as Dworkin describes it. If those people are entitled to treat that uncertainty as having been provisionally resolved by the decision of a court, as they must if the decision is to play any part in establishing a life in common, then they must treat the decision of the court as authoritative in the Razian sense, as pre-empting their own consideration of the merits of the case and the principle or principles at stake in it. Were it otherwise the decision would lack any communal significance, any imaginative resonance, for those whom it is supposed to serve. And of course if ontological uncertainty is not in fact ruled out and moral pluralism is put back into the mix, as many believe that moral realism requires it be, then the

Dworkinian position becomes indistinguishable from that offered by legal positivists.[2]

44. A defender of the Dworkinian account might possibly seek to address these objections by embracing the abyss—that is, by developing and radically extending Dworkin's initial parry to the claim that there must be something for law to decide. Law's authority, it might be said, cannot be a matter of decision because there is in fact nothing at all for courts to decide, either ontologically or epistemologically. The opinions expressed by courts and embodied in their judgments have no greater status than the opinions of those to whom law is addressed, though admittedly people often act as if it were otherwise. The opinions of courts may be more likely to be sound than the opinions of the rest of us, as it so happens, but we owe them no deference by reason of that fact, even *prima facie*. On the contrary, it is part of the civic duty of those who are subject to law, directly or indirectly, to determine its content for themselves and so to consider critically, even sceptically, the claim of any court or commentator to have identified that content correctly on their behalf. Only thus can the subjects of law maintain their autonomy, indeed their rationality. It might be further pointed out that nothing less is demanded of them by the Razian account, which expects the subjects of law to determine for themselves whether the authority that law claims for its requirements is in fact justified.

45. All this is true enough, up to a point only. What it neglects is that an abandonment of the claim to epistemological authority cannot be reconciled with either the central tenets of Dworkin's account or the necessary ambitions of any account of law and legal system. What it overlooks is that the superficially similar assessment called for in the Razian account is fully compatible with the recognition of the authority of law, ontologically and epistemologically, as the assessment described above is not. There are at least three flaws in this kind of last-ditch reading of Dworkin's account. First, as noted above, it is implausible to think that a legal system could conceivably lack the ambition to shape and direct the conduct of those to

---

[2] At which point the decision of courts must again be treated as authoritative, either in the Razian sense, of creating exclusionary second-order reasons that pre-empt the consideration of the relevant first-order reasons by inhabitants of the jurisdiction, or in the sense Stephen Perry has proposed, of zero-weighting those first-order reasons. See Perry, 'Second-Order Reasons, Uncertainty and Legal Theory', 62 *Southern California LR* 913 (1989), and Raz, 'Facing Up: A Reply', 62 *Southern California LR* 1153 (1989).

whom its laws are addressed, that courts could be content to express judgments as to the state of the law without claiming any authoritative status for those judgments. It is entirely true that in the Razian account the addressees of law are expected to question the authority of law, as part of their autonomy and rationality, but what they are expected to question is the law's claim to pre-emptive status and not, other than consequently, the substance of what it calls upon them to do. Questioning of the former kind is compatible with recognition of law's authority because it is compatible, in part at least, with allowing the law to think for one rather than thinking for oneself, so allowing the addressees of law to reap the benefit of reliance on the thought of others, as embodied in law, when and where that benefit exists.[3] By contrast, direct questioning in each case of the substance of what the law calls upon one to do is incompatible with the justification of the law's authority, and hence of its practical existence in the rational landscape of a life in common.

46. Second, this reading of the Dworkinian account would render the application of force by those in authority unjustifiable, contrary to Dworkin's claim that the fundamental obligation of any legal system, and by extension of any sound explanation of a legal system, is the justification of its use of force. Enforcement of the law would be unjustifiable because in the absence of any authoritative status for the pronouncements of legislatures and courts, there would be no acknowledged legal record in terms of which force could possibly be justified; the familiar enforcement of law by those in authority (the police and other officials) would be nothing more than the unwarranted enforcement of one person's reading of the law (that of a judge, say) against another reading that was no less valid, or at least that was bound to be treated as such.

47. Third, and most damagingly, this reading would violate the central ambition of the Dworkinian account, which is to explain law as the best possible interpretation of sound government of a particular social and political culture. The law as identified by its manifold interpreters could not satisfy the requirement of either fit or justification (for there would be no legal record in the jurisdiction to fit or justify), and so would be incapable of describing or yielding a life in common, just because it would be incapable of identifying common

---

[3] For further consideration of this superficially paradoxical feature of Raz's account, see Chapter 5, The Service Law May Offer to Life in Common.

principles of governance. Collective moral life, in the form of law, would be as fragmented and disparate as an assemblage of the various individual moral judgments of those who would be regarded, on any other analysis, as the addressees of law. Once again, the problem is not one of moral pluralism, which has been bracketed for these purposes, but of moral error. Where decisions have authority, epistemologically at least, they are capable of yielding government, however misguided, however wicked that government may be. Where decisions have no epistemological authority, and yet are vulnerable to errors of many kinds and thus open to multiple renderings, there is no possibility of government in terms of them and hence no possibility of a life in common, at least to the extent that a life in common depends on law.[4]

48. And yet, sound as I take these criticisms to be in themselves, it seems to me that they perhaps miss what may be the deeper point and function of Dworkin's account (even if Dworkin himself would not have recognized or endorsed it), which, it might be said, has to do with capturing, vivifying, and projecting for a particular culture the kind of rational beguilement that begets and constitutes what we take to be collective imagination. As Dworkin himself maintains, his jurisprudence is but a more abstract instance of the account of law it sets out. One way to understand this claim is to see both levels of that account of law as elements in an imaginative exercise, in which the possibilities for rational action confronting a particular people are envisioned and the ways in which those possibilities might be played out are contemplated so as to lend narrative power, and thus the appearance of rational pre-eminence, to a particular course of action that is in fact no more rationally compelling than a number of its rivals. Law as Dworkin understands it is indeed like literature in this regard. Such exercises of imagination have the feature that if and to the extent that one is prepared to believe them they become true by virtue of that belief, or more precisely by the vindication of that belief. Once we commit ourselves, actually or imaginatively, to the course of action that imagination (ours or another's) captures and

---

[4] On the understanding of law offered by legal positivism, namely that the validity of law depends on its sources alone, judicial decision is not similarly vulnerable, because even where its claims to authority are morally unsound what it requires remains law. Of course, decisions as legal positivists understand them are vulnerable to any uncertainties in the rules of recognition and in the substance of what those rules require. Both of these, however, are marginal, and so do not undermine the possibility of law.

vivifies in this way, the fact of our commitment rapidly lends rational force to that course of action, so conferring on the course of action the rational priority it initially only pretended to. Put succinctly, the truth of such imaginative exercises, such as it is, stems from their appeal and its embrace, not the other way round. Once the rational appeal of a course of action has been acknowledged and acted upon, the investment in that course of action, the history it gives rise to, and the commitments it entails lend that course of action rational priority over its rivals, by making it, for a time at least, the most fruitful course to pursue in terms of the realization of value, even though that was not the case when it and rival possibilities for action were originally contemplated. Perhaps, then, the account of law that Dworkin offers can be most fruitfully understood as an invitation to a community to embrace the imaginative priority that it lends to the courses of action that the scheme set out in it purports to identify.

49. There is some cultural basis for regarding Dworkin's account as itself an imaginative enterprise proposing a particular role for law in collective life, quite apart from the imaginative resonance it has had for many audiences. It is surely no accident that the account is not simply a jurisprudence for a particular legal culture but an explicitly American jurisprudence, for the United States has achieved its remarkable supremacy in part at least by a process of beguilement, by convincing people, at home and abroad, that the ways of life that it endorses and embodies are rationally superior to their rivals. There is a good deal to be said for this way of proceeding, given the alternatives, and something also to be said against it, but whatever its merits, the cultural narrative that the United States has proposed and beguiled much of the world with is indisputably the narrative of empire, advancing and embodying assumptions of rational priority, and Dworkin's account can plausibly be seen as charting the role that law might be called upon to play in the imaginative construction of that narrative and that empire—as the title of his best known book makes clear. Critics of empire, of course, emphasize the extent to which such narratives downplay the role of force in the achievement of empire, and critical legal scholars similarly fasten on Dworkin's account as concealing what they take to be the role of force in the articulation of law's empire. Other critics, those who see and take seriously the role played by imagination (in conjunction with will) in the articulation of a particular moral and political vision, might similarly take issue with the priority that the account more or less

silently confers on one prospective legal narrative rather than another. All this lends some plausibility to the idea that Dworkin's account is best interpreted as an imaginative proposal that rational priority be conferred upon the understanding of law that it describes, rather than as an analysis of social practices that discerns that priority.

50. Plainly, however, this is not the way in which the account understands itself. The significance of imagination in practical reasoning, as I have explained it, depends upon the fact of moral pluralism—a fact that Dworkin denies—both in the identification of law (where rival rational courses of action are available to the law-maker) and in the application of law (where those rival courses and others confront the addressees of law). Rather more unfortunately, perhaps, it is not a way in which the account can hope to be successfully understood. There are at least three reasons for this. First, as I have already emphasized, the account lacks the internal resources needed to identify a course of action that could be lent the weight of imaginative possibility, unless it were to be reconstructed so as to give judicial decision a significance that Dworkin would deny it and that would be at odds with the fundamental tenets of his position. Second, the account looks for the raw material of imaginative vision in the wrong place, namely in the record of past action that constitutes what Dworkin describes as pre-interpretive law—a record that is in fact the reflection of past exercises of reason, will, and imagination acting in concert to yield decisions in courts, in legislatures, and in society at large. Such a record could serve as the foundation for a subsequent vision, of course, but it is not itself a vision in the absence of the imaginative act that would make it so. Hercules could choose to make it so in the realm of law (or Dworkin himself in the realm of jurisprudence), but the vision thus generated would gain its shape and character at the hands of the visionary, in the manner observed by legal positivists, and would only then and by that means gain the prospective and purportedly pre-eminent quality that is essential to a political vision that would define and shape a life in common. Third, and most revealingly perhaps, imagination can do no more than play its part in ensuring the endorsement of the requirements of law by the addressees of law. It does nothing to preclude the need for that endorsement. Imagination on the part of a political actor, be that actor a legislator or judge, promotes the requirements of law in the minds of its addressees by lending those requirements a gloss that makes them appear more rationally compelling than they actually

are. It cannot, however, go beyond promotion to make the purchase, so to speak; in itself, it lacks the capacity to secure the compliance that it seeks. Something more is needed.

51. How then is the gap between imagination and action to be bridged, in one life or in many? Start with the individual case. When we are confronted by rival, incompatible courses of action, no one of which is rationally superior to the others, we may proceed by an arbitrary exercise of will, deciding because decision is called for, without pretending to ourselves or to others (except after the fact) that the course of action we have decided upon has any rational priority over its rivals. Alternatively, we may proceed through the exercise of imagination, calling various possibilities into mind and then tracing their prospects in a way that ultimately invests one of them with a narrative power (itself deriving from but not wholly accountable to rational phenomena) that the others lack, so lending the one upon which we have imaginatively fastened the appearance of rational priority.[5] In doing so we bridge, in the very act of imagination, the motivational gap that would otherwise exist between the course of action envisioned by our imagination and action itself, because the rational priority that the imaginative narrative confers (or appears to confer) upon the course of action that it describes is all the warrant that the action needs (*pace* Bernard Williams). Action in such cases, as in all others, follows from the force of reasons without the need for the exercise of will (at least on the part of the virtuous).

52. The transfer of these phenomena to the setting of a life in common alters their shape and the character of their operation. Because there is no such thing as a collective will, the role of force in securing courses of action that describe and shape a life in common is as explained above. There must be at least two initial exercises of will in such cases: the first on the part of those who determine the requirements of law and the second on the part of those who decide to abide by those requirements. If those two exercises are to be aligned with one another by reference to will alone, then a further exercise of will is needed on the part of those who determine the requirements of law, in the form of enforcement of those

---

[5] For further consideration of the ways in which imagination can be exercised in a manner that is essentially rational yet less than fully accountable to reason, and of the political capital that can be made of that fact, see paras 53–4 and 60–4.

requirements, although in many cases even that will not be sufficient to secure compliance. Can that further exercise of will be avoided, or is force fundamental to the operation of a legal system? Is it possible for an act of imagination on the part of one person (the legislator) to generate the resources needed to secure compliance by other people (the addressees of law) with that which the act of imagination demands of them? Because there is no such thing as a collective imagination, the separate minds of the addressees of law cannot go through the imaginative exercise that lends a law the appearance of rational priority, either in concert with one another or with the mind of the legislator. On the face of it, and apart from the question of force, all that is accessible to the addressees of law is the rational appeal of the law and any weight that may be lent to that appeal by the exercise of their own imaginations—an exercise that inevitably leads different minds in different directions and so fails to describe a life in common. Hence the gap between imagination and its implementation in collective life.

53. The answer here is that if and when the rational priority of laws over their rivals has been bestowed upon (or apparently bestowed upon) them by the imagination of those who have decided upon them, and the political vision that such imagination yields, compliance with those laws depends either on enforcement (as previously discussed) or on the skilful presentation of those laws, and the courses of action they describe, as embodiments of political vision and imagination (secular or religious) that the addressees of law are invited to endorse as their own, in endorsing as their own the politics of which those laws are a part—not of course by rational reflection and the exercise of their own imaginations, but in response to the many familiar strategies of beguilement, some open, some covert, some attractive, some repellent, that are regularly called upon by leaders, good and bad, as a means of persuading a populace to embrace a certain politics without due regard to the question of its rational standing. When those strategies are successful, a political vision is embraced by enough people to establish a life in common, without recourse to force or the degree of individual reflection that would divide. The price, of course, is proper scrutiny of either or both the vision itself and the particular laws it is alleged to entail.

54. This sort of exercise is a standard, possibly paradigmatic feature of political life, but it is not distinctively political, for political

beguilement is but an instance of a broader phenomenon of the seduction of imagination by the power of imagination—not simply through the articulation of a compelling narrative, but in the many various tropes that are called upon to entwine and embed that narrative in the imaginations of those to whom it is directed. That phenomenon is most obviously played out in literary fiction, where readers are drawn into a narrative and its modes of presentation in such a way as to make the author's imaginings theirs and, simultaneously and reciprocally, are invited to clothe and develop that narrative for themselves, by calling on the power and character of their own imaginings in such a way as to lend the narrative a particular flesh of their own, so that the experience of it on any given occasion is the outcome of a collaboration between author and reader, rendered somewhat differently for each reader and every reading. Something similar takes place in the enveloping darkness of the cinema, where the power and scale of photographic images, and their arrangement in cinematic language, draw the viewer into the screen in such a way as to make the viewer's imaginings one with what is projected there, as Buster Keaton famously noticed and dramatized in *Sherlock Jr* (and, in doing so, added yet another layer of narrative and imagining). The salient difference between these aesthetic journeys and political journeys is that politics must provide a common ground onto which people can project their own imaginings in the conviction that those are also the imaginings of the politician, whereas in literature the imaginings of the reader need not acknowledge the imaginings of the author—to the extent that the role of a reader may ultimately subsume that of the author in the experience of reading, yielding what may come close to being entirely different literary journeys for different literary travellers as the author more or less drops away. Because the imaginings of a politician are in the service of a life in common, they are necessarily less permissive, less accommodating than literary imagination. Yet one is bound to notice that reciprocal imaginings take place even in politics, to the peril of a life in common, when political citizens behave like readers or moviegoers and so take the imaginings of a political vision to be what their own imaginings would have them be, and accordingly project their own, manifold imaginings into the superficially unifying vessel of a political vision. Politicians in turn very often notice and trade dangerously on this reciprocity, by rendering their political vision in terms that are sufficiently capacious and flexible as to encourage reciprocal imaginings, and so promote the promise of a life in common where the ground for it does not yet and may never exist.[6]

55. In order to secure its implementation, therefore, in law and otherwise, a political vision needs to be explicit about its galvanizing power and the capacity of that power to make real the rational priority of the vision in question over rival courses of action, rival directions for communal life; further, it needs to present itself as what it will become if and when it is endorsed by its addressees: namely, the collective vision of the community. To succeed in this, however, political vision must not go so far as to undermine the rational priority that it claims for itself and what it requires in law, as it would do if it was overly explicit about the role of political imagination in constructing that priority. It must strike a careful balance, in which the truth of rational priority is insisted upon while its imaginative status is simultaneously acknowledged. Put from the opposite perspective, political vision and the laws that are informed by it must be self-consciously inspirational and recognized as such, while insisting that their rational feet are planted firmly on the ground. When political vision does this successfully compliance with the law follows, in just the same way that it does in the individual case, and the exercise of force becomes unnecessary, simply because there is—as far as anybody is aware—no longer a rational gap to be bridged between the requirements of law and compliance with them, other than in marginal cases of non-conformity.

56. The successful operation of such a political vision, it should be noted, is not necessarily preferable to the use of force as a way of securing compliance with the law. The workings of a political vision are typically more insidious than the use of force, and for that reason a political vision can be more damaging than force to the rationality of its addressees, suborning the exercise of their imaginations to its own as it does.[7] When politics invites a population to make its imaginings theirs, it displaces the manifold imaginative exercises that

---

[6] I have spoken of political life here in terms of politicians, legislatures, and the electorate, but political life also embraces other forms of legal narrative, authors, and audiences, most obviously the narratives of barristers and the judiciary in the formation of the common law. This helps to explain the appeal of case law to lovers of literature, its narrative impact on the lawyers who read and take part in it, the connection of barristers and judges to actors and dramatists, and the soundness, up to a point, of Dworkin's claim that law is like literature.

[7] I am here speaking pejoratively of both force and imagination, because I am seeking to compare the dangers of yielding to each of those in general and in their own right. It

would otherwise have taken place in that community, so limiting both the variety of options there and the independence and worth of the ordinary minds that would have canvassed those options. The use of force shows a certain respect for at least the preliminary conclusions of other minds, however brutally it may try to alter them; by contrast, the process of beguilement works deeper, seeking to prevent other convictions from ever arising in other minds. As history has shown, the consequences of beguilement, for minds and bodies alike, can be utterly devastating. It is dangerous to let another do one's thinking for one—the more so when that other is in a position, as a government is, to do the same for others and then to vindicate, with large and often deadly resources, the policy that it has secured endorsement of in this way, in the assurance of public quiescence as to both the wisdom of the policy and the absence of alternatives to it.[8]

57. So the connection between law and collective action, between law and a life in common, depends upon the presence of reasons and putative reasons beyond those that are embodied in the content of law. It follows that accounts of legal positivism are typically incomplete in that, no less than anti-positivist accounts, they look to the content of law alone for the reasons law provides, or more precisely may provide. Given value pluralism, it takes rather more than this to yield action of a kind that will establish a life in common, for good or ill. Compliance with the law, of a kind that will secure a life in common, requires an act of endorsement on the part of the addressees of law, itself predicated upon, first, a recognition

---

is true, of course, that in some, perhaps many, cases such yielding is a good idea, because in those cases what one yields to is, at a minimum, rationally permissible. When that is not so, however, the question is which, of force or imagination, presents the greater danger, or more precisely just what kind of danger is presented by each.

[8] My emphasis throughout this book will be almost exclusively on the constructive rather than the destructive implications of the exercise of imagination in the implementation of a political vision. This one-sidedness in the narrative should not for a moment be regarded as a reflection of reality, for the social and political history of the twentieth century in particular has made us all too aware of the vulnerability of our imaginations, and the consequent corruption of many social and political missions, some tyrannical and some not, to forces such as fear and hatred. A distinction needs to be drawn here, however. Although I will not spend time exploring the phenomenon, there can be no objection to an appeal to imagination as an arational aid to decision in bad circumstances. If one is confronted by two bad options one is fully entitled to choose whichever of those options one finds the most imaginatively appealing, or least imaginatively repugnant, perhaps because one sees less to fear or hate in it. Concern arises, therefore,

of the rational appeal of the law's requirements (or more precisely a belief that those requirements are rationally appealing); second, an embrace of the imaginative narrative that presents that appeal as rationally pre-eminent; and/or third, a prudential reaction to whatever enforcement measures have been attached to the law's requirements by legal authority, and indeed, by social practice—all of these combining in different measures in the minds of different actors in the face of the same or different laws, and consequently in the social and legal practices of different societies that are marked by different degrees of conformity and anarchy in their populaces and so marked by the different balances to be struck in each between the roles of force and social convention in securing compliance.

58. There is much in Dworkin's account that both captures and embodies, elegantly and imaginatively, the role that may be played by political vision[9] in securing a life in common. Yet there is a fundamental gap between any plausible reconstruction of Dworkin's account and a sound account of the role played by imagination in enabling law to describe and shape a life in common, which stems from the account's mishandling of each of the three constituents of action, in one life or in many: reason is identified with past practice, or at least with the best elements of past practice, thereby immunizing that practice and its future import from full rational scrutiny; imagination is also identified with past practice, thereby limiting the imagining of a political future to the implications of the past, be they rational or irrational; while the role of the will, both in the making of decisions by legal authorities and in the endorsement of those decisions by their addressees, is altogether ignored, or more precisely is confined to cases of irrationality on the part of those to whom law applies.

59. Put more broadly, the tensions and difficulties in Dworkin's account stem largely from the imperial character of its ambition, namely its attempt to build into a scheme for the identification of law everything that commends law to us, its addressees. Even its

---

as and when recourse to imagination leads a political authority and its subjects from arational to irrational reliance, as it does when the basis of fear or hatred (for example) is neither rational nor arational (in the latter case, when the irrationality of the fear or hatred informs not merely the selection but the content of what one endorses). See further at paras 64 and 154.

[9] A political vision that may be exercised by legislator or judge: see Chapter 5, sections B3 c) and d).

two-part test of fit and justification, which might be said to go some way to marrying the pull of imagination and of reason respectively, cannot capture all that commends law to us, for—quite apart from the account's mishandling of those two aspects of law's appeal to us—it entirely neglects the role of the will.[10]

60. Yet to stop there is to say rather too little about the nature of imagination, and so fail to distinguish fully, in something like the Dworkinian manner, its rational and arational dimensions.[11] Let me begin with the former. When we anticipate in our mind's eye the possibilities that are latent in a course of action, and trace

---

[10] There is something of an interpretive puzzle in Dworkin's account, which stems from its ambiguous, possibly equivocal attitude to value pluralism. On the face of it, Dworkin rejects value pluralism, as indeed he is bound to do by reason of his belief in a single right answer and of law that exists waiting to be discovered, in advance of, and without the need for, any decision that would make it what it is. Yet what place can there be for a criterion of fit as well as a criterion of justification in the absence of value pluralism? In a monistic moral universe, the only possible function of a criterion of fit would be to accommodate moral conclusions that fell short of making the society in question and its governance the best they could be. To explain: if and to the extent that only one conclusion could possibly fit (because it fitted best), the effect of a test of fit would be to pre-empt the issue of justification and so ensure that law was less worthy than it ought to be (apart from cases in which justification would yield the same conclusion; that is, cases in which the society in question was already the best that a society could be in that respect). Dworkin cannot have that in mind. Yet is there any other reading he could endorse? If more than one conclusion could fit, it could only be because fit itself is a matter of kind as well as degree (which would be to accept value pluralism), or because fit is a threshold issue, beyond which all possibilities are either equal in fact (which is implausible) or ought to be treated as such (why so, and if so, why not so for the outcomes of the test of justification as well?). What is more, if fit was understood as either of those things, as a matter of kind, or at least as independent of the values taken into account in considering justification (so as to preserve the independence of the two questions), there would be significant scope for conflict between the claims of fit and justification in any assessment of the content of the law, and a corresponding need for decision to resolve that conflict. That too would be to accept value pluralism. Yet if value pluralism is accepted, justification would have to precede any consideration of fit, and both questions would require a decision in order to yield law. The ambiguity surfaces elsewhere, particularly in Dworkin's handling of the relationship between law and literature. Why is more than one author engaged in the creation of a chain novel, or more precisely, why should writers embark upon the project of a chain novel? It is true that co-operative endeavours can help to eliminate error, but chain novels do not involve co-operation of that kind: they are the products of serial solo authorship. It is also true that co-operation can enable a task to be completed more quickly, but that is not normally the point of writing a chain novel. The obvious answer is that each author is expected to bring his or her vision (and will) to bear on the problem of the narrative's direction in ways that the other author might not have contemplated but that are no less rewarding for that, thereby multiplying the possibilities of the novel and the challenges for each ensuing author. Yet that answer again presupposes value pluralism.

[11] On the idea of arationality, see Chapter 5, para 116, note 9.

their contours with a view to better apprehending them, we very often do so in a way that is fully in accordance with reason precisely because it is guided by reason. Sometimes that guidance is conscious, as when we deliberate, in light of our understanding and our experience, on what might follow from certain actions and commitments, with a view to achieving a proper appreciation of the nature and depth of their rational pull. Sometimes the guidance is unconscious, as when the course of our imagining naturally pursues a rational path just because our understanding and experience have over time shaped our powers of imagination in such a way as to ensure, in certain relatively practised settings at least, that our unreflective exercise of our imagination is rationally informed. In these cases, and with these resources, imagination strengthens rather than supplements our rationality. It has no power, no special capacity, with which to overcome conflicts of reasons, because its role is to track reason.

61. Plainly, however, that is not the full story of imagination and what it has to offer us, as the artefacts of imagination make clear. Every creator and consumer of narrative is aware of, and bound to negotiate, the fundamental difference between life recounted as fiction and as fact, despite the many powerful overlaps that exist between the two, the support that they offer one another, and the impossibility of ever completely disentangling them. Ordinary life is bound by the claims of reason in certain basic ways that fiction simply is not. We are genuinely surprised when ordinary life takes on the character of fiction, and correspondingly disappointed when fiction seems as ordinary as life. This is not just a matter of the stuff of fantasy, of elves and unicorns and other imaginary creatures, or of people flying and animals talking and other imaginary capacities—cases in which the world as we know it has been manifestly altered and extended. Rather, it is the stuff of even such prosaic ventures as the naturalistic novel, in which fiction seeks to portray the world exactly as we know it, albeit with a view to heightening our understanding of certain aspects of it.

62. There is something like an underlying clarifying quality to all fiction that seems to proceed from its capacity to manipulate (or, more fairly, to alter) the circumstances of reason in two key respects. The first of these respects, stemming from the basic fact that fiction depends on language (of whatever kind), is to be found, in part at least, in the notorious capacity of language to bewitch the intellect, as Wittgenstein put it—a capacity that in spoken and written

language finds its purest expression in the art of rhetoric, but which is everywhere latent both in the distance between words and the various matters that each of them is capable of referring to, and in the further and only partially consequent ambiguity of meaning that is ever-present in the use of words and the ways in which they are arranged and might otherwise have been so. In ordinary life, as nearly all of us ruefully recognize, there is a familiar cycle through which an apparently great idea becomes mundane, as we become aware of the idea's inherent flaws, adapt it to overcome those flaws as best we can, and thus step by step gradually secure some measure of truth at the expense of clarity and strength of vision, thereby rendering what was initially inspiring ordinary. How tempting, and how far the stuff of our dreams and our fiction, to break this cycle by eliding, through various half-knowing strategies of self-deceit, at least some of the difficulties that reason would have us recognize, and thereby allow ourselves to be correspondingly bewitched and inspired. Language is a principal, though far from the only, source of such bewitchment. Our minds seem additionally to be distinctively susceptible to certain narrative structures—sometimes on aesthetic grounds, sometimes on psychological grounds, to take but two relatively familiar examples—and skilled purveyors of narrative, be they novelists, film-makers, playwrights, or politicians, know how to couch particular narratives so as to reach particular audiences, in ways that achieve the most compelling balance, for that audience, between truth and fiction. The simplest explanations are the most truthful, we are often told—so pointing to the appeal of the reductive—or if not the simplest, the most elegant, or the most coherent, or the most native, or sometimes even the most emotionally satisfying. In all these and other ways the power of imagination is called upon, at its best, to enlighten by distorting. In playing this reshaping role it can often make a course of action appear to be more rationally compelling than it is in fact, just because the enlightenment that it suggests is, at least in part, rhetorically rather than rationally grounded.

63. The other respect in which imagination is able to manipulate the circumstances of reason finds expression in the capacity of narrative (played with in both directions by novelists) to be purposeful, a capacity that stems from the way in which the elisions and simplifications that fiction makes possible are able to diminish the claims of rival courses of action supported by rival reasons. In life it is reasonably rare to be able to do no other, but in fiction it

is something close to characteristic. The point of many fictional narratives is to explore what such a destiny might look like (whatever the source of that destiny might be), or, in more contemporary hands, to undercut and play with an audience's expectations of that sort of destiny. Imagination has a capacity to delineate the contours of a course of action in such a way as to make them seem more sharply defined than their rivals, and the effect of that sharpness is to lend the course of action in question the appearance of a special richness and so to invest its claims with the appearance of a greater rational weight than the claims of their rivals, as if they were commensurable with their rivals when in fact they are not. The nearest physical analogy I can think of is to the relationship between focus and visual richness in the appreciation of an image. When one's eyes are poor, or the image that one is contemplating has been badly reproduced, the consequent lack of focus robs the image of much of its tonal richness. It appears muddy and dull, or *unsaturated*, to put it more technically. Think of the shift in aspects of Monet's painting as his cataracts advanced. When one's eyes are good or one's glasses are new, however, and the image before one has been crisply reproduced, colours become deeper and the greyscale acquires a luminous quality. Definition heightens contrast, and contrast alters perceptions of colour and tone.

64. These distortions of imagination tread the line between the arational and the irrational. To portray a course of action as rationally superior to its rivals when it is not is to betray reason in the portrayal but not necessarily in the consequent pursuit of the action, provided that both the action and its rivals are rationally permissible. Yet once a pattern of acceding to such betrayals has been established, subsequent betrayals can all too easily infect the choice of which action to pursue and thereby become damaging to the choice as well as to its analysis, so that a life in common that is made possible by a surrender to the appeal of a political vision is inherently morally vulnerable, just because its participants are apt to lack a critical perspective upon what the law is asking of them that is necessary to protect them (as far as any critical perspective can) from acceding to what should not be acceded to, as has already been noted.

5

The Service Law May Offer to Life in Common

65. The limitations inherent in the law's ability to engender collective action underpin the soundness, indeed the wisdom, of the reservation that Raz attaches to his account of the service conception of authority. The normal justification of any authority (including the authority claimed by law), as he explains it, is that we do better by acceding to its demands than we would by consulting our own judgement, both assessed according to the same standard. When any given claim of authority is justified in this way we have reason to do what the authority requires, just because the authority requires it—unless, Raz adds puzzlingly and apparently paradoxically, there is reason to decide the matter for ourselves. The puzzle is this: how could compliance with the law be at once preferable and not preferable to the exercise of our own judgement? The paradox: how could we begin to answer that question in any given case without foregoing the benefit that law is said to offer those who conform to its requirements without exercising their own judgement as to whether those requirements are rationally preferable to the conclusions of their own judgement?

66. The paradox, it seems fair to say, can be more or less readily dissolved by reference to the resources of Raz's own account: in the face of authority the exercise of individual judgement acquires, *prima facie* at least, a new object in place of the reasons that would otherwise govern it—namely, the claim of the authority to be in a position to create directives that amount to exclusionary reasons in what it calls for and to whom it applies. It is that new object, rather than

what it calls for, that one ought to question. Put crudely, one ought to question the directive of a legislator in much the same way that one ought to question the directive of a doctor, or indeed any other person who tells one what to do and not to do, not by undertaking the same diagnosis as the legislator or doctor but by questioning the rationality of their authority to make a diagnosis that seeks to exclude one's own rational diagnosis, in general and/or in the particular case. That is but a sketch, of course; clearly a great deal more would need to be said to give proper flesh to such an explanation and to colour it with the sophistication it requires. Nevertheless, in the present setting the problem of the paradox, important as it is in principle, can be set to one side on the ground that the resolution of the paradox is ancillary to the issues under consideration here. The puzzle, however, remains.

67. Yet in fact in the puzzle can be found the beginnings of an explanation of what law can and cannot do for us. As it stands, at least on the face of it, the service conception of authority is incomplete in two ways. First, it draws attention to, but does not expand upon, the question of what the law cannot do for us. Second, it says nothing about the extent to which the role played by law, and the service rendered by its authority, could be performed no less well by other social forms and practices. Just what is it that the law can and cannot do for us, and when is it that whatever it can do for us is superfluous at best?

A. Concepts of Law

68. In considering questions such as these we necessarily call upon a concept of law, or, to be precise, perhaps more than one such concept. There is no alternative. It is of course entirely possible to apprehend the world directly, without the mediation of concepts; to dive into the water and be refreshed without invoking the concepts of diving, water or refreshment. As far as we know, this is how other animals live all the time. It is how we ourselves live a good deal of the time, depending on our circumstances and our temperament. But in the balance of our lives we call upon our stock of concepts to describe the topography of our engagement, direct and indirect, possible and actual, with the landscape of value.

69. Broadly speaking, two dimensions of our engagement with that landscape are mapped by concepts. We call upon concepts first as an aid in the assessment of value and disvalue themselves and second in the identification of the bearers of value and disvalue in our lives—some of which are created by human beings and other animals in the form of artefacts and practices, some of which are naturally occurring, a few of which are co-extensive with a particular value or disvalue, but the great mass of which are capable of giving rise to a complex array of values and disvalues in the lives of those who engage with them: some forgotten, some yet to be discovered or invented, some accessible to human beings, others not. Our purpose in calling upon concepts is two-fold: first, to enable and to structure reflections on our engagement with value, whether before or after the fact; second, to guide our engagement with value in those settings where that engagement is self-conscious. Of course, this picture is complicated by the fact that concepts are themselves part of the landscape of value that they describe, and so are in their turn objects of reflection and sources of guidance in our engagement with them as well as with what they refer to.

70. In contemplating the practice of law, therefore, we necessarily call upon one or more concepts of law, because that is what contemplation involves, and in so doing very often reflect upon and seek guidance from the concept that we call upon. But that is not all, for it is not merely contemplation that brings a concept of law into play; on the contrary, reference to a concept of law is fundamental to the practical operation of law, given that engagement with law—as distinct from engagement with coercion or with social mores (both of which may operate through law without taking on its name or character)—is by its nature self-conscious and hence guided by a concept of itself. We can pay attention to law as a distinct practice, as we are bound to do in engaging with it, only by recognizing it as law, and in recognizing the practice as law we necessarily call upon a concept of law. It follows that engagement with law is not one of those cases in which not understanding the concept of a practice, or not paying attention to that concept in one's engagement with the practice it refers to, may better secure the fulfilment of the values that the practice is capable of giving rise to.

71. Of course, noticing this much does not take us very far, because it raises, only to leave unanswered, the question of the nature, degree, and depth of understanding of the concept (or

concepts) of law that successful engagement with the practice of law calls for. How well do we need to understand the practice of law, in its generality or in its particularity, in order to be properly guided by it—that is, in order to be so guided as to arrive at a life in common, and ideally a good life in common? On the face of it, that question would appear to yield different answers in different settings. Just what does that tell us? Is the issue indeed, as it appears to be, one of different degrees and depths of understanding of a univocal concept of law, or are different concepts of law at stake in those different settings?

72. The concept of law is typically treated as univocal in the setting of reflections on law that seek to distinguish (and sometimes to merge) its role in our lives, its value and disvalue, from those of certain practically and conceptually allied and overlapping phenomena. In employing the definite article to speak of the concept of law, Hart took as fundamental the generic contrast between the claims of laws, of whatever kind, and the claims of force and of morality, as captured in his three basic questions: How does law differ from and how is it related to orders backed by threats? How does legal obligation differ from and how is it related to moral obligation? What are rules and to what extent is law an affair of rules? There is certainly much to be discovered by thinking of law in this univocal way, not least of course with the assistance of the analysis undertaken by Hart himself, most notably in his celebrated *The Concept of Law*. Yet there are many other questions—subsidiary in some senses yet primary in others—that would appear to draw upon multifarious concepts of law: that is to say, that do not merely draw attention to rival univocal concepts of law, one of which is said to offer a superior explanation of law as a whole, but rather draw attention to the different types of law that can be said to fall within any univocal concept of law, and to the different types of issues that laws (of different types) seek to address.

73. Against this latter line of thought, of course, there is a persistent strain of scholarship, extending back to Austin, that operates to the opposite effect and so seeks to develop the implications of a univocal understanding of law beyond the three recurrent issues that *The Concept of Law* sought to pursue (and others akin to them), so as to see individual instances of law as but law writ small and their identification as a jurisprudential project, or at least the necessary consequence of the same. To put it in Austinian terms, on this view

the varieties of law are but the varieties of command, coupled with the varieties of sanction that may be called upon to back them up. To put it in Dworkinian terms, there is no distinction between law and the law; both are to be determined by looking to the requirements of integrity, the difference between them being merely one of scale.

74. Yet as contemporary studies of the practice of regulation have made clear, law is not only enormously various, but is to all appearances fundamentally so. The study of its varieties, and the goals they embody, is on the face of it the study of the different values that those varieties can give rise to, and of the rationality of the connection between certain governmental ambitions (which themselves embody particular values or clusters of values) and particular legal strategies for their realization. Indeed, that much might be said to be implicit in the two basic varieties of law that Austin and Hart famously drew attention to, namely laws that are duty-imposing and laws that are power-conferring. At stake in those two types of law, *inter alia*, are the values of order and of autonomy, and the strategies for their achievement in the setting of a life in common.

75. The relatively straight-forward claim being made here is that there are evidently a great many ways of conceptualizing law, each of which has its own rewards. To think of law univocally, as Austin, Hart, and others have done, is at best to gain one insight at the expense of others; at worst it is not only to conflate insights but to insist on their conflation. In particular, to think of law univocally is, I will suggest, to miss many of the implications of the rational claim that law has upon us, implications that only become fully visible by calling upon ways of thinking about law that are capable of distinguishing one context of law-making from another in terms of its rational pull, and so are capable of distinguishing the varying problems of rational action that different contexts of law-making may give rise to. Of course, the reverse is also true: to insist on distinguishing certain contexts of law-making is to miss the overarching rational claim or claims that law can make upon us, some in common with its alternatives, others in contrast to them, which only become visible in the recognition of law's unity, and hence in the concept of law that embodies that unity.

76. It follows that in considering the roles played by reason, will, and imagination in describing and shaping a life in common through the medium of law, it is necessary to establish whether those roles, and the balance to be struck among them, hold more or less constant

for all laws—so that the lessons to be learned about them are lessons about the concept of law, understood univocally—or whether the apparent variation in those roles, and in the ways they are balanced against one another, is ultimately a reflection of different (sub-)concepts of law: that is, of different types of law and the different types of issues that laws (of different types) seek to address, in relation to any one of which reason, will, and imagination may have different roles to play, different balances to be struck among themselves.

B. Different Laws as Different Catalysts for a Life in Common

77. What matters as a starting point for the present discussion, then, it will be clear, is the particular varieties of law, and of governmental ambition that they are expected to serve, that interact with the roles played by reason, will, and the imagination in the exercise of practical reasoning toward a life in common. If and to the extent that law is a practical reason for a body of people, it is a reason of a special kind—namely, one that is capable of functioning as a reason embedded in common practice, which in turn calls for, in relation to any particular law, a variable interplay of reason, will, and imagination in the minds of the addressees of that law; the balance depending on the law, the context, and the governmental ambition at stake.

78. This is not to claim that the prisms of reason, will, and imagination, and the varieties of law that their admixtures give rise to, have any particular priority over other ways of understanding law, either in logic or importance, apart from their ability to offer illumination and guidance in relation to certain governmental ambitions and the extent to which those are fulfillable, without more, by the rational account that can be taken by the addressees of law of a scheme of exclusionary reasons (as well as by the irrational reactions it may inspire). The many varieties of law, as well as the unity of law that binds them to one another, and the many ways of thinking about law we call upon in the identification and analysis of these are but more or less distinctive vehicles for the realization of value by human beings in the setting of a relatively fluid and heterogeneous social practice, all of which can be thought of compendiously as instances of an overarching concept of law such as Hart had in mind,

but each of which further marks a distinct aspect of that practice, its associated artefacts, and the particular values and clusters of values that those give rise to.

79. The following sections will examine certain varieties of law as if they were paradigmatic; varieties of law in relation to which reason, will, and imagination, respectively, and their admixtures might be thought, by some at least, to be crucial to their capacity to function successfully as practical reasons for a successful community—that is to say, as reasons that are capable of establishing, with appropriate support, their pre-eminence over their rational rivals and so capable of establishing a life in common. Of course, apart from the first, these varieties will in fact be paradigmatic only for certain communities, and the corresponding cultures, and accompanying rational and irrational traditions and convictions, that describe and define them. Were it otherwise, the appeal of these varieties would be universally assessable in terms of rationality alone, and the rational pre-eminence of any law over its alternatives (ignoring rare cases of equality) would be knowable to all in advance. That being so, the identification that follows of laws that are said to embody certain types of appeal can be no more than suggestive at best: true of and for some communities and cultures but not others. Those who disagree with my selection should simply think of a different selection that can plausibly be thought of as paradigmatic of these types of appeal in and for their particular community and culture.

1. Authority as Perfecting Reason

80. To begin with the most straight-forward case, the exclusionary claim of reason upon the addressees of law is at its purest when the very identification of what the law requires in itself renders rival courses of action in fulfilment of the same set of values rationally ineligible. As Raz might put it, in such a case the service conception of authority tells us all we need to know about the laws in question, for it establishes that their rational claim upon us is not only justified but pre-eminent. Take the familiar illustration of certain rules of the road. All members of a community of drivers have reason to proceed safely and rapidly along the roads, and in doing so to negotiate the potential hazard of oncoming traffic successfully. If and to the extent that an anarchistic way of satisfying that reason is unavailable to them, those drivers have reason to settle authoritatively, *inter alia*,

on a particular side of the road to drive on. It matters not which side. The value of a law prescribing left rather than right, or vice versa, is that it establishes authoritatively a preference for one side of the road rather than the other for the community of drivers it claims to govern. Tellingly, in doing so it renders driving on the opposite side of the road rationally ineligible in and for that community, subject to two classes of personal exception, in aid of which, it will be noticed at once, force must be called into play. Otherwise the significance of this category of laws in the establishment of a life in common is that such laws lay down rules, the content of which (and its authoritative determination for the governance of a particular community) is all the warrant the laws in question need to establish a life in common in the domains they address. No reference to will or imagination is needed to secure their priority over their rational alternatives.

81. The first exception to this is the case of the irrational driver—the person who drives down the middle of a two-lane road, straddling the white line, because he or she believes it to be safer there. The possibility of a sanction may be more rationally transparent to such a person than the rule of the road itself (though he or she may well be impervious to both), and if and to the extent that that is so, the attachment of a sanction to the rule of the road may enhance the rational pull of that law for that person. How weighty such a sanction would need to be to be rationally or irrationally effective, and whether the necessary weight would be justifiable in terms of its impact on liberty and other aspects of human well-being, are familiar concerns in the analysis of the moral implications of the enforcement of law. That aside, there is little to be said about this category of exception, given that it is premised on conduct that is not fully susceptible to rational analysis and explanation. It does nothing to undermine the claim that laws such as this rule of the road need nothing other than their status as law, and the authority that embodies, to render their alternatives rationally ineligible.

82. The second exception is the case of the contrarian driver, the person who wishes to drive on the other side of the road from that adopted by the general community of drivers just because it has become the wrong side of the road in that community: in other words, not because the person in question has reason to regard driving on the other side of the road as rationally superior for the community of which he or she is a member, for the law has indeed and for the time being made that option rationally ineligible there,

but because he or she has reason to regard that side of the road as a rationally superior avenue for himself or herself on a given occasion—perhaps because it offers an easy way of getting past traffic going in the same direction in a setting, such as a divided highway, where passing is not permitted; perhaps because he or she is a bloody-minded person who regards rule-breaking as an aspect of his or her autonomy.

83. There are two things worth noticing about this latter class of exception. First, it verges on the irrational: passing where passing is not permitted is very seldom a good way of proceeding safely and rapidly along the roads, while driving on the wrong side of the road has only very tenuous connections to the vindication of personal autonomy (even granted that rule-breaking for its own sake can be an aspect of autonomy), given that there are far better—that is to say, genuinely offensive—rules available to break. Second, the significance of this exception is that it does not affect the rational ineligibility of alternatives to the general rule, given that the nature of the general rule is such that the value at stake in it can only be realized if the rational superiority of that rule over its alternative is not only endorsed but bound to be endorsed by all (rational) drivers in the community, including those who break it even as they break it. In other words, this class of exception not only implies endorsement of the rational superiority of the general rule, but actually trades on that endorsement for the value of the antisocial action undertaken in breach of the general rule. It is contrarian behaviour as complementary antidote, rather than as fundamental challenge to the rational pre-eminence of the general rule.

84. Laws like these, in relation to which nothing other than their status as law is required to render alternatives to them rationally ineligible, would appear to constitute a significant yet relatively circumscribed category of law, an important but far from dominant aspect of any legal system, contrary to the assumption of certain commentators that reason alone, at least when specified with the aid of official determination, is normally sufficient to explain the authority of law.[1] In fact, the purity of that claim is established only when rationally eligible alternatives to what the law requires either do not exist

---

[1] Alternatives are rationally ineligible, of course, only to the extent that the law succeeds in establishing and maintaining its authoritative status; otherwise we would need to look to some other authority (be it embodied in an institution or in a practice) for a resolution to problems such as that of co-ordination.

or can be regarded as functionally equivalent to one another in terms of the value that the law exists to serve. In practice, that is rare in any setting where the difference drawn by the law is other than trivial.[2] By contrast, however, the opposite situation, where what a given law requires is rationally impermissible, rendering any one of a range of alternatives to that law rationally mandatory, would appear to be relatively common. One need only think of oppressive legal regimes and the many discriminatory (and much worse) edicts they have laid down. Such edicts are sometimes secured by force (for example, by fostering a climate of fear that may be sufficiently powerful as to engender compliance and even acquiescence from the victims of the edicts in question) or by beguilement (for example, by fostering a public culture that is itself bigoted, or at least that is prepared to be passive, oblivious, or unwittingly compliant in the face of what an oppressive legal regime has called for). In either case reason, without more, tells decisively against what the law demands.

2. Authority, Reason, and Will

85. Laws such as these may be usefully contrasted to the central prohibitions of the criminal law, the value of which is securable *pro tanto*: the more widely that fundamental and, let us assume, sound criminal prohibitions are endorsed as rationally superior to their alternatives, and are acted upon accordingly, the better the prospects will be of a worthy life in common in the community in question (assuming that the community includes at least some who would otherwise undertake what the criminal law prohibits, as it surely must if the criminal law has any effect as a deterrent). Nevertheless, the bare existence of these prohibitions does not in and of itself render their rejection as rules rationally ineligible. It is true that some minimum level of endorsement as rationally pre-eminent is necessary to the practical functioning of these prohibitions as community rules, as proved to be the case in the prohibition of alcohol and may now be proving to be the case in the prohibition of certain other drugs. It does not follow that such endorsement need be universal or that it preclude the existence and consequent recognition of rational

---

[2] The claim clearly cannot be sustained for all co-ordination rules, and hence its scope should not be thought to map onto the extent of co-ordination problems and the law's response to them. For further explanation see the discussion in paragraph 87.

alternatives. On the contrary, it is worth noting that these laws are regarded as central prohibitions of the criminal law not only by virtue of what is at stake in their compliance or breach, but by virtue of the level of sanction that is attached to their breach—a level of sanction that suggests, among other things, the limited prospects for a life in common that would follow from the rationality of their content alone, and so implies a consequent need to bolster the rational claim of that content with the supplemental (or even alternative) rational pull of a powerful sanction. Powerful sanctions could only be otherwise explained by a human tendency to exhibit greater irrationality in regard to these prohibitions than in regard to other laws.[3] In fact, it is far from clear why people should be particularly muddled in the face of central prohibitions of the criminal law; by contrast, it is all too understandable why people should be rationally attracted to the possibility of acting in contravention of them.

86. The rational difference at stake between these two classes of criminal law, the one typified by certain rules of the road and the other typified by the fundamental prohibitions against murder, rape, theft, and the like, is the difference between the logical and the contingent ineligibility of what they prohibit. The prohibition against murder, even when understood in all its detail, as embracing every possible element of the offence and every possible defence to it, does not render murder rationally ineligible, as a number of familiar scenarios make clear—the most currently prominent of these being that of euthanasia. One common response to such deficiencies, if that is the right word for them, is to seek a corrective amendment in the law of murder, so as to permit, for example, euthanasia. Sometimes that is indeed what is required. Yet one is bound to notice that any such amendment would give rise to its own alternatives (drawing the line between permitted and impermissible conduct in a different way, embodying different principles perhaps, or different interpretations of the same principle)—not all of which would be rationally ineligible, given that an amendment to such a law normally has no capacity to alter the general character of the ineligibility at stake, which in this case would remain contingent rather than logical.

---

[3] Powerful sanctions also have expressive implications, of course, an issue that will be addressed later. In the meantime, it is worth noting that in terms of compliance there is not necessarily more at stake in the breach of these laws (driving on the wrong side of the road is liable to kill or injure) and even if there were, it is not clear why more should be required to prevent it.

87. It is for this reason that the project of amending the content of the criminal law so as to make alternatives to it rationally ineligible is admirable only up to a point. Ultimately the contingency of the law's requirements, in many if not most cases, must simply be accepted, given the relatively coarse-grained character of a general rule, however qualified it may be, and the immensely fine-grained and various character of much of moral life. Rules of the road and the fundamental prohibitions of the criminal law are alike in the first respect; what distinguishes them is the second. Driving on one side of the road rather than the other is one of those relatively straight-forward cases where the rational possibilities are extremely limited in the first place; where those possibilities are equally capable of satisfying the value that is to be secured by the law; and, most importantly, where the authority of law has been exercised so as to lend one of those possibilities a rational pre-eminence that it correspondingly denies to the others, thereby rendering those others rationally ineligible in that community. That is true not only of certain rules of the road but also of a good many of the detailed provisions of the regulatory state, which consist in the same sort of specification, say, of the precise diameter of particular pieces of plumbing pipe, or the R-value of building insulation, or the rate of VAT on particular goods, or the age of first school attendance, and all the other fragments of the vast assemblage of state prescriptions of process, conduct, capacity, and status that characterizes contemporary government. It is not the case, however, with the fundamental prohibitions of the criminal law or, indeed, many other socially reforming laws. There the rational possibilities are multiple in the first place, typically secure quite different values, and cannot be rationally diminished by the authority of law so as to make the course of action that the law calls for rationally pre-eminent in all settings in comparison to its rivals.

88. Many criminal prohibitions, most notably that against theft, are plausible instances of prohibitions that there may be good reason to breach, by certain people or in certain circumstances. We can all think of good reasons to steal, justified instances of theft, that are not recognized as such by the law. Yet it may strike some as quite profoundly counter-intuitive—and what is more, offensive—to suggest that there could ever be rational alternatives to the criminal prohibitions against rape or sexual assault, that is to say that it could ever be morally permissible to do what the law on rape or sexual assault forbids. Perhaps that is so. Perhaps the law in those cases indeed leaves

no rational alternative to compliance with its requirements; its only failure, therefore, would be in what it fails to prohibit and thus tacitly permits. If that is true, those laws would belong in the first category, together with certain rules of the road and other specifications of the regulatory state. Yet it is also possible that the rational ineligibility of alternatives to compliance with the prohibitions against rape and sexual assault that sustains our intuition in this respect is indeed contingent, but the circumstances in which the ineligibility would not apply are simply beyond our present imagining, given our deep commitment to ensuring that the prohibitions against rape and sexual assault be established and interpreted in such a way as to emphasize the wrongness, and hence the irrationality, of certain conduct within the scope of those offences that in many settings was, until quite recently, regrettably but commonly regarded as entirely rational. After all, if the ineligibility at stake were genuinely logical in character, one would expect to be able to imagine, relatively readily, the impossibility of its not applying, as one can in the case of certain rules of the road. In fact, however, it seems as difficult to imagine the rational ineligibility of an alternative to the prohibitions against rape and sexual assault as to imagine its rational eligibility. Yet in both cases the inability to imagine is only a weak guide to the impossibility of existence, and so is compatible with contingent ineligibility. Part of the point of laws such as these, surely, is to take a socially defining moral stand, to declare to be unacceptably irrational in a particular community damaging conduct that many there have been all too willing to make a rational case in favour of, and all too successful in vindicating that case. If such a case had no plausible rational foundation, there would be less need to take a vigorous stand against it.

89. As the presence of their strong attendant sanctions might be taken to imply, therefore, it is the rationality of many breaches of the fundamental prohibitions of the criminal law that makes an element of force necessary to the successful functioning of those prohibitions as catalysts for a life in common. Arguably, it is recognition of that fact that makes accounts of law that emphasize the use of force, such as that of Austin, persuasive (to the extent that they are persuasive). Force is crucial to the rational pull of many laws, or, as Austin might have put it, to the sovereignty of their requirements over their rational rivals. That is not to say that Austin was correct to believe that the presence of a sanction is essential to the claim upon us of

even fundamental criminal laws. Hart was entirely right to think, for the reasons he gives, that the rational claim of such laws (though he would not have called the claim rational) is complete without the presence of a sanction. Where Hart surely erred was in thinking that sanctions are necessary only for the ill-intentioned, and thus necessary to the existence of a legal system but not to the existence of law. In fact, they are also necessary in addressing the well-intentioned, and so are as necessary to the existence of even fundamental criminal laws as catalysts for a life in common as is the rational appeal of the prohibitions that they lay down.

90. Yet force has its limits, for the self-preserving reason in favour of compliance to which it gives rise in those to whom it applies is only one reason among others. Those who are confronted with the possibility of a sanction may well find it rational to embrace the risk of that sanction for the sake of what is to be gained, directly or indirectly, from breach of the prohibition to which the sanction is attached. That is why, without the presence of some other factor supporting it, it is only the most brutal force that can be counted on to ensure a high degree of compliance with criminal prohibitions, and with the regime they help to sustain, because only that level of force strikes at the preconditions of any and all value in a life—namely, life itself and the basic capacities that make life an apt vehicle for the realization of value. Even then, given that enforcement of penalties is never guaranteed, many prospective law-breakers will regard the risk of incurring the penalty as incommensurable with the benefits of breach, as governments of all kinds have discovered to their cost.

91. It follows that there is a vital role to be played by social and political imagination in the securing of morally contestable laws, such as the central criminal prohibitions, if a life in common is to be established in terms of the values they seek to secure—an exercise of imagination that is typically embodied in the expressive dimension of such provisions. If a particular community is to have any hope of achieving a social order that is relatively free of, for example, intimidation, rape, and the imposition of bodily harm, as the community in question understands those things, then it must call in aid a political vision that at once transcends, and so embraces, something broader than the specific requirements of the laws forbidding those forms of conduct, informs the meaning of those requirements as we would have it, and finally extends their implications to other, cognate aspects of human relations—an exercise of imagination

that both inspires the enactment of the laws in question and helps to secure compliance with their terms, and that typically comes to be embedded, as I have said, in the expressive dimension of those laws. So we enact (or perhaps I should say maintain, so as to avoid an assumption about legal history) laws against rape in part to prevent rapes, but in part also to secure a social climate that is antithetical to sexual abuse of all kinds and, more generally, to other forms of degradation of women (and in certain settings men), and further to signal and so to foster a broad social commitment to the well-being of women more generally, and by extension to the well-being of others whose lives have historically been diminished in the way that the lives of women have been.

92. It is important, however, not to be too quick at this point, not to fall into the thought that there is any ready identification on the one hand of the use of force with the project of compliance, and on the other of the invocation of political vision and imagination with the expressive dimensions of law and the projects of cultural engineering that those dimensions of law may assist in securing. Those two superficially paired features of law and a life in common (force and compliance, imagination and expression) simply do not map onto one another. As has already been emphasized, force does not necessarily secure compliance, for there is very often good reason to do other than that which force would have one do. Nor does compliance necessarily require force, for it may be no less effectively secured through the workings of political imagination, in the manner previously described. Force in its turn has many implications (expressive, *ex post facto* justice-based, and so on) in addition to the degree of compliance that it may secure (and the costs attendant upon securing it by that means)—implications that are often drawn upon in the construction of a political vision that invokes the use of force for its expressive significance. So we are familiar with political visions in which calls for increased penalties are a central feature—from those on the right who emphasize public crackdowns on crimes of certain kinds, often those committed by the socially marginal, or the rapid deportation of asylum-seekers, to those on the left who call for heavy sanctions against polluters, or other ways of using penalties as a means of stigmatizing corporate wrongdoing in a way that trades on public suspicion of corporate activity. Once again in turn, and as was also emphasized previously, when called upon as a method of securing a life in common, the exercise

of political imagination and its projection in the form of a political vision can have significant coercive implications, for the success of such a vision depends on the displacement—as far as is necessary to the achievement of a life in common—of the imaginations of all those who embrace it.

3. Authority, Reason, and Imagination

93. The rational eligibility of what may amount to a potentially troubling range of alternatives to even the central prohibitions of the criminal law—troubling both because of the attendant moral cost it may entail and the social consensus it may undermine or even preclude—means that if the law is to secure a life in common in those respects it must go beyond its rational claim upon us, and the normal justification of its authority which that gives rise to, so as to call upon force or imagination in the ways just described. In recognition of this, criminal prohibitions very often rely not only upon sanctions for their breach but upon their expressive character, and the political vision that is embedded there, to shape public opinion in such a way that the addressees of those prohibitions internalize the political vision in question and so find themselves governing their subsequent behaviour in light of that vision without the further guidance or direction of the law. For most people, or at least for most of those people who attend to the law when contemplating actions that are governed by it, that is how the prohibitions function as practical reasons.

94. This kind of expressive legislative strategy, whether at the hands of elected representatives or of the judiciary, is at its most explicit and most unadulterated, however, in domains other than the criminal law, namely those domains of contemporary law-making, human rights law being the most prominent example, that self-consciously seek to build a better kind of society—a better kind of life in common—by altering the attitudes of the addressees of law in ways that alter their subsequent relations to one another—not merely or even principally in the activities directly regulated by the laws in question (so as to secure absence of discrimination in employment, or provision of services, for example), but in those domains of social interaction in which people regulate their own lives, domains that the law might well be constitutionally incapable of regulating directly. By this means—that is, by capitalizing upon the law's

capacity to inspire the imaginations of its addressees—human rights provisions can help to secure, indirectly and over time, a society in which people express proper respect for one another in all their dealings with one another without being specifically required to do so by law. Indeed, it might be thought that it is just this kind of expressive ambition and approach that helps to distinguish the project of human rights from its otherwise closely allied legal and cultural forebear, the project of civil liberties.

95. The expressive approach at work here is something that has become close to necessary in the world we live in today, made necessary not only by the character of human rights law and similar provisions (which taken by itself would simply bracket the question of the need for such laws) but, more profoundly, by the underlying concern that those laws seek to address: namely, the challenge of creating a life in common in circumstances of diversity, where values that are incompatible with one another, or at the very least that sit uncomfortably with one another, are embedded in attendant social practices which, in their turn, help to constitute distinctive, potentially competing ways of life—ways of life that must then not merely co-exist but also discover and maintain among themselves a sense of common purpose, one of sufficient degree and depth as to ensure that they and the pluralistic society that they constitute flourish, separately and together. In such a project, force and reason can have only supporting parts to play. Something more must be called upon, namely imagination and the politics in which it is embodied.

a) Force and Imagination

96. Begin with the question of force. While there can be no doubt that prohibitions and their attendant sanctions are an integral aspect of human rights laws, laws such as those forbidding discrimination (be it on the basis of sex, race, religion, or some other ground), their significance is limited by the fact that when those laws are responded to directly, as they present themselves, they are for the most part insensitive to the wider political ambition that typically underpins them, and to that extent irrelevant to the addressees of that ambition. The *prima facie* focus of anti-discrimination law, for example, on forbidding discrimination in employment, or accommodation, or provision of services, and on backing that prohibition with appropriate sanctions, is not driven principally by the sense that those domains are where the problem of discrimination actually lies. Rather it is

animated by a sense that it is there and only there that the problem can be remedied directly by law, with the aid of sanctions, and by the further and more fundamental sense that action there will inspire action, in all probability more significant action, elsewhere. Law cannot do more than this, however much it might like to, because law cannot compel the extension of the values that animate anti-discrimination provisions, and others like them, to domains that do not fall within both the legitimate and the effective scope of law as a social practice.[4]

97. Part of the reason for this, of course, is the familiar point that it is impossible to compel belief by force. In itself, however, that would simply prompt the question of why the law should want to be in the business of compelling belief, rather than action, in these respects. After all, most legal prohibitions, paradigmatically those embodied in the criminal law, are concerned not with whether people *believe* in engaging in theft, or assault, or murder, or rape, but whether they actually do those things. Why should belief have a significance in relation to human rights laws that it lacks in relation to other prohibitions? The answer would seem to be that in the setting of human rights and similar laws it is typically attitudes rather than actions that concern law-makers most, and attitudes concern law-makers because of a disjunction between the ambitions of government in these respects and the capacity of law to fulfil those ambitions directly, either through reason or through force.

98. Some reforms in some societies, many in the world we live in today, require a shift in popular attitudes, not only as a means to an end but as a constituent of the end, perhaps even as an end in itself. Part of the reason for this, as I have already suggested, is that it is only through a change in popular attitudes that political influence can be extended to domains beyond the proper reach of the law—that is, to those domains, however extensive they may be, in which people are bound to govern themselves. If a government, and the political vision that it embraces and embodies, hopes to alter behaviour in domains that, for reasons of political principle or practical effectiveness, are beyond the law's capacity to regulate, then it must proceed indirectly, by seeking to alter behaviour in domains that the

---

[4] The domain within which the law is both legitimate and effective varies somewhat from culture to culture, depending on the political morality present there and the extent to which the population is law-abiding.

law can regulate in such a way as to generate attitudes that will carry the social change in question elsewhere, so that extra-legal actions become the law's emissaries. In such circumstances, an enlarged sense of political ambition (and the dependency of certain forms of social change upon that enlargement) is coupled with a recognition of the effective limits of the law, and hence of effective government through law.

99. More fundamentally, however, when what is at stake in a political vision is a value or set of values such as those that are collected under titles like human dignity, or concern and respect, that ambition can only be fulfilled, and those values realized, by people who have the right attitude. The values typically collected under titles like dignity and respect turn in large part on the ways in which people think of one another and the ways in which their thoughts are expressed, implicitly and explicitly, rather than on the actions that those thoughts may give rise to. (This is not to deny that it is also possible for thoughts of a certain kind to become reified in conventions that an actor may participate in without ever thinking in the way that the convention implies; in such cases the attitude is no less present, but the actor evinces it unwittingly.) In effect, for law-makers and for the new, pluralistic society that they are seeking to build, the attitude becomes the prize. To a very large extent, actions in these respects matter just because they are expressive, consciously or unconsciously, of attitudes. Yet coercion cannot on its own compel a shift in attitude. It can do so only by becoming an element in a larger expressive enterprise, in which the imposition of a penalty is part and parcel of a denunciation of those attitudes that fail to embody the respect that the law-maker is seeking to engender (in this case the respect owed to other ways of life), and that fail to acknowledge the dignity of the people who pursue those ways of life. That is why coercion has a much less significant role to play in the achievement of a pluralistic society than it has in securing the central prohibitions of the criminal law, where this logic is reversed and by and large actions rather than attitudes are the law-makers' prize.

b) Reason and Imagination
100. Yet what of reason? Is it not the case that discriminatory practices are irrational? Shouldn't all rational people perceive and act upon the non-discriminatory conviction that animates anti-discrimination legislation? If so, shouldn't reason do all the work of

spreading the word, so to speak? If that is the case, does it not make sense to think that the law's proscription of discriminatory practices is directed only to the ill-intentioned and negligent, and therefore confined to the domains that the law seeks to regulate directly, domains in which the law's proscriptions can be more or less fully secured by coercion? Whatever people have thought at various times in various places, could it ever in fact be rational to discriminate? The answer to this last question is: no and yes. The no aspect of the answer is straight-forward and familiar from the points just made. Part of the challenge that arises from the need to see that a commitment to non-discrimination is internalized very broadly by the members of a diverse community is the institutional one already described, stemming from the constitutional limits (in the broadest sense of the term constitutional) on what the law can legitimately seek to achieve. Implicit in this way of understanding the challenge of overcoming discrimination is a working belief in the irrationality of discrimination. To the extent that the belief is sound, as in many respects it is, reason does indeed do all the work that is needed, so that the assistance of imagination is not required (constitutional limitations aside) except in relation to the recalcitrant and irrational, some of whom may find an imaginative appeal more persuasive than the threat of a sanction. (The practice of political correctness—in its North American form at least—which is often called upon to deal with the recalcitrant and irrational stands somewhere between imagination and force in its persuasive stance and legislative status, in that it is a publicly inspired form of private enforcement.)

101. Yet there is more. In fact, and as in the case of serious criminal prohibitions, perhaps disturbingly, it is not always irrational to discriminate, for two reasons. First, the most blatant cases of racial segregation and apartheid aside, discriminatory practices, as much as the non-discriminatory practices that the law seeks to promote in their stead, are typically embedded in broad networks of more extended social forms and practices that, taken as a whole, are not necessarily less legitimate than the networks of practices to which they stand in opposition. Even where a way of life is fundamentally committed to respect for the diversity in its midst, and so can properly regard itself as non-discriminatory, it is bound to make choices—with or without deliberation—that embody different conceptions of that respect and what it calls for, and hence different conceptions of non-discrimination, each of which gives rise to different, potentially

conflicting practical conclusions—some of them interstitially distinct, others more fundamentally so—about the proper shape of a pluralistic society and the legitimate role of the state in helping to direct and foster it. There are many possible ways in which to construct a diverse society, each of which is bound to be understood and evaluated as a package, given the mutually supporting character of its elements, and—further and more troublingly—each of which contains elements that can be reasonably objected to as discriminatory when viewed in isolation (or from the context of a rival package) but that can be regarded as legitimate when viewed in the context of that package as a whole and the distinctive approach to the achievement of social unity in circumstances of diversity that the various elements of the package serve to constitute. So, for example, it is possible for a society committed to diversity to regard the practice of discrimination as either a reciprocal or a non-reciprocal phenomenon; to think that the correction of discrimination can legitimately include actions that in other social orders would be regarded as discriminatory; to be neutral, approving, or disapproving of any tendency toward the assimilation of differences in the long term; and so on. To the extent that these approaches to the accommodation of diversity, and their many variants, are legitimate, reason does no more to commend one form of pluralism, with its attendant package of practices, than another. From the point of view of reason, all are legitimate, all are flawed. Part of the project of a pluralistic society, and part of the role of the members of such a society, is to bring imagination (and indeed will) to bear upon the development and evolution of a particular scheme of diversity that will thenceforth stand as its contribution to human possibility in that respect.[5]

102. The second reason it is not always irrational to discriminate is more profound: discrimination can actually be constitutive of a genuine good. Contrary to what is generally assumed, there is rather less distance between a discriminatory and a discriminating mind than meets the eye or leaves one comfortable. Indeed, something close to the discriminatory is a necessary precondition of the discriminating. There are two aspects to this claim. First, human diversity, and the manifold ways of life that have to co-exist successfully in order

---

[5] For a more extended consideration of the connection of anti-discrimination rules to the project of multiculturalism see Raz, 'Multiculturalism: A Liberal Perspective' in his *Ethics in the Public Domain* (1994) at 162.

to cater adequately to that diversity in any given community, are not the only possible ends in terms of which a legitimate and successful society can be constructed. As I have emphasized elsewhere, the fact of value pluralism does not entail the goal of a liberal culture.[6] On the contrary, unity, closure, and the exclusion of strangers have been the building blocks of many sound communities, most of them small in scale, but not all so. Such communities, unfashionable and uncommon though they may be today, are paradigmatically stable, inflexible, rooted, and unaccommodating and, strikingly, make use of those characteristics not simply to impose a disability on those of their participants who cannot flourish under such conditions (though that does follow), but as a resource from which to fashion a distinctive, insular set of social goods, forms, and practices which, at their best, can be rich and rewarding—and more notably, perhaps, which are quite beyond the creative grasp of more contemporary, dynamic, fluid, restless, and open societies. This is not to overlook for a moment the terrible price that is very often paid by people in those communities who can find no place there for ways of life, and attendant practices, that are essential to their flourishing. It is only to point out that the price can sometimes be worth paying, in the limited sense of being partially offset by the realization of genuine goods that would not exist were it not paid, and to the limited degree of diminishing rather than degrading the existence of those who cannot flourish fully in terms of such goods or the conditions that sustain them. It is further to notice, self-critically, that those societies that are committed to pluralism and diversity similarly exact a price from their participants, despite their overt promise of inclusion—namely, the price paid by all those whose flourishing depends upon participation in ways of life and attendant practices that are rooted and enduring, and that cannot survive in conditions of transience and flux. We all need to remember that there is more than one way to make a misfit, and few if any ways to avoid doing so. Liberal cultures, and the misfits that they give rise to, can claim only one fundamental advantage over their conservative rivals, although it is an important one: by the nature of their convictions, they do not pursue their ends to the point of bigotry or brutality, at least as long as they are true to themselves, as so often they are not.

---

[6] 'The Art of Expression', in *Independence of Mind* (2006) at 19. William Galston takes the opposite view in *Liberal Pluralism* (2002).

103. The second aspect to the claim that discrimination can be constitutive of a genuine good follows from the first: paradoxical as it might seem, there could be no practice of inclusion without the presence of practices of exclusion to sustain it, no pluralism without the fact of its denial. Variety in human affairs is a consequence of creativity in isolation, so that the cultural variety that makes a multicultural society possible is necessarily created and sustained by the ongoing presence of monocultures elsewhere, and the inflexibility and closure that characterize them.[7] Just what does this tell us? Issues of international responsibility aside, it reminds us that there is always room for rational challenge to a multicultural project on behalf of participants in subcultures that are in need of reconciliation to that project, who may well be committed by their way of life, or some significant aspect of it, to a monoculture of the kind just described—indeed, who are bound to be so committed if and to the extent that the subculture to which they contribute and upon which they draw is not itself liberal in its outlook, as typically it is not. Sometimes the answer to such a challenge is that the subculture in question, or more precisely the relevant aspect of it, is not viable without the support of social forms and practices that are not and could not be made available in the setting of a pluralistic society. That is the kind of answer that one might give to proponents of arranged marriages in Western societies, for example. More often than not, however, there is as good reason to lean one way as to lean the other on questions like these, to favour the subculture as to disfavour it. As claims to self-government regularly insist, it is entirely possible to isolate certain dimensions of the project of a life in common, so as to leave those dimensions to local ordering (as in a federal structure), to private ordering (by the guarantee of fundamental rights and freedoms, which often are but need not be individual let alone individualistic), and to many other emerging ways of calling into question the conventional association of a life in common with a unitary state and a single source of governance. To the extent that such isolation is possible, monocultures are viable in the midst of diversity.

104. All this means that reason cannot tell us whether to be multicultural, which way to be multicultural, and how far we

---

[7] For fuller consideration of this point, see '(In My) Solitude' in *Independence of Mind* (2006) at 60.

ought reasonably be expected to temper a multicultural commitment. The point of dwelling at length on these facets of the issue of non-discrimination and multiculturalism is the plausibility of the thought they give rise to, that in regard to such matters the content of law alone embodies a claim that defeats all rival reasons and so is enough to determine the actions of all rational people and yield a life in common for the community that those people seek to constitute, leaving the irrational to be dealt with by measures of enforcement. If that thought were correct, nothing more would be required. No recourse would need to be had to the resources of imagination, to the appeal of a political vision. Yet in fact neither the thought nor the conclusions it gives rise to can be sustained even in this apparently persuasive case, where they would appear to be at their most plausible.

105. At least, so I am claiming here. Perhaps I am wrong. Were my claim to be mistaken on the facts, however, so that the alleged rationality of a degree of dissent from policies of non-discrimination and multiculturalism is misconceived (as a great many would insist), it is nevertheless clear that the challenges for the construction of a life in common to which the example of non-discrimination purports to draw attention hold true wherever there exists more than one morally permissible course of action that a significant proportion of a community's membership could reasonably elect to pursue. How frequently is that? Very frequently indeed, it would seem, given the facts of value pluralism, human diversity, the diversity of goods, the diversity of social forms and practices, and the coming together of all these in many contemporary societies as the consequence of extensive and ever-expanding patterns of migration and communication.

106. Of course, as I noted above in considering the role played by the will in establishing a life in common, not all laws seek to describe and shape a life in common, and so not all laws require enforcement. Particularly in a liberal society, law may not only tolerate but actually encourage a diversity of responses to its provisions. Yet that is true less often and less fundamentally than one might naturally take to be the case, even in a community that is constitutively committed to the recognition of autonomy. Western societies are not in fact indifferent as to whether wills are made or contracts are signed (to take two illustrations made familiar by Hart), as they would largely be if they were to go no further than enacting the relevant power-conferring rules. In practice, a good part of a common

law court's concern in the adjudication of contracts, for example, is not simply to make sure that the rules of contract are functional and appropriately upheld, so as to confer power successfully, but to see that the practice of contracting itself is suitably fostered, whether that be by ensuring certainty or ensuring fairness in the articulation and development of the power-conferring rules that sustain and shape the practice. Western societies are committed to promoting the practice of contracting because they take it to be a fundamental component of the multitude of profitable exchanges between strangers on which their commercial and financial well-being is founded, and further because they regard the power to decide whether or not to enter into a contract as a significant aspect of the personal autonomy that they seek to promote in their populations and in terms of which they themselves are defined.[8] Rather more is needed to secure this practice than the bare provision of rules that confer an effective power to enter into contracts and the rational claim that the presence of those rules makes upon their addressees. Neo-Austinians have long maintained that something is missing from accounts of law that fail to capture this fact, and believe that what is missing is the role played by the element of force that they allege is implicit in a judicial determination of the nullity of a contract. But in fact the missing ingredient in accounts of law that focus primarily on the content of law and its rational claim upon us, in this case on the power-conferring rule that enables the formation of contracts, is not force but imagination.

107. These are but tentative and, I hope, suggestive illustrations. People will inevitably disagree as to just which laws fall into this category, yet the category itself seems clear enough for all that. Laws that fall within it do so because they rely to a great extent on imaginative appeal, and the political vision embedded there, to shape opinion in such a way that their addressees are able, indeed likely, to govern their behaviour in light of that vision without the further guidance or direction of the law. As I have already observed in relation to the fundamental criminal prohibitions, for most people, or at least for most of those who attend to the law when contemplating actions that are governed by it, that is how the prohibitions function as practical reasons. Yet this gives rise to a paradox, at least on the face of it, for when law depends on politics for the achievement of

---

[8] For an illuminating account of the value of contracting see Dori Kimel, *From Promise to Contract* (2003).

its ends, it comes close to obviating its function as law in doing so. Put shortly, once politics has done the work of shaping opinion to a certain end, the claims of law to the same end would appear to be superfluous. The resolution to the paradox lies in distinguishing two modes of law-making, which are aligned with but do not quite map onto the distinction between legislation and adjudication, in relation to which political vision, and the imaginative claim it makes upon us, is either extrinsic or intrinsic to the content of law itself. The nature of that resolution tells us something significant about the relationship between politics and law, and in particular about the nature and limits of the doctrine of separation of powers.

c) Extrinsic Imaginative Appeals

108. The most straight-forward way to explain this is by returning to the initial, basic question of the role of law in a life in common. What is at stake in a project of government is the realization of a public culture, a culture secured through the collective endorsement of certain values to a degree sufficient to sustain the existence of a life in common. In a small community, a village perhaps, such a culture would be liable to evolve organically, to be secured instinctively and incrementally, so that denizens would, through their constitutive understanding of one another and their environment and through a constant process of accommodation and mutual alignment, come to act considerately in the broadest sense of that term, so that the flourishing of their fellows became an aspect of their own flourishing and each showed respect of the proper kind for the needs and aspirations of those others with whom he or she was bound to interact. In a setting of that kind, government beyond self-government might hardly be required. At least, that is the way such a culture would work as long it was working successfully; one is bound to notice that the denizens of a village are also capable of being insensitive and intolerant of one another's needs and aspirations.

109. In a community made up of strangers as well as familiars, however, a common culture must by and large be established deliberately rather than discovered naturally, making it necessary to develop and communicate the grounds on which appropriate respect (and consequent concern) for one's fellows turns. This implies, of course, that new social structures, or those that for whatever reason find themselves in flux, are more likely than their predecessors to need the presence and support of law in order to secure

a general public culture and a life in common. Sometimes this involves no more than communication to a population of the relevant information—for example, placing a 20 mph sign in a residential area, or warning graphically that children or elderly people may be crossing the road there, in awareness that otherwise members of the community would not be liable to know of such people or their needs. In cases like those, the attitudes that make such information relevant, and that will ensure that it is properly acted upon, can be assumed to be more or less in place. At other times and in other settings, however, the relevant attitudes may well not be in place, or at least cannot safely be counted upon, and so must be inculcated, perhaps insisted upon. That requires the contribution of imagination, as well as of reason and force, in the manner previously described. Yet if and to the extent that law requires a public culture to build a public culture, in any particular respect, its role would appear to be redundant, and the familiar anarchist claim that law is an unnecessary means to a state of order and community that could be better achieved without it would appear to be correct. Unless, of course, there is a way for law to establish the very politics on which its successful functioning depends—that is, to build the foundations on which it rests.

110. Where law is made by legislatures (or their delegates) and its ambitions are promoted by politicians (and indeed other public figures or institutions, such as non-governmental organizations), it is often the case that the imaginative vision that is required to make a law functional also makes it to a large extent superfluous. Examples of this phenomenon are all too familiar, for they are part of the fabric of scepticism and disappointment that has, in recent years, come to clothe the democratic project and the laws that are the paradigmatic product of its reason and its will. Many of the most significant changes in social attitudes toward formerly oppressed ways of life, in the West at least, bear an uncertain relationship to the laws that are said (usually by lawyers) to have prompted them. Was it the law that led many Western societies to think more positively of homosexuality, or did a change in attitudes to sex and sexuality there prompt the change in the law? And if the answer is, as it would appear to be, a bit of both (first one leading, then the other), just what could the law have done on its own, without the presence of the social and political vision that, if fully effective, would ultimately have made law unnecessary?

111. The preceding analysis suggests a number of possibilities that add up to a significant but modest role for law. Law can attend to details, because it is better at specification than is political vision; law can often help to secure compliance in the face of at least a limited degree of resistance and dissent, because compliance may depend on force, and law is a necessary condition of the use of force in any society with a developed judicial system and a consequent separation of powers (though not a sufficient condition of its effectiveness, as has already been noted); law can play an expressive role in the furtherance of a political vision, by lending its imprimatur to a political project undertaken independently of law; law has the capacity to be more stable and enduring than most political visions, and so is in a position to preserve at least the outlines of a political project long after the political momentum that inspired it has disappeared; law can put an end to the disabilities (of capacity, for example) that law itself has created; and from time to time law can serve as a catalyst for a change that it lacks the capacity to deliver on its own, so shading into the expressive and the political and thereby becoming a partner in the project of, for example, enhancing respect. These things matter, sometimes greatly so, but they make of law a supporting player in a wider project of social and political vision, much of which makes law unnecessary and indeed might well be marred by the intervention of law.

112. In cases like these, the political vision in question precedes, anticipates, and largely subsumes the law. If the vision is potent enough it will render the law redundant, even where the law embodies expressive aspects that might otherwise have done the imaginative work that the building of community in circumstances of rational and practical diversity requires. Such cases of political vision can be contrasted with others, however, in which the vision is intrinsic rather than extrinsic to the content of law and the process by which that content is determined. Where a political vision is intrinsic to law, as it may be in either legislation or adjudication, law makes an imaginative claim upon us in and through the very gesture by means of which it makes its rational claim upon us. This is not merely the usual politics by another means but politics of a special kind, one that only law can play. It is, for the most part, the politics of the judiciary, and the ability of judges to play it well constitutes a central part of the value that law in general and adjudication in particular is capable of bringing to a society and its governance.

d) Intrinsic Imaginative Appeals

113. When a society, and its scheme of governance, assigns to the courts and to the judiciary, or leaves to them by default, responsibility for the articulation of legal obligations of whatever kind, it does so for reasons in addition to, and to some extent in contradiction of, the reasons commonly identified in analyses of constitutional law: namely, that the judiciary is the governmental institution best placed not so much to identify or secure the law through its powers of reason and will but to exercise imagination of a distinctive kind, one that gives rise to certain possibilities and closes others off with respect to the obligations in question. That exercise of imagination, and the rational priority it asserts, is to be found not so much in the *ratio decidendi* that, strictly speaking, constitutes the law that arises from adjudication—though it may well be present there—but in the balance of a judgment, the narrative of which, particularly at the appellate level, often (though not inevitably) calls upon that very repertoire of tropes, previously described, that makes possible the seduction of imagination by imagination. What is distinctive in the judicial setting is both the nature of that repertoire (which in any given jurisdiction is described and shaped by the institutional character of the judiciary and the culture of adjudication there) and the nature of the audience for legal judgments (which at its narrowest is the community of legal officials that Hart spoke of and at its widest is a public culture in which adjudication and judicial reasoning have become a feature of public discourse and communal self-understanding, in the way that Dworkin has attended to and sought to capture).

114. In setting out what are generally known as their reasons for judgment, judges call upon all the familiar resources of reason, subject to certain modifications that stem from their institutional role. Some aspects of reason, most notably those collected under the rubric of the rule of law, are the peculiar preserve of the law, its distinctive contribution to the realm of rationality. When judges invoke those aspects of reason they are being rational in ways it is not open to the layperson to be, and so have greater resources available to them with which to reach a reasoned conclusion than do the rest of us. Other aspects of reason, however, are correspondingly denied to the judiciary, on the grounds that their content is at odds with the institutional role that the courts are expected to play in the governance of society. Justice is not blind, as it is so often depicted, but it is blinkered. Many matters that are morally salient are irrelevant

in adjudication, and regrettably, judgments that mistake the true implications of that fact may well treat as irrelevant further matters that are in fact legally relevant as well as morally salient. This means that an ordinary citizen, or another source of law, may well have access to reasons that a judge lacks; this explains, at least in part, the frustration experienced by many lay observers—and indeed by some legislators—with certain outcomes of adjudication that ignore factors which appear to be morally inescapable. Within the rational domain so delineated—enhanced on the one hand and diminished on the other—a judge may well find sufficient resources to yield a determination in the case before him or her, if and to the extent that the adjudicative reasons that tell in favour of one conclusion defeat all others. More often, however, he or she will have a decision to make, and so will have to reach beyond the domain of the rational without betraying it.

115. Sometimes such decisions are established by fiat, frankly or otherwise. First-time readers of law reports are often struck by the brevity of the argument with which a decision is supported. A judge will typically describe the alternatives before the court at considerable length, by reference to the arguments presented by counsel, the precedents that support those arguments, the principles and traditions that inform those precedents, and so on. All these are part of the culture and tradition of adjudication, evidence of the concern and respect that the courts are committed to showing to those who appear before them, as well as to those whose well-being is at stake in what they decide. Yet, just as typically, little is then said by the judge as to why one set of reasons should prevail over another so as to yield one conclusion rather than another, simply because there is little that can be said within the resources provided by the rational repertoire to which judges have access.

116. More commonly, judges seek to highlight the rational appeal of the decision that they have reached by employing certain arational[9] techniques, once again frankly or otherwise. First-time readers of law reports are similarly struck by the degree to which many

---

[9] Strictly speaking, appeals are rational, irrational, or more commonly some mixture of the two, in which the rational dimensions of an appeal serve as a cloak for one or more irrational considerations that, given the features of human psychology, individual and collective, exert a pull upon an audience that buttresses the claims of rational considerations to a degree that may be crucial to the success of the appeal. It is not possible for an appeal to be rationally inert (unless it is unintelligible) and so strictly speaking it is not

judgments are couched as something close to moral fables, in which the facts of the case become the crucible for a narrative that the author of the judgment addresses to a particular audience in terms that the audience in question is likely to recognize and respond to. There may be several such audiences available for a judge to take account of, depending on the legal and political culture in which he or she is operating. The most immediate audience is the community of legal officials, ranging from other members of the judiciary—be they fellow members of an appellate panel or judges who will subsequently be expected to take account of the decision—to members of the wider legal profession, such as lawyers and the police, who may likewise be called upon to refer to the decision in their future pleadings or practice. That immediate audience of officials has been traditionally receptive to the distinctive values and reasons, already referred to, that are the domain of law and the legal community—values and reasons such as certainty and faithfulness to precedent. Judgments that seek to appeal to that community tend to emphasize those values and reasons, to the point of treating them as having a pre-emptive character that in fact they lack, thereby presenting them as determinative of a conclusion that they actually have no capacity to determine by virtue of their rationality alone.

117. In certain cultural settings, however, where law and politics are close fellows, there may be a wider audience for adjudication present in the non-legal community, so that a judge comes to function as something of a public intellectual and his or her reasons for judgment, or portions of them, become capable of entering the wider public culture, where they can help to shape the politics that determines a decision's reception and influence. Those audiences may well

---

possible for an appeal to be arational. In what follows, however, I use the term arational to refer to ways of describing and developing the implications of a proposed course of action, a course of action that is neither defeated by nor victorious over the rational claims of any rival course of action, that encourage an audience to make the mistake of regarding that course of action as rationally pre-eminent. The course of action is no less rational for this way of presenting it, of course, and the decision to pursue it remains rational by virtue of that fact, but the considerations that tell upon a particular agent's mind may be either rational (detailing the course of action without attempting to present those details as defeating rival claims) or irrational (involving irrational considerations, or representing rational considerations as rationally determinative when they are not). I want to draw attention to the possibly irrational basis of a preference, and the vital role that it can play in the construction of a life in common, while being clear that such a basis does not affect the rationality of either the course of action or its preference. Hence the use of the placeholder reference to arationality.

be unreceptive or even hostile to the values that hold imaginative appeal for the community of legal officials, and for that reason the narrative and vocabulary of a judgment that is directed at audiences beyond the legal community will shift so as to take on a shape that will resonate in a lay setting, instead of or in addition to the resonance it may have in the legal realm.

118. Begin with the most contained case. In certain adjudicative settings, such as that in England and Wales, where the workings of the common law are not a standard part of political discourse, the appeal is not so much to the wider public culture as to the lay understandings of the legal community, those parts of a lawyer's mind and judgment that the blinkers of justice would normally exclude from consideration in reasoning toward a judgment, or toward the understanding of a judgment. When Lord Denning distilled his language to the elemental, so as to suggest the simple common sense of what he had to say; when he invoked folk understandings in something close to folk idiom ('It was bluebell time in Kent'; 'The avoidance of tax may be lawful, but it is not yet a virtue');[10] when he appealed to ideas of justice that embraced the morally salient in all its richness and insisted on their legal relevance, he drew upon a distinctive and politically effective repertoire of imaginative resources in an attempt to persuade lawyers to think less like lawyers, and thereby endorse conclusions that were not merely no more rationally compelling than their rivals, but that would actually have been ruled out of consideration by any conventional focus on the distinctive rational domain of the law. In doing so he came close to inverting standard judicial practice, by claiming pre-emptive character for a set of non-legal values and reasons—a character that they in fact lacked just to the extent that the rhetorical exercise that he engaged in was necessary.

119. It is worth noticing that much of Denning's effectiveness derived from the skill with which he was able, in a manner characteristic of political vision, to be self-consciously inspirational while in the same breath insisting that his rational feet were more firmly planted on the ground than those of the judges with whom he took issue. Much the same technique can be found in American adjudication; think of Cardozo's handling of the issue of liability to an unforeseen rescuer: 'Danger invites rescue. The cry of distress is the summons to relief. The law does not ignore these reactions of the

---

[10] Hinz v Berry, [1970] 2 QB 40; *Re Weston's Settlements,* [1969] 1 Ch 223.

mind in tracing conduct to its consequences.'[11] However, it is in the realm of constitutional adjudication, principally though not exclusively in the United States, that the blending of rationality and arationality is at its most sophisticated and disarming. In that setting the considerations that must be taken into account by appellate courts, particularly in the adjudication of issues raised by bills of rights, are notoriously abstract and conflicting, to borrow the terms of Finnis's analysis of the problem of practical reasonableness; the consequences of deciding one way or another are very often of large political and cultural import; there is no algorithm available with which to determine the outcome; and certain familiar judicial techniques are ruled out by the institutional setting, so that a decision cannot be arrived at by fiat, or by more or less explicit appeal to a political vision in the Denning manner.

120. When conflicts of values are writ large and deep in the fabric of a political culture, and it falls to the courts to resolve them, as constitutional law very often requires, the role played in that resolution by judicial will, and indeed by imagination, must be correspondingly discreet, given that the readiness of an idea's opponents to yield to what they deeply object to can only be discovered in the primacy of the reasons in favour of that idea, or such appearance of that primacy as the judicial imagination can conjure. That holds true whenever the comprehensive use of force to compel acceptance of the idea has been ruled out, and whenever explicit appeals to political vision have been similarly excluded, not simply because they would be incompatible with the role of the judiciary—for the proper role of the judiciary is itself a matter of debate—but, more importantly, because the conflicts of values that are in need of resolution in such a setting have by this stage—the stage at which they are being adjudicated upon by the highest court in the jurisdiction—become a conflict of political visions, which the courts must find a way to transcend by whatever sleight of hand they can come up with, rather than allowing themselves merely to echo and thereby reproduce. The wider public that the courts must reach and persuade in this context is keenly alive to the possibility that political vision of an all too familiar kind may have played a determining role in adjudication, and is as ready to discredit a judicial outcome on that basis. *Brown v Board of Education* could not have hoped to persuade its audience of its conclusion

---

[11] *Wagner v International Railway,* 232 NY 176 (1921).

had it not made its understanding of equality appear to be rationally inevitable, and correspondingly downplayed the role played in the decision by imagination and by will.

121. Dworkin would have it, of course, that the US Supreme Court's understanding of equality in *Brown* was indeed rationally inevitable, and a compelling instance of law as integrity, as a sound application of his criteria of fit and justification, in his view, would clearly demonstrate. In maintaining this, Dworkin has at least two irons in the fire. On the one hand, he is concerned to establish that there is, or should be, a fixed approach to adjudication, one that when properly applied will yield what is, at any given time and place, a fixed answer to the question of what (the) law is. The soundness of that claim was considered earlier. On the other hand, and underpinning that claim, is endorsement of the view that it would be improper for judges to reach conclusions on the basis of will, or imagination, or any combination of those two powers. In this respect, Dworkin undoubtedly reflects, perhaps capitalizes upon, a view widely held in the body politic, at least in the United States. Yet in fact this underpinning of his account of law is as vulnerable to challenge as are the terms of the account itself. Judges are confronted by a range of rationally permissible conclusions and a host of possible approaches to the problem of deciding among those conclusions, the approaches to decision-making varying with, without ever being settled by, the culture, the audience, the temper of the times, and ultimately the proclivities of the judges in question, or more broadly of the courts of which they are members. The consequence of this realm of possibility is that adjudication is unavoidably political, as reasoning is necessarily supplemented by the exercise of imagination and will—an exercise that, when conducted properly, is rationally licensed and constrained, but seldom rationally determined.

122. Of course, even if true, that fact might be a matter for regret, an inescapable falling away from an ideal in which the judiciary is apolitical and the relationship between the judicial and legislative branches embodies the doctrine of the separation of powers. In truth, however, the kind of politics actually practised by the judiciary helps to make the law the rich, diverse, complex domain that it is, channelling and nurturing as it does the fine-grained, multifaceted web of social forms, practices, and convictions that the courts address and engage with in their processes and their decisions, thereby enabling the common law, and the community it serves, to arrive

at resolutions that could not be arrived at by either the usual politics or their disdain. *Brown v Board of Education* is just one of a plethora of successful instances of this.

123. Just what is this politics, then, that is the exclusive preserve of the judiciary, and what might be thought to be distinctive and potentially valuable about it? The answer is a familiar and perhaps a disappointing one. In the main it is nothing other than the politics that each of us knows from our experience of legal practice, and what is distinctive and potentially valuable about it is nothing other than what distinguishes the common law and its creation through adjudication from legislation and its enactment, and makes the common law as we experience it the repository of remedies that only it could have supplied. Some aspects of that distinction would hold true of adjudication and legislation wherever they are practised. Yet those need not be the most telling or the most valuable aspects of what judicial politics has to offer in any given jurisdiction. The very variety of possible approaches to adjudication, described earlier, and of the factors that influence the choice among them means that it is impossible to say much that is uniformly true about the character of adjudication in this respect. In certain settings its politics may be of marginal significance, or of interest only to the legal profession, and so of little import or concern to the population at large. In other settings, notably that of the United States, its politics may be of great cultural import, and the subject of much public debate. This way of putting things, evasive though it may seem to some, should not be mistaken for a mere gesture at an explanation. Rather, it is a way of capturing a claim that the description of adjudicative politics in any particular jurisdiction is entirely knowable, indeed entirely familiar and accessible to the lawyers who practice there, but at the same time very largely local and contingent, precluding any ready extrapolation from the practices of one jurisdiction to those of another. Just what kind of description might be offered in local and contingent terms in a particular setting is a matter that I will return to; first, it is necessary to take account of an objection of principle.

e) The Separation of Powers

124. Surely, it might entirely reasonably be objected, there is a very great deal that can, and ought to, be said about the politics of the judiciary, and its propriety or lack of it, in terms of the doctrine of the separation of powers. On a strict reading of that doctrine, the

judiciary is barred from engaging in politics of any kind; even on an indulgent reading, the judiciary is barred from engaging in the kind of politics engaged in by legislators, and the ability to know and respect the difference between the two kinds of politics is essential to any enforcement of the bar. Arguments along these lines might be advanced from either end of the political spectrum—from the left as an objection to any politics that is undemocratic, as the politics of the judiciary certainly is, and from the right as an objection to any conception of adjudication that would permit judges to reach conclusions on a basis other than that of rationality, and of legal rationality in particular, without the sort of exercise of imagination that would prefer one conclusion to another that was no less rationally qualified.

125. It is certainly true that there must be some separation of the powers of the judiciary from those of the legislature, for without some distinction of function there would be little if any point in distinguishing the institutions. Yet it does not follow from this either that a functional distinction, necessary as it is, need take the form of the distinction between the political and the non-political, or that it need be clean, unambiguous, unadulterated, without any overlap of functions between the judiciary and the legislature. On the contrary, it is quite implausible to think that a public institution such as the judiciary could possibly conduct itself in a way that did not have political overtones, and quite natural to think that two sets of decision-makers, engaged in the development of the law for the common good as best as they respectively can, should act in ways that, while respecting the relative independence and distinctiveness of their roles, from time to time attempted to best fulfil their separate remits each by taking on aspects of the other, without going so far, of course, as to become the other, even temporarily. Part of the reason for such an overlap is the difficulty of drawing clear distinctions in practice, but part also is what would be lost by doing so even if it could be done.

126. Put succinctly, the judiciary engages in politics, of a kind that is at once distinctive to the judiciary and overlapping with that engaged in by the legislature, and is indeed bound to do so, just as and when it falls to the courts to articulate a governmental agenda that depends upon the exercise of imagination for its realization in the shape of a life in common. In certain cases, such an agenda may be assigned to the judiciary for other reasons, so that the politics necessarily involved in delivering the agenda is a consequence possibly

to be regretted, as I have already noted. On the other hand, the agenda may be assigned to the judiciary for the very reason that the kind of politics that the judiciary will bring to bear upon it, given the institutional character of the judiciary in the culture in question, is the kind of politics that the assigning body wishes to see attached to that agenda: perhaps because the politics of the judiciary will serve the agenda best; perhaps because that is how the agenda is bound to be served in the culture in question, given other features of the culture; perhaps because a community has simply made that choice, directly or indirectly, consciously or unconsciously, as a matter of historical circumstance. Considered from the opposite perspective, the judiciary could only avoid engagement in politics of this kind (or reliance on fiat in its place) if its agenda were fully identifiable and realizable without any reference to imagination, which, following the arguments previously developed, would be the case only if the jurisdiction of the courts were confined to the consideration of issues in relation to which authority could perfect reason. In fact, however, issues of that kind, where a choice is made among options that are equal in terms of the value that the law-maker is seeking to serve and hence realize in a life in common, typically fall within the province of the legislature, while appellate courts for the most part operate in realms where the exercise of imagination is essential.

127. I emphasized earlier the difficulty of saying very much in principle about the distinction between the politics of the judiciary and those of the legislature, but at the same time emphasized that there was a good deal to know and say about the distinction contingently and locally. In the particular setting of Anglo-American jurisprudence, for example, where the distinction is between the practices of common law adjudication and those of legislation (primary and subordinate), it is noticeable that the exercise of imagination is built into the fabric of the common law and its adjudication in a way that it is not built into legislation. In the common law, particularly at the appellate level, the distinction between what is part of the *ratio decidendi*, and therefore law, and what is *obiter dicta*, and therefore not law (though susceptible to being given special weight in subsequent decision-making), is not always sharp—sometimes deliberately so, with the consequence that the imaginative cast that informs the judgment as a whole cannot be confined to what is *obiter*, but instead seeps into the *ratio* so as to lend it certain expressive implications, with their attendant political appeal. Those who read

judgments, it should be remembered, read them as a whole, often argue about what is and what is not part of the *ratio* (by drawing on different strands of the judgment as a whole), and, particularly at the highest level of judgment—that emanating from a supreme court or its equivalent—are often prepared to treat as legally significant judicial observations that plainly form no part of the *ratio*, simply because they plainly had no bearing on the outcome, perhaps were even made in dissent.

128. That kind of continuity between law and the reasons for its existence is largely missing from legislation, where the distinction between what is enacted as law and the debates and other pronouncements that surround and shape that enactment is typically much sharper. That is not to say what would be clearly untrue: that those who read legislation never turn to surrounding materials, such as working papers, or the statements of a sponsoring legislator, or what was said in the course of debate in a legislative chamber; that they never use such materials to argue about the meaning and content of law. Legislation, like most other human artefacts, is open to interpretation, and there are more or less recognized rules about what extrinsic materials can properly be turned to in the course of interpretation, rules that in the Anglo-American common law world permit consideration of the range of materials just referred to—though there are also, of course and in turn, further arguments about the content of those rules and their own proper interpretation. It is to say, however, to put it at its simplest, that one does not read legislation in the same way that one reads a judgment, and one aspect of the difference between the two ways of reading is the difference in continuity, in each of those settings, between law and what are presented as its reasons for being.

129. That difference is noticed and traded upon by judges and legislators alike, so that judges typically exercise imagination in a low-key way that promotes continuity between a *ratio* and its setting, while legislators trade on the lack of continuity between legislation and its enactment to make the circumstances of enactment politically charged in a way that the terms of legislation themselves could never be. On one side of the divide the contrast is minimized, on the other it is maximized, in both cases so as to further the impact of an imaginative appeal in the context in question, and by doing so to promote the prospects of the life in common that both institutions are committed to securing.

130. The pattern of influence runs in both directions. Judges act as they do not as a matter of subterfuge but because it is in the nature of reasons for judgment that the distinction between *ratio* and *obiter* is not capable of being rendered in a way that is particularly sharp, so that continuity between the two, including continuity of imaginative appeal, is natural and inevitable. Just as a judge would never explicitly step back to identify what is *ratio*, so he or she never need declare that at a certain point imagination, rhetoric, and other like forms of persuasion are at an end. By the same token, but from the opposite perspective, the terms of a statute are fundamentally distinct from the circumstances of their presentation and debate in which the case for them is made, in all the ways that a *ratio* is not, and so are by and large free from political vision, apart, of course, from that which has attended and supported them in presentation and debate—some elements of which, it is true, may be called upon in their interpretation, but the most explicitly political of which will be ignored. The consequence is that the lack of continuity in the legislative setting has the effect of exaggerating the distinction between law and its reasons for being, so that debate becomes highly political while the terms of the statute are largely, though not entirely, stripped of imaginative cast.[12] The politics of the judiciary, it follows, is naturally tacit, or, as its critics might put it, insidious (just because its presence cannot be acknowledged, even by its practitioners, without undermining the very nature of adjudication, and the subtlety of the relationship that the nature of adjudication establishes between *ratio* and *obiter*), while the politics of the legislature is just as naturally explicit. The assignments of tasks and roles that a society makes to the courts and to legislatures respectively are accordingly made with that fact in mind, so that the courts are typically asked to take responsibility for

---

[12] It is true that some sort of political vision is embodied in the names and preambles of certain statutes, but it is also true that those names and preambles are typically disregarded in any exercise of statutory interpretation. What remains, of course, is the expressive dimensions of a statute, such as those considered earlier in relation to the fundamental criminal prohibitions. Tellingly, however, those dimensions are accessible only through an exercise of interpretation which, at least in Anglo-American legal culture, it falls to the courts to undertake, through a reading of the statute that draws in part—and to the limited degree that the courts are prepared to regard as permissible—on legislative debates and similar materials; in part on wider considerations of policy and principle, including the realm of legal rationality to which the courts have special access; and finally on the arational resources that are needed to reach a determination in the face of alternatives each of which is no less rationally appealing than the other.

matters that are best handled in a way that makes politics tacit rather than explicit. Just what those matters are varies from culture to culture, but they typically include matters in relation to which explicit politics would be likely to yield the wrong conclusion (perhaps an intemperate one) or no conclusion at all (where a society is deeply divided on a particular issue).

131. It might be thought that a politics of the judiciary, whatever potential it might offer for the realization of a life in common, is nevertheless inherently to be regretted and avoided where at all possible, given that the ideal of justice that it is the duty of the courts to safeguard and advance depends upon absence of bias in favour of any participant in the proceedings, and of any convictions on the part of the judge that would lead to such bias or be equivalent to it, or be reasonably perceived to be so. If and to the extent that politics is a matter of bias, therefore, as it most certainly is when advancing and relying upon arational considerations in order to favour one conclusion over another, it would seem to follow that the courts should avoid politics for the same reasons that they should avoid bias. Yet that is too quick a conclusion. Just as the politics of the legislature avoids service of particular interests not by ensuring that interests are never served, but rather by ensuring that all interests that could conceivably be served in the matter being legislated upon are properly heard—whether by being voiced directly in debate in the legislative chamber, or by being voiced indirectly in one or more of the various fora that support legislative debate—so the politics of the judiciary avoids bias not by blindness to politics and its imaginative potential, but by full attention to the arguments of the parties before the court and genuine open-mindedness as to the outcome. Clearly that is a far from straight-forward task, and between the extremes of what is obviously and obviously not bias there is ample room for disagreement as to the extent to which a judge is entitled to approach a decision with certain of the convictions that will determine its outcome already in place in his or her mind. The existence of such disagreement, however, tends to confirm rather than contradict the legitimacy of the basic practice of judicial politics, as something to argue about and to negotiate rather than as something to eradicate.

132. This is not to suggest that politics on the part of the judiciary is never objectionable, let alone to propose that it should be unconstrained. When a judge falls more or less in love with his or her own voice, as Lord Denning might be thought to have done, and

as other judges have certainly been led to do by that familiar degree of vanity that is all too often the consequence of judicial independence and isolation, he or she is very liable to mistake the arational significance of the imaginative enterprise that he or she is engaged in for rational significance—in just the way that the consumers of his or her judgment are expected to do—and, worse, is liable to come to believe that this supposed rational significance is a product of his or her own special mind, or culture, or profession. A belief in the special rationality of one's own mind or culture is something that Lord Denning may indeed have succumbed to, in his evident confidence in the superiority of his common sense and of his Englishness; belief in the special rationality of one's own profession is something that may have been succumbed to by those of Denning's judicial peers who allowed themselves to be convinced of the rationally pre-eminent character of legal reasoning, or at least of certain facets of it. As I have already noted, it is often thought by lawyers, so much so as to be a relatively common form of professional conceit, that legal rationality is somehow more rational than other forms of reasoning; less policy-driven perhaps, less political, as if that were either true or a virtue. Of course, it is simply not so: where more than one set of reasons is relevant and applicable, one aspect of reason is no better than another, even in a courtroom, other than by stipulation—although one may well be more successful rhetorically than another, at least in the context of particular judgments that are directed to specific audiences in specific settings.

133. It is worth noticing, however, that these sorts of errors are objectionable, not so much because they involve the practice of politics on the part of members of the judiciary as because they involve a damaging degree of self-delusion on the part of a politician, an affliction that legislators and their political leaders are just as prone to as are judges. It is all too easy to be seduced by the power of one's own imagination and the flourish of one's own rhetoric; political history is littered with the names of those who have become so, and consequently disfigured by the price paid by them and by others—usually and more painfully by others—in terms of hope, virtue, and the good.

f) The Price of Imagination
134. Quite apart from the question of the separation of powers, however, there is indeed a real price to be paid for this kind of exercise

of imagination in law-making, whoever the law-maker may be. Just because the role of imagination in the project of law is typically tacit rather than explicit, as in most cases it has to be if it is to be successful in its objects, the exercise of imagination as typically generates, and indeed trades upon, a significant degree of ambiguity as to the function of law and the value that law can bring to the realization of a life in common. Laws that are informed by imagination, whether extrinsically or intrinsically, must inspire, in ways that are arational, so as to establish the primacy of what they require over alternative, no less rational, courses of action, and yet must at the same time insist upon the full rationality of what they call for, so as to distinguish their claims from others that lack proper rational foundation—in awareness, however, that a genuine appreciation of the full implications of their rationality would undermine the very primacy that their arational appeal attempts to secure. This kind of endeavour can only be successful through a rhetorical sleight of hand the consequence of which is to create in the addressees of law conflicting understandings of its nature, and misguided expectations of its possible outcomes.

135. When law becomes reliant for its success upon the exercise of imagination, either intrinsically, as is typical in the practice of adjudication, or extrinsically, as is typical in the practice of legislation, it harnesses the power of imagination to present a conclusion in terms that suggest that the conclusion is identifiable by force of reason alone, contrary to what is in fact the case. There are two ways in which the addressees of law might reasonably regard this claim as credible, so as to allow themselves to be seduced by it; two kinds of story that they might tell themselves to explain it in rational terms, bearing in mind the limited degree of reflection they are likely to give the matter, granted their endorsement of a legal authority that they otherwise have reason to accept as justified. On the one hand, they might believe, at least in the context of adjudication, that the force of reason, without more, is capable of yielding a conclusion that the courts are in a special position to identify. In some cases, of course, they are correct to believe this, for the judiciary has, by virtue of its legal education, special access to the resources of legal rationality and, by virtue of its professional experience and constitutional status, a heightened ability to employ those resources successfully. When those special skills are harnessed to that special body of knowledge in the circumstances of a courtroom, the application of

legal rationality can indeed yield a conclusion that would otherwise be inaccessible. Alternatively, the addressees of law might believe, particularly in the context of legislation, that authority is capable of perfecting reason by the force of will and the consequent fact of decision. In some cases they are right to believe this too, for the reasons previously set out—cases such as those when an authority determines which side of the road to drive on.

136. In believing either of these things, however, in such a way as to take their implications to extend to laws generally, and in particular to laws that rely for their success upon the exercise of imagination—as they must if those laws are to establish a life in common—the addressees of law make the very mistake made by many analysts of law, which was earlier referred to, of conflating the separate phenomena of reason, imagination, and will, and the distinct roles which each of those phenomena play, or more precisely are capable of playing, in the formation of a decision. Of course, that is precisely what the exercise of imagination, and its attendant political vision, calls upon the addressees of law to do, and that is why the success of that exercise depends upon a rhetorical sleight of hand—one that disguises even as it displays the arational dimensions of the appeal that is being made. Participants in the practice, both the makers of law and its users, in effect become collaborators in a piece of collective self-deception as to the nature of law and the role it is capable of playing in the construction of a life in common. The price paid for this deception in any particular context is a function of the various expectations that come to be generated in this way, and the political implications of their disappointment, as and when the deception is unmasked.

137. Certain audiences expect law to be as effective everywhere as it is, or at least is capable of being, when it specifies—that is, when it aims to perfect reason by making precise what reason renders only imprecisely. In doing so they make the mistake of extrapolating generally from their experience of law in a context where its rational significance is relatively transparent, that of specification, and accordingly expect law to function in the same way and to be effective to the same degree in all other contexts. This is a false extension: because the law is good at making things happen through precision, it must be good at making things happen generally. That is far from the case when imagination needs to be turned to, for a political vision may obscure but cannot fully disable the rational

appeal of rival courses of action.[13] The failure by the addressees of law to recognize this fact is precisely what enables imagination to do its work, of course, often for the good, but it is at the price of confusion and misguided expectations. The consequence of that failure of recognition is that audiences make the mistake that they are invited to make by the terms of a political vision, and so attribute to law generally what is in fact true of only specifying laws; very often look to law for the wrong things; and seek to achieve through law what cannot be achieved through law, or at least cannot be better achieved through law than by other means, and may in fact be worse achieved. In doing so they are not merely disappointed, though they certainly are that. More important, perhaps, they embrace an outlook that diminishes the rational status of those who would disobey the law, or otherwise object to its terms, by regarding such people as irrational—in the manner of those who would drive on the wrong side of the road—rather than as what they are in fact: namely, attentive to reasons that have no lesser claim upon them than the reasons that have been embodied in law. By the same token, they diminish their own rationality by allowing themselves to mistake the appeal of the arational for the appeal of the rational. When things go well, this results in support for a course of action that is no better but also no worse than its rivals. When things do not go well, it results in support for a course of action that reason would reject.

138. Other audiences, with like understandings of law in terms of specification but different political convictions, notice the imaginative cast that has attended judicial determination of the laws in question, take that cast to be illegitimate (because it violates their sense of what law is and how it ought to be identified), and as a consequence make the mistake of condemning those laws as tainted by the presence of the political vision that imagination is embodied in, failing to recognize that laws very often, perhaps typically, cannot secure their claim upon us by force of reason alone, and that a good many of the laws that they themselves would be ready to commend rely for their capacity to establish a life in common on just that imaginative cast. Both audiences, sharing as they do an exaggerated view of the significance of legal rationality, are overly deferential to the legal profession and its values. The ideal judge does not have the powers of Hercules, and so has no capacity to resolve fundamental

---

[13] See later in this section (147ff) for full consideration of this point.

conflicts of values. He or she differs from the rest of us only in the possession of access to a small additional arsenal of reasons, those that have been born in the domain of legal practice or that have acquired distinctive colouring there—an access that is purchased at the expense of access to reasons that the rest of us have access to, but that are ruled out of consideration by the terms of judicial office. To be a judge is to be in a distinct realm of rationality, but not one that is overall better resourced than any other. Reasoning in the setting of adjudication makes the resolution of some issues more possible, that of others more difficult.

139. Confusion and misguided expectations yield their own distinctive disappointments, of which those just considered are but examples. More important, however, they derive from a rational misunderstanding that generates disappointment of a deeper kind. The role of imagination, in one life or in many, and of the narrative power that the exercise of imagination finds expression in and through, is to foster the belief that one possible course of action possesses greater rational weight than its rivals. In the life of any one person, that belief can often be vindicated by a degree of investment in the course of action, because investment, through various forms of commitment, typically enlarges the implications of a course of action, and hence the value that can be realized from its pursuit, while correspondingly diminishing the attractions of its erstwhile rivals. If and to the extent that such investment is pursued, it soon comes to be the case that the attractions of rival courses of action can only be realized in one's life through a process of disinvestment from what one has already committed oneself to and a subsequent reinvestment elsewhere. The greater the investment in one's present commitments, of course, the more costly and traumatic the process of altering them in this way. If one is either fortunate or far-seeing, deepening commitment brings deepening rewards; if one is unfortunate or myopic, however, it brings only entrapment, by rendering alternatives to it inaccessible or unaffordable. In practice a person's life is typically enriched in parts and impoverished in parts by entanglement in the toils of its long-term structure and goals. Of course, the distinction between what is enriching and what is impoverishing in one's life is slightly less clearly demarcated than that description in terms of separate parts might suggest; in fact the satisfactory is rarely perfectly satisfying, the unsatisfactory

rarely completely unsatisfying, for each usually contains within itself aspects of the other.[14]

140. In the life of a community, however, the exercise of imagination, and the projection and endorsement of a political vision in which imagination is embedded, has different implications, in terms of commitment to a course of action and the rational pull of alternative courses of action, because of the difference between what is excluded in terms of possibility by personal and collective commitments respectively. When endorsement of a course of action is fostered in a community through the projection and subsequent embrace of an imaginative appeal, that endorsement, and the assumption of rational priority that it trades upon, can indeed be vindicated by collective commitment to that course of action, but in a manner that only roughly parallels the vindication of choice that can follow from individual commitment. As a communal commitment to a course of action, and to the set of beliefs that warrant it, deepens over time and through various modes of implementation, the course of action comes to be constitutive of certain social forms and practices, which then, in their turn and in their own right, direct and shape future endorsement and development of the course of action. It is in this way and by these means that law and politics can help to bring about and sustain social change. When their imaginative appeal functions successfully, so as to become embedded in social forms and practices, they do not merely change society; in sympathetic circumstances they can give birth to new engines of social change that are able to operate, to consonant effect, long after the law's own appeal has dimmed, after its claims have become superfluous, even after its terms have been altered or repealed. Quite apart from their dynamism, however, quite apart from their continuing capacity to deepen their grip and extend their reach, the social forms and practices that law has inspired shape the possibilities for action of those who fall within their embrace, in good ways and bad, by making alternative courses of action less rational courses to pursue, simply because they are less productive of value in that setting than their rivals, whether in one life or in many.

---

[14] For a more extended consideration of the shaping of the pursuit of value by personal commitment and goals in life see Macklem and Gardner, 'Value, Interest, and Well-Being', 18 *Utilitas* 362 (2006), particularly at 374ff, and Macklem, 'Choice and Value', 7 *Legal Theory* 1 (2001), particularly at 27ff.

141. Yet there are two ways in which the shaping influence of social forms and practices is avoided—one in principle, the other in practice. Not all people fall within the embrace of a social form or practice, because not all people are bound to participate in all social forms and practices—though all are bound to take rational account of them—and not all those who are bound to take rational account of them need take account of them in the same way. That is the crucial difference between individual commitment and collective commitment, and it stems from the different finitudes that govern the life of one person and the lives of many. In the collective setting, some people commit themselves to a social form or practice (and to one or more of the possibilities to which it gives rise), and some dissent; some commit themselves whole-heartedly, some with regret. This is not just because some people are irrational, and so irrationally dissenting or regretful. Put to one side cases of irrationality and, for the time being, cases of those whom the social practice (and the law that has inspired it) makes no claim to govern. Those cases aside, there are typically good reasons to dissent and to regret, and strikingly, they are none other than the very reasons that sustain the appeal of alternative courses of action and the alternative social forms and practices that those courses of action might have given rise to; the very reasons that the exercise of imagination, and the political vision in which it has been embedded, has portrayed as inferior to those that it has sought, more or less successfully, to endorse and give effect to.

142. Begin with the practical realm. The claims of undefeated reasons lose none of their force for not having been attended to and acted upon.[15] On the contrary, they are in as good a position to make their claims upon a community that has endorsed their rivals as upon any other community. What the fact of collective commitment changes is the implications of acting upon those reasons in the

---

[15] It might be thought that this is true not only of undefeated reasons but also of defeated reasons. If I were to give the last indivisible bit of food to the hungrier of two people, I would still have reason to be concerned at the hunger of the other person, and so would have reason to find a way of meeting that hunger on another occasion, and reason to feel pain at not being able to meet it more immediately. What I have in mind here in distinguishing defeated and undefeated reasons is that in the case of rational defeat the reason to feed the second person is deprived of its force in relation to the last bit of food by the stronger claim of the hungrier person, while an undefeated reason would continue to insist that it should have been preferred, and its insistence would be no less rationally compelling than the insistence of the reason that had been preferred,

face of that commitment. Where the claims of reasons of a particular kind run counter to, or at least sit uncomfortably with, prevailing social forms and practices and the reasons to engage in them, one is bound to respond to those claims as something of a dissenter, whether on one's own, as a member of a recognized counter-culture, or as a member of a more or less alien minority culture. In some respects this may diminish or even eliminate the value of engaging with those reasons in that context; in other respects, however, it may actually enhance that value, or more precisely some dimension of that value. Where a course of action, and the reasons to undertake it, run contrary to the reasons to do what law and society expect or encourage, any pursuit of that course of action will lack the support of certain social forms and practices—those that depend on general endorsement, which may be crucial to the realization of at least some part of the value that the course of action is capable of giving rise to, and so make the course of action less worth pursuing or not worth pursuing at all. On the other hand, the force of undefeated reasons can still be felt and responded to through all those social forms and practices that are consistent with marginalization and dissent. The power of those reasons—and the inability of the exercise of imagination on the part of officials, and of the political vision in which it is embedded, to inflict any kind of comprehensive defeat upon them—poses a continuing threat to the construction of a life in common, sometimes for the good and sometimes not. Unlike the individual case, where commitment to a course of action very often fully precludes a subsequent commitment to its rational rivals, in the collective setting a commitment to a course of action by some people does not usually preclude a like commitment to a rival course of action by others.

143. In many ways we approve of dissent of this kind, and of diversity of opinion and practice, and for good reason. Some forms of dissent are internal, and so constitute a challenge to a legally inspired and broadly endorsed social form or practice; others are external, and so limit the reach of an accepted social form or practice by proposing and helping to sustain alternatives to it. Internal forms of dissent can be valuable even when they are misguided, for all the reasons offered

and so would lose none of its force as a result of its legitimate neglect. Thanks to John Gardner for raising this point, although I should make clear that he seems to differ from me on the underlying issue of the character and significance to be attached to the fact of rational defeat.

by Mill and those who have followed in his wake—reasons that have to do with the value of a critical mind and all that such a mind can give rise to. External forms of dissent can also be valuable, partly for the same sorts of reasons and partly because they frequently sustain alternative ways of life, with their own distinctive social forms and practices and their own potential for value; value that is accessible in and through that way of life and not elsewhere, value on which the success of certain lives in that society depends. These are the reasons that sustain and justify the space and commitment that many contemporary societies offer to multiculturalism, as well as to certain microcultures in their midst, be they aboriginal, nomadic, religious, ethnic, linguistic, or some other.

144. So far do contemporary Western societies approve of such practices of dissent, internal and external, that significant strands of the law there are dedicated to protecting and fostering dissent. The protection of internal forms of dissent, through the legal entrenchment of freedoms of belief, conscience, and expression and to a lesser extent of freedoms of association and assembly, has become something of a modern commonplace. The protection of external forms of dissent, though more recent, is now well entrenched and still in the course of development. In doing these two things, of course, the law quite deliberately undermines its own projects, including its most basic project of articulating and establishing a life in common. There is no natural or inevitable equilibrium between dissent and what it opposes, and communities often find themselves frustrating their own endeavours in both directions at once, caught between the value of what they are seeking to build and the various values of opposing it. Their resulting sense of disappointment, however, is born of something greater, something deeper, than the basic practical frustration born of conflicting ambitions.

145. When law depends upon the exercise of imagination, and the political vision in which imagination is embedded, for the purchase it obtains upon a particular community—or at least upon enough of that community to sustain a life in common—it claims in doing so that the course of action that it calls upon the community to undertake is one that is rationally determined rather than what it is in fact—a course that is merely rationally eligible—and so claims that any dissent from that course of action is either irrational (though possibly valuable nonetheless) or rational but entirely alien, so as to be incompatible with pursuit within that community. This is, among

other things, a piece of deceit (though it is, when more or less freely subscribed to, as much self-deceit as anything else), however worthy its outcomes may be, and when it is exposed as deceit, as sooner or later it is bound to be by the evident viability and rationality of the practices of dissent that law itself typically encourages, it engenders a perception of corruption on the part of its purveyors and a sense of betrayal at their hands. A greater authority is being claimed for the law's requirements than is warranted, and when that fact is recognized the disenchantment that follows very often becomes a disenchantment with political authority itself: that is, with law and with the political institutions and political processes (such as democracy) that make and recommend it.

146. When this second form of practical disappointment is combined with the form of practical disappointment considered earlier, that which follows from the frustration of certain public objects as a result of the endorsement of conflicting strands of public reason (those in support of a particular course of action and those in support of dissent from it), the two forms of disappointment reinforce and compound one another to yield a relatively familiar contemporary malaise. Law, as it turns out, is not terribly good at doing many of the things it is currently asked to do (which is in part why imagination is so often looked to); imagination is accordingly called upon to promote the law's requirements, but in that characteristically beguiling way that both conceals its role and strips away that concealment, a piece of *legerdemain* that succeeds only intermittently and provisionally; governmental regulation that is promoted by those means inevitably gives the impression of being at once ineffective and corrupt; and the upshot is a growing and entirely understandable disappointment in law, in its institutions, and ultimately in the democratic project itself (or other mode of government if and when that is the context). Although the evidence at present is speculative and ultimately anecdotal, this seems to be in many ways the temper of our times, in what appears to be a period of transition in Western liberal cultures in which the values of the rule of law and of democracy are promoted and emphasized with increasing frequency, while the regimes that espouse them are increasingly identified with incompetence and deceit, and the general public's underlying faith in and commitment to both more or less visibly ebbs away.

147. Underpinning these two forms of practical distance from what the law requires, be it the awareness of a lack of rational

pre-eminence in what the law calls for and the political detachment which that may give rise to or the rationality of practices of dissent from its claims, is the other, more profound way in which the shaping influence of social forms and practices is avoided: that of distance in principle. The claim of reasons upon us is in no way lessened by our neglect of them, or our inability, all due attention having been paid to them, to realize them in the course of our own, necessarily limited lives. We notice this most readily, of course, when we see those reasons acted upon by other people, and in doing so come to appreciate, in the setting of other lives (be those lives consonant with our own or alien to us), the value that acting upon those reasons is capable of giving rise to. The deeper our understanding of those other lives, the greater our empathy for their distinctive meaning and structure, the more we appreciate values that we have not committed our own lives to, and in doing so recognize the claim of reasons that we have not ourselves acted upon. Yet we need not always look to the lives of others, for we may notice the claims of reasons that are alien to our lives just as powerfully through contemplation of the kind of people we are, the kind of lives we have led, and just what we might have been and done had our choices and circumstances been other than they were. Our awareness of these competing claims upon us—those we have honoured and those we have neglected—and the continuing vitality of both is the setting for a familiar cluster of rational reactions, of which the most notable perhaps is that of regret.

148. To put it in somewhat romantic terms, roads not taken still have their call. Their destinations continue to beckon to us long after any turning to them has been missed, all the more powerfully sometimes when the turning is well past, or indeed was never present for us. Even quite young people are entirely familiar with the pang. These are the things we might have done, the lives we might have led, though we might have had to be other people in other times and places to have done them or led them. It can be irrational to dwell unduly upon such matters, if to do so would have the consequence of undermining worthwhile projects in which we have invested ourselves, but it is no less irrational to overlook them, or to discount their claim upon us by regarding it as having been rendered irrelevant by the commitments we have made or have been led into. On the contrary, our awareness of those reasons in many ways provides the surest path to appropriate reflection upon the kinds of people

who we are and the kinds of goods that we have committed ourselves to, and the value and disvalue of being such people and having such commitments.

149. In the collective setting of the law, and of a life in common that is arrived at with the assistance of law, our awareness of the claims upon us of reasons that are in one way or another inconsistent with the forms and practices of our society (forms and practices in which we are more or less engaged and through which we are more or less bound to pursue those aspects of goodness in our lives that depend on the support of prevailing forms and practices) brings home to us the contingency of our present way of life, individual and collective, and the dependency of its goodness on the goodness of forms and practices to which it is more or less hostage for its viability, but over which our reason and our will usually have only marginal influence. This contingency stems from the fact that the continued existence of such a way of life, one that reaches beyond what reason and will can command unaided, depends upon either the continued vitality of the imaginative vision that gave it birth or a widely held commitment to the preservation of existing social forms and practices, either or both backed up by the force of will and whatever instruments of coercion it may have at its disposal. Given the natural dynamic of all political visions, it is in the end only social conservatism, and the possibility of embedding a particular political vision in the social forms and practices that are secured through such conservatism, that can ensure the survival of forms and practices that there is as good reason to reject as to endorse. In a social and political order such as that which prevails in the West today, where robust questioning of existing social forms and practices, the fostering of diversity through the support of a number of alternative social forms and practices, and the encouragement of dissent from both the dominant social order and its alternatives are all prominent, there can be no more than a faint prospect that the forms and practices which a particular political vision has secured sufficient endorsement of to ensure a life in common that is patterned on its terms will long endure. That is particularly so when the life that is being recommended by those means is reformist and dissolving, while the attitudes needed to ensure its survival are anti-reformist and conservative.

150. It need hardly be said that there is little that can or should be done about this. Life is, among so many other things, a fragile, fluid enterprise, and the vulnerability and transience that mark the lives of

each one of us are inescapably writ large in the life in common that all of us both contribute to and draw upon in the course of our elemental pursuit of goodness, separately and together. Yet, that having been said, there is still something that is worth taking note of here, and bearing in mind when we contemplate different kinds of politics and what each of them offers and asks of us. The more ambitious our politics, in reaching beyond the basic project of articulating, through the precision of law, those aspects of a life in common that can be rendered rationally pre-eminent through the exercise of reason and will alone, the more we must call upon political imagination and vision and look to their seductive force for the successful construction of the kind of life in common that by its nature can only be cast in those nebulous terms—a life that is all too soon bound to belie its carefully contrived appearance of solidity and inevitability as and when the population to which it speaks and seeks to embrace becomes aware of its contingency and fragility, through awareness of the host of reasons that tell against it. How should such a population respond, if and when it finds itself in that predicament? For some people, the contingency and frailty of such ways of life are in themselves sufficient reasons to restrict the common project of law and governance to the relatively minimal terrain of what follows from reason alone, with the support of the will, and to be cautious about any wider kinds of ambition, of the kind that can only be secured through reliance upon the call of imagination. However, that conclusion certainly need not and usually should not follow. Great good can be achieved through social constructions that are fundamentally vulnerable, and a refusal to stake a social order, or significant parts of it, on any such fragile ventures would lead us to miss much of what an enlightened politics can achieve—most notably perhaps many of the very real virtues that characterize contemporary Western societies at their best; those virtues, for example, that express and embody a broad respect for human diversity. We need to remain aware of the price of imagination, but in so doing we should not neglect its promise.

C. Different Kinds of Life in Common

151. I have spoken so far as if the relationship between a life in common and the various pulls of rationality, of will, and of imagination held more or less constant across different lives in common, varying

only with the character of their legal and political missions, which might be focused to greater or lesser degree on matters that could be enforced by rationality, will, or imagination respectively. Yet of course that is not the case. Lives in common vary not only in their character, in the special sense of their distinctive social and political missions, but also in their scope, their depth, and their degree of self-consciousness. Indeed it might be said that this further fact is part and parcel of a wider understanding of the character of any particular life in common, wider than I have taken account of so far. That being the case, the sufficiency of the rational pull of the law (to take but one example) for the achievement of any particular life in common varies from legal system to legal system, depending on the full meaning and ambitions of life in common there, and so may or may not require the support of will and imagination for its realization in any given respect. That is to say, a particular society might accept the limited degree of commonality that rational attention to the law gives rise to, whether broadly or in specific settings. Depending on its self-understanding and aspirations, and on the character and convictions of its population, that community might be capable of accommodating the consequent degree of dissent, either in the relevant respect or more generally, and even if not so capable might believe that the dissent in question should be tolerated, short of course of the point of dissolution of the community, in that respect or more generally. Still, that much having been granted, there is no reason to think that what is sufficient to constitute a life in common maps in every case onto the degree of compliance that follows from attention to the rational pull of law alone, and so no reason to think that will and imagination are not necessary partners to law in the shaping of life in common in every legal system—albeit along different lines in different societies, those lines varying with the extent to which the societies in question are committed to life in common, of whatever kind, and the extent to which they are further committed to the role of governance in bringing that commonality about.

152. To put it in metaphorical terms, the topography of a life in common has three dimensions rather than two. It not only occupies certain territories (two-dimensionally), but does so with varying degrees of density and flourishing. In any given respect, and sometimes in them all, lives in common can be either thick or thin, and the particular domains in which they are one rather than the other of those things may vary from place to place and time to time. What is

more, it is possible to have different views of the husbandry of a life in common, and of the ways in which the full achievement of such a life, be the life thick or thin, is best brought about. The consequence in practice of the existence of these variables is that there are three distinct and interoperating planes in which lives in common may be registered and differ from one another: that of subject matter, that of degree of observance, and that of the culture of their proper creation.

153. The first plane of commonality, that of subject matter, gives rise to different patterns of reason, will, and imagination in the achievement of life in common in different societies as and to the extent that those societies commit themselves to particular ends that by their nature, and by the nature of the population to which they are addressed, are realizable through reliance on the pull of one or another or some particular combination of those three factors. Projects that emphasize the value of co-ordination, for example, and projects that emphasize the value of certain shared attitudes typically call for different patterns of implementation in terms of the weight of their appeal to the several forces of reason, will, and imagination. That much is implicit in all that I have previously said and so needs no further consideration here. Yet those same projects may also vary in their scope—that is, in the degree to which the goals that they embody seek to embrace a population (some people, all people, some people in particular), and in the fullness of the commitment that they seek to secure on the part of those whom they aim to embrace. That fact gives rise to a second plane of commonality, that of degree of observance.

154. Again, there is not much more that can be said about this plane of commonality other than to notice that high degrees of observance typically depend (that is, depend in all cases other than those in which a high degree of observance follows from attention to reason alone) upon strong appeals to will and to imagination. It follows that liberal cultures, those that tolerate and even celebrate significant degrees of non-observance, will typically make the weakest of such appeals, while authoritarian cultures will make the strongest. What this suggests is that there is something of a reciprocal link between authoritarianism and recourse to the pull of imagination (and to the techniques of beguilement) in the project of establishing or seeking to establish a life in common. Imagination, just as much as force, is the necessary instrument of a high degree of compliance,

the degree that goes beyond whatever would follow from the appeal to reason alone. Hence the importance of image-making as much as force in the construction of certain totalitarian societies, and hence also reason to take note of, and to be wary of, the authoritarianism that may well be latent in certain appeals to the imagination in the construction of what are otherwise liberal, democratic societies. I noted earlier the dangers of recourse to imagination in constructing a life in common in relation to certain subjects; the additional thought here is that this danger extends also to certain degrees of observance in a population, in relation to subjects that would not otherwise depend for their appeal on the pull of imagination.

155. The third plane of commonality is in some ways perhaps the most interesting, although again there is not a great deal that can be said about it in this setting, beyond recognizing and taking due note of it. One of the ways in which lives in common can differ from one another is in the understandings that they hold of two quite closely related ideas: that of the quality of community as a community and that of the modes of its construction, be the latter conscious or unconscious. These ideas differ from one another principally in the direction of their influence. On the one hand, a community may tend to see itself as a community of a certain overriding character, and this self-understanding may entail a commitment to being the kind of community that can be arrived at by one or another, or by some distinctive combination of, the forces of reason, will, and imagination, which would mean being the kind of community that is as a result committed to certain ends and not others. Such a community would not discover its nature through reflection on commitments independently arrived at, but rather would discover its commitments, in whole or in part, through reflection on its nature. So, for example, a community might be committed to seeing itself in terms of conservatism or change, pragmatism or idealism, happiness or virtue; different goals, and hence different calls to the forces of reason, will, and imagination, would follow from those different self-understandings.

156. On the other hand, a community may tend to see itself as a community that is distinctively committed to a certain mode of self-construction. Self-understanding of that kind entails an approach to the process of governance in that community that is self-consciously driven and animated by one or more of the forces of reason, will, and imagination at the expense of the others—that

is, to being the kind of society that sets out self-consciously to shape itself, predominantly if not exclusively, as a rational construct, a construct of the imagination, or a construct of the will, and then, and derivatively, to goals that are consistent with those modes of construction. Part of the mythology, as well as the reality, of a life in common is the extent to which it sees itself as being generated by the forces of reason, will, and imagination respectively. So, for example, a community might see itself in technocratic terms (as being shaped, for example, by supposed principles of economic efficiency), or in atavistic terms (as being shaped, for example, by the imperatives of history, tradition, or text), or in terms of aspiration (as being guided by openness, fluidity, and a sense of possibility).

157. In these as in the other ways described, lives in common exhibit different balances in their dependency on the forces of reason, will, and imagination, some derived from the particular details of their agendas and others derived from their characters as communities, real or imagined, chosen or received. Yet, as I suggested at the outset of this section, it is difficult, indeed close to impossible, to believe in the practical possibility of a community the contours of which were derived from attention to the claims of reason alone. Will and imagination are ever present, albeit in different patterns in different places.

6

Appreciating the Limits of the Service Conception of Authority

158. The preceding, extended consideration of the roles played by imagination and will in enhancing the rational appeal of a very significant range of the claims that the law may make upon a population in order to secure a life in common has emphasized the extent to which the service conception of authority quite self-consciously falls short of fully accounting for the resources that are needed to ground collective action in many of the most familiar instances of law-making. According to that interpretation of it, the service conception, and its attendant understanding of the normal justification of authority, presents a picture of law in which the addressees of law are offered recommendations for action that fall well short of being fully determinative of a life in common. The consequence of that shortfall is that those who are subject to the authority of law very often, perhaps typically, find themselves in the position of having more reasons available to them than they need in order to act, and so just as often find themselves faced with good reason to choose between complying and not complying with the requirements of law—a predicament that is in a great many cases a very good thing from the perspective of autonomy, but is nevertheless, and by the same token (though not necessarily in the same settings), a bad thing from the perspective of a life in common, simply because the choice that it gives rise to is bound to be exercised differently by different people even when those people are fully rational and so can be expected to act fully in accordance with reason. This is not to suggest that the service conception is in any way flawed because it yields

such a shortfall. On the contrary, it might be thought to be one of the strengths of the service conception that it is capable of recognizing and capturing the shortfall of reason in determining collective action, and the predicament that gives rise to.

159. An aside, before going further, to clarify the premises of the discussion in this section and the reasons to engage in it. There is an assumption at work here, or perhaps I should say something of an underlying conviction, that I have not addressed in the text so far and that I should make clear that I will be quite consciously setting to one side in what follows. Many believe that there is a general (moral) obligation to obey the law, one that may be overcome only in special circumstances—classically, those of conscientious objection and civil disobedience. A great deal has been written about the moral foundations for such a general obligation and as much about the moral circumstances in which the obligation might be overcome. Yet I have said, and will continue to say, nothing about these questions here, not merely because the literature on them is already large and the arguments concerning them well rehearsed but, more to the point, because the questions are rendered moot, or at least collateral, by the premises of this project. I am with Raz in believing that the obligation to obey the law is in fact piecemeal rather than general, and it is that belief that makes it sensible for me to be concerned to explore the challenges for a life in common of a moral world in which the law, lacking the rational weight of any such general obligation, must very often compete for attention with other reasons for action for the claims it imposes upon its addressees, and so as a consequence is bound to assert the primacy of the obligations that it seeks to create through alliances between such reasons as it may give rise to and the powers of will and of imagination, in all the ways that I have sought to describe. The logic of a general obligation to obey the law, by contrast, is to distil the claims of any other rival undefeated reasons into the categories of conscientious objection and civil disobedience, and then to manage the pull of those other reasons in the various ways that those two special categories call for and subject to the terms that they impose. Few if any of the problems that I am seeking to explore would arise in such circumstances. In fact, one way of thinking of the entire project of this book is as an endeavour to develop a fully worked alternative to the idea of a general obligation to obey the law and its recognized exceptions. How might the piecemeal acquire something like generality, so as to facilitate, perhaps enable, a life in common?

160. On the other hand, and in contrast to most of the literature on the general obligation to obey, the challenge to the service conception mounted by Darwall and the other commentators noted in the paragraph which follows has rather different implications. If sound, it would support the idea of a general obligation to obey the law by means of a repudiation of the service conception of authority, and thus by means of a repudiation of the distinctive view of the nature of law's rational claim upon us that gives rise to space and purpose for the operation of will and imagination in the project of governance. That consequence makes the question of the soundness of that particular challenge—that is, the soundness of that particular way of thinking of a general obligation to obey the law, be that soundness in whole or in part—clearly pivotal to this project, and thus deserving of careful examination as part of its course. It is, as I see it, a matter of defending the premises of the project against what purports to be a fundamental challenge to them, and that in doing so offers what I take to be very rich and revealing arguments to that end.

161. To return to the discussion, then, for a number of recent commentators the service conception is vulnerable on precisely the opposite ground from that which I have sought to explore. As they see it, the normal justification of authority warrants not too much but too little. It provides no adequate justification, they contend, for a whole range of more or less familiar pieces of law-making, and more profoundly for the various institutions whose proper role it is to make laws and which in consequence properly claim authority for what those laws require. It follows that, if adhered to in principle or in practice, the service conception would leave the addressees of law deprived of those forms of guidance that do not meet its terms, and thereby deprived of elements of governmental direction that are essential to their collective well-being. The true justification of authority should be looked for, these commentators suggest, in the constitution of authority, rather than in the reasons that the exercise of authority helps to secure conformity with on the part of its subjects.[1]

---

[1] See Stephen Darwall, *The Second Person Standpoint* (2006), Scott Hershovitz, 'The Role of Authority', 11 *Philosophers' Imprint* 1–19 (2011), Stephen Perry, 'Political Authority and Political Obligation' in *Oxford Studies in Philosophy of Law: Volume 2*, ed Leslie Green and Brian Leiter (2013) 1, and Joseph Raz, 'The Possibility of Partiality' (a draft paper once available on his website: see footnote 5). From the point of view of Raz's critics on this question the service conception warrants too little with respect to legitimately constituted authorities, but it might also be thought to warrant too much to the

162. This critique, it will be seen at once, amounts to a fundamental challenge to the service conception's tacit understanding of the proper relationship between power (imaginative as well as coercive) and reason, a challenge that can be evaluated from a number of perspectives. First, what forms of guidance does the service conception actually fail to warrant? Do they include anything that is valuable, or more precisely, anything that is essential to the achievement of a worthwhile life in common? Second, and from the opposite perspective, could those forms of guidance that fall outside the service conception (just because they do not satisfy the normal justification of authority) ever be legitimate, and if so, on what grounds and in what circumstances? These two questions address the nature and the extent of the reasons captured by the normal justification thesis, and seek to assess the significance (if any) for a successful life in common of whatever considerations the application of the normal justification thesis might fail to capture. In that sense, the questions could be said to be Razian in outlook.

163. A further two questions adopt a rival, what might be called constitutional, perspective on the same problem—the perspective urged by these commentators—and so look to the connections between authority, however it may have been constituted and without regard to what it requires, and right reasoning toward a life in common. Third then, and in that vein, does the service conception appear to offer less in the way of guidance than these commentators have in mind just because the kind of guidance and the kind of authority that they are looking for is simply not rationally available in most cases, no matter how the authority in question may have been constituted, and no matter whether the authority it purports to exercise is epistemic or practical? Fourth and finally, is it possible for an illegitimately constituted authority to exercise authority legitimately, let us assume as and when the normal justification thesis is satisfied, and conversely for a legitimately constituted authority to exercise authority illegitimately, let us assume as and when the normal justification thesis is not satisfied (all due regard having been accorded in each case to the legitimacy of the constitution of the authorities in question)? Are we not, in certain cases at least, free, perhaps even

extent that it locates authority in persons or institutions that have not otherwise been legitimately constituted as authorities. Perry in particular pursues the latter point, which I address in Chapter 6C 'Alternative Authorities, Alternative Regulation' at para 198ff.

bound, to obey illegitimate governments and to disobey legitimate ones, all due allowance having been made for the particular moral circumstances of their constitution? More probingly, if the answers to those last questions are in the positive, as the rhetorical cast of the questions suggests, can they be understood as anything other than answers, however limited, to the problem of identifying legitimate authority? If not, does it follow that it is a mistake to regard the identification of legitimate authority as an all-or-nothing matter, in the constitutional manner?

A. Limits to Guidance

164. Begin with the second, most straight-forward question. The service conception of authority treats as illegitimate any exercise of authority that calls upon a person to do something that he or she has no good reason to do, where a reason to do something is understood to include, at the most immediate level, all that is in that person's interests, as a distinct person and as a social being, and at a more remote level all that is valuable in that person's hands, whether or not it is in his or her interests.[2] Could it ever be legitimate for an authority to expect anything more? By definition, the notion of legitimacy that is being claimed and referred to in this setting could not merely echo the service conception of authority, and so could not be tied to, equated with, the reasons that could possibly have a bearing—direct or indirect—upon the person in question's life, for all such reasons are registered by the service conception and the normal justification thesis. What is at issue in the challenge, therefore, is the legitimacy of any considerations that are not so registered. Nor could the notion of legitimacy that is being referred to include reference to reasons that the authority might have to expect the person in question to contribute to a good that is in no sense in his or her interest, or even to a good that brings no value to his or her life, for those two species of reason are also registered by the normal justification thesis. That leaves only one possibility, namely that the claim to be exercising authority legitimately is based on something other than the reasons

---

[2] For a fuller consideration of the relationship between value and interest, see Macklem and Gardner, 'Value, Interest and Well-Being', 18 *Utilitas* 362 (2006).

that govern the lives of those over whom authority is exercised, as indeed it so often has been in practice—some consideration such as the embodiment of national will or the expression of public imagination, perhaps—so that it would be a mistake to expect authority, in its constitution or its operation, to be nothing other than responsive to the reasons that its subjects respond to. Yet that is quite plainly not what these critics of the service conception of authority have in mind. They are not in any sense in favour of fascism or demagoguery. Their intuition, rather, is that the normal justification of authority fails to capture central aspects of the democratic project, and of the distinctive approach to a life in common that democracy seeks to foster, all of which are supported by reason, though they may well be less than fully determined by reason. Which returns us to the first question: what, if any, valuable forms of guidance does the service conception actually fail to warrant?

165. In considering this question it is difficult to escape the sense that a good deal of the concern felt by critics of the service conception of authority and the normal justification thesis stems from a relatively parched understanding of the nature of the reasons that govern and direct a person's actions in the ways that the service conception seeks to draw attention to. There seems to be a lingering suspicion on the part of these critics that the reasons that apply to a person are more or less confined to what is in his or her interest, where the idea of an interest is itself conceived narrowly, to exclude the flourishing of social forms and practices that have no direct bearing on that person's well-being, or more broadly on the success or failure of his or her life. Those social forms and practices would, in the view of such critics, include in particular the establishment and exercise of democratic authority and the value that such an authority is capable of embodying and giving rise to, significant parts of which may be difficult to trace in the contours of individual interest, narrowly understood. Were any of those things the case, then the normal justification thesis, and the service conception of authority that it relies upon, would indeed fail to capture much that is valuable and necessary to a successful life in common. Yet they are plainly not the case. What is more, if they were mistakenly understood to be the case in any particular setting, the consequent shortcomings in the operation and application of the service conception of authority would be a function not of the concept of authority itself, but of the understanding of reason to which it referred and upon which it

relied. The remedy for those shortcomings would rightly be looked for by revisiting the too limited understanding of reason that was being relied upon, not the notion of authority that quite properly insists upon rational reliance. Once reason is rightly understood to be a function of value (complex and multifaceted as that function may be), it follows that virtually nothing of value that is applicable to the life in question could ever be overlooked by a sound application of the normal justification thesis and the underlying service conception of authority.[3]

166. Yet this, of course, is precisely the claim that critics of the service conception of authority are seeking to dispute, in particular, through reference to the range of goods that they believe a soundly constituted authority is uniquely capable of giving rise to, pre-eminent among them the transcendent good of its own distinctive method of constitution and consequent capacity for direction. Authorities, it is commonly believed, have a right to rule, which entails a correlative obligation to obey.[4] What is in question is the particular quality of that right and the source of its limits. There are two perspectives from which that question can be addressed. From the first perspective one may ask: Is the normal justification of authority liable to attribute authority to the wrong persons? Can it distinguish properly between those who have the right to rule and those who do not? Is satisfaction of the normal justification thesis sufficient to ground a duty of the appropriate kind? Conversely, when authority is exercised by those who possess a right to rule, does the normal justification thesis invite us to look for the source of rightful authority in the wrong place: in the extent to which compliance with the authority's directives tends to satisfy the reasons that otherwise apply to the people to whom the directives are addressed, rather than in the obligation to accept such direction that appears to a number of commentators to follow from the very existence of the right to rule, which in its turn would follow from the legitimacy of an authority's mode of constitution and the faithfulness of that authority's conduct to the terms of its constitution? For those who have sought to challenge the service conception of authority in this way, the favoured proving ground for their contention has been Raz's long-standing claim, currently tentatively withdrawn, that the

---

[3] For an account of the presence of values without reasons, see Gardner and Macklem, 'Reasons', in *The Oxford Handbook of Jurisprudence and Philosophy of Law* (2002) 440, at 455–7.

[4] Though see Edmundson, 'State of the Art: The Duty to Obey the Law', 10 *Legal Theory* 215 (2004).

normal justification thesis explains and warrants the exercise of epistemic authority.[5] According to that claim, one of the most common and most important instances of authority, and the attendant right to rule and obligation to obey, is the case of expertise, where the authority's judgement pre-empts our own as and when it knows better than we do with respect to what it requires.

167. Suppose, to modify an example offered by Stephen Perry, a public authority advises foot travellers to follow a certain route, or to follow a route with certain goals in mind and certain precautions in hand, be it a scenic route, a challenging route, a route for those who are less than fully agile or who tire easily, a quite possibly dangerous route, or a potentially safe route.[6] In assessing the significance of this advice and determining the appropriate rational response to it, a number of questions would need to be addressed, the most prominent of them being whether the public authority has any expertise in routes of these kinds and so has any business in offering advice on how to travel them; to what extent the public authority's advice is applicable to certain species of travellers, and so applicable to oneself if and to the extent that one belongs to that species; and whether the 'advice' is properly understood as obligatory or permissive, however the public authority may have seen it. All these are ways of probing the expertise of the authority and one's own need for expertise of that kind, and ultimately of answering the question of whether the authority's advice should be regarded as authoritative in this setting. According to the normal justification thesis, a positive answer to those questions yields the conclusion that the advice of the authority pre-empts one's own judgement on the matter, and leaves one rationally obliged to adopt its judgement instead.

---

[5] Raz appeared to doubt the soundness of the application of the service conception to epistemic authority, in terms that went beyond what he had said in 'The Problem of Authority: Revisiting the Service Conception', in the final section of 'The Possibility of Partiality', a draft paper that was for some time available on his website. The paper was never for citation and has since been removed from the site, so the position that I am tentatively attributing to Raz should be treated as a hypothetical position taken by Raz'.

[6] Perry's example, put forward in his paper 'Political Authority and Political Obligation', involves hypothetical advice as to the safe transportation of a dangerous substance, and the alleged inability of the normal justification thesis to distinguish among government obligations to follow that advice, government recommendations to do so, and a friend's recommendations to do so. My own response to the example is that it shows, first, that something more than a recommendation is normally called for on the part of those who have the relevant expertise in transporting dangerous goods, given the risk to others that is present in such cases; that the combination of the presence of expertise in

168. In recent writing Raz himself has doubted this conclusion, in the face of challenges to it by Stephen Darwall in particular. As Raz might now put it, epistemic authority is something of a misnomer, because expertise on any given matter does not, Raz now believes, in itself provide a rational warrant of any kind for allowing one's own judgement of the matter to be pre-empted, and as a consequence cannot serve as the basis for a sound claim to practical authority. Once the expertise has been established, so as to indicate, for example, which particular route the less than fully agile person should follow, the expert is in no better position to direct the conduct of a less than fully agile foot traveller than is the traveller who has been informed of the expert's conclusions. Raz concludes that no legitimate practical authority can be based on superior knowledge alone, contrary to what he previously maintained. This disables Darwall's challenge, but at a price. Darwall's position, it will be recalled, is that the normal justification thesis is not satisfied in such situations, and yet state claims to authority in those situations are plainly legitimate, or at least are capable of being so. If the legitimacy of those claims cannot be explained in terms of the service conception of authority, then authority must be understood in some other way, most plausibly in what I have described (a couple of paragraphs ago) as the constitutional manner. Raz's riposte, that there is simply no authority in such situations, undermines not only Darwall's position but significant aspects of what was once his own position. Authority can do much less for us than we have thought. In cases where authority rests on superior knowledge alone, authority can inform, but having done so it thereby and to that extent ceases to be our guide.

169. Is this too quick a conclusion? Raz's work is so thoughtful and so rigorous that one ought to reflect extremely carefully before raising such a possibility, even in defence of Raz's own ideas. On the other hand, Raz has clearly erred in one setting or the other,

one person and the need for reliance on that expertise in another person (based on the absence of like expertise) rationally obliges the latter to heed the former; and that while a *claim* to authority is necessarily prospective and intentional, the *fact* of authority is often retrospective and even accidental, established only once authority has been earned by the combination of its justified exercise and a subsequent acceptance of that exercise by a person in need of authority of the relevant kind, a person who in that act of acceptance properly subjects himself or herself to the authority and through that gesture helps to constitute the authority as an authority, however partially, contingently, or temporarily.

then or now, and since his former position is more consistent with the picture of law as I understand it and have tried to set it out, the possibility that the former position is in fact the correct one—albeit helpfully illuminated by his recent reconsideration of it—seems well worth exploring. Is the role of epistemic authority exhausted (so to speak) once it has yielded a complete epistemic basis for action, or does epistemic authority survive as something of a supervisory overtone in the operation of practical authority, in a manner that distinguishes it from purely practical authority in a number of significant respects, which Raz and certain of his critics have now drawn attention to, but that does not distinguish it from practical authority in respect of what makes both authoritative?

170. The issue, in short, is whether epistemic authority is capable of yielding a sufficient epistemic basis for action in regard to whatever it is an authority in respect of, all other considerations having been controlled for. Is it possible to know something indirectly, through reliance on the expertise of an authority, in the same sense (if not by the same means) that one knows it directly, so that once one knows whatever it is the voice of the authority then drops out of the practical picture, other than as an element in the record of the means by which one came to acquire the information that was needed in order to act? If so, then an epistemic authority is plainly not a practical authority. Or does reliance on the authority continue to be one's guide in what one does on the strength of its expertise, so that epistemic authority continues to be a necessary, governing presence in one's reasons for action and one's scrutiny of those reasons, both prior to the action and in the course of it? Is that presence necessary in order to pre-empt one's own direct visitation of the epistemic reasons that underpin the action, and hence the reasons to doubt what the authority has claimed an expertise in respect of?

171. As the exchange between Raz and his critics has revealed, there are significant differences between epistemic authority and practical authority, most notably in the ways that their rational status as authorities may be established or undermined. Rational achievement is a possible consequence of the exercise of practical authority but the source of epistemic authority. One can become a practical authority without there being any evidence that one's exercise of that authority is or will be sound, but one cannot so become an epistemic authority. Conversely, rational failure (say, a failure to secure compliance or co-ordination) may undermine practical authority (if

it is widespread, for example) but rational failure (say, evidence of epistemic error) necessarily undermines epistemic authority, *pro tanto* at least (and by extension undermines claims to practical authority to the extent that they are based on epistemic authority). In short, rational success and failure go only to the effectiveness of practical authority, but go to the very constitution of epistemic authority.

172. On the other hand, and on the face of it at least, there is a significant degree of overlap between the two forms of authority—enough, one could reasonably maintain, to make the description of epistemic authority sound rather than a misnomer. Each form of authority provides, in the exercise of its authority, reasons for action or for belief, or claims to do so. Each thereby seeks to pre-empt the reasoning, practical or epistemic, of those who fall within the scope of the authority's claims. According to the service conception of authority, either form of authority is rationally justified if and when due attention to its claims enables one to comply more fully with the reasons that otherwise apply to one. Yet in both cases of authority the requirement of due attention gives rise to the apparent rational paradox considered earlier—that one cannot review the soundness of the authority's claim, as rationality requires, without forgoing the rational benefit that submission to the authority is capable of giving rise to in terms of the reasons that otherwise apply to oneself.

173. Those various forms of overlap having been acknowledged, however, it remains the case that merely to suggest that epistemic authority has a supervisory role to play in actions undertaken on the strength of it is, on the face of it and without further elaboration, either conclusory or mysterious. What could that supervisory role be, all relevant information having already been imparted? How might one test for the presence of such a role? To offer a response in somewhat less mysterious terms, the suggestion is that the underlying role of epistemic authority in inspiring and supervising action is simply one, underpinning dimension of the role that a critical intelligence properly plays in reviewing the soundness of the ends that one is committing oneself to, the effectiveness of the means that one has chosen to realize those ends, and the broader consonance between the values of ends and of means in sustaining action. In the course of that review it will typically be necessary to make reference to the epistemic basis for one's action, and in doing so in the specific setting of action that is predicated on epistemic authority one is bound

to make reference to what the authority has proposed, upon which one relied in committing oneself to the action, and upon which one continues to rely in continuing in the action. It need hardly be said that reviews of this kind must be reconciled with the requirements of action, and so are likely to be intermittent rather than continuous. Were it otherwise, one's capacity for action would be significantly undermined by second-guessing. Indeed, the reviews might not even take place, either as a result of inattention or in recognition of the fact that any review in the course of the action might undermine the action's value. Yet those caveats, important as they are, do not in themselves tell against the role of epistemic authority and its significance, for they would hold as true had one played the role of epistemic authority oneself, and so had thought for oneself from the outset.

174. How might one test for the continued presence of epistemic authority in actions that are taken on the strength of it? It seems to me that there are at least two plausible ways of doing so. The first would be to take seriously the possibility of believing otherwise, of believing that epistemic authority is exhausted and so drops out of the picture once its conclusions have been adopted. According to that line of thought, one should believe what an epistemic authority expects one to believe just because one knows it to be an authority on the matter, and one should then act in accordance with one's beliefs in the standard manner, authority aside. The problem with this picture, it seems to me, is that one's beliefs in such a situation are not free-standing in the way that they are when one acts in the standard manner, authority aside. Rather, they depend from the outset, and continue to depend throughout the course of actions taken in reliance upon them, upon the prop of authority. Strictly speaking, they are the beliefs of the authority, and so become and remain one's own beliefs only derivatively and dependently. One believes in their content if and to the extent that one believes, and continues to believe, in the reliability of the authority that has identified that content, and if it is necessary that one believe in that content as a basis for undertaking actions on the strength of it, or for continuing in those actions, as is commonly, perhaps typically the case, then it is necessary to regard the source of the belief as an epistemic authority, and to continue to do so, just to the extent that the belief in question informs and justifies one's actions.

175. A second way of testing for the continued presence of epistemic authority in actions that have been taken upon its recommendation is allied to the first. In what way, it might be queried, should a belief that is predicated upon the pronouncement of an epistemic authority be challenged? What question would one rightly ask oneself in examining the soundness of one's basis for consequent action in such a situation? What should one demand of oneself as one struggles, let us suppose, along a very rough path that had been authoritatively pronounced to be suitable for the less than fully agile? Should one ask oneself 'What was I thinking of?' or should one ask oneself 'What was the authority thinking of?' And if the former (as indeed seems entirely sensible in certain settings), would one's question, suitably refined, not be, 'What was I thinking of in taking the authority's word for it?' In blaming one's own judgement, should one not blame one's reliance upon the judgement of another rather than one's own enquiry and reflection? Could one intelligibly even begin to do the latter, strictly speaking, there having been in fact no enquiry or reflection of one's own—at least, none that related to the roughness of the path as opposed to the wisdom of the authority on the point?

176. These questions are only superficially rhetorical, for they return the argument to the familiar paradox that arises, or appears to arise, epistemically as much as practically, whenever reliance on authority needs to be reconciled with a commitment to rationality. How can one obtain the benefit of an authority while preserving the exercise of one's own judgement in the matter, and the value that arises from that exercise? The answer, in principle, is that one does so by questioning the authority's claim to be an authority in the matter rather than by questioning the substance of what the authority has claimed to be an authority in respect of. It is only where one seeks to do the former by means of the latter that the paradox becomes real. The further and apposite question in the present setting, however, is whether and in what ways the problem of reconciliation differs when the matter in relation to which authority has been asserted is epistemic rather than practical. The answer would seem to be that in every case, whether epistemic or practical, one needs to ask oneself whether the status of the authority is a deserved one, and in the epistemic setting it may sometimes be more difficult to do this without addressing the substance of what the authority has proposed or required (thereby undermining the potential value that reliance on the authority is capable of giving rise to) than is the

case in the practical setting. What is more, given that the knowledge to which epistemic authority lays claim is always present in advance of the exercise of that authority, there may be a greater temptation to challenge epistemic authority in this kind of self-defeating way than there is in the setting of purely practical authority, where the particular forms of co-ordination that practical authority makes possible (to take but one obvious illustration) do not exist apart from the presence of and reliance upon the authority. Yet, real as these difficulties would seem to be, their place in the operation of epistemic authority merely restricts rather than precludes the benefit that epistemic authority is capable of bringing to the exercise of practical reasoning.

177. If that description is sound, however, it lends epistemic authority something of a fragile quality, which may on the face of it seem at odds with what many commentators take to be the essential character of authority, as fundamentally pre-emptive, determinative, and compelling. Yet the burden of the argument that has gone before, in its general outline and in its details, is to suggest that authority, of whatever kind, is in fact fundamentally contingent and vulnerable, notwithstanding the pre-emptive character of its claims. If that argument is sound, there should be nothing terribly surprising in the recognition of the tentative, incomplete shape of epistemic authority, for it would follow that a degree of fragility is in the very nature of authority, though the specific character of the contingencies to which any particular authority is subject is liable to take a somewhat different shape in cases of epistemic authority than in it takes in cases of purely practical authority.

178. Yet suppose, for the sake of argument, that I am wrong in all that I have maintained in this section, and that there is indeed a fundamental distinction to be drawn between epistemic and practical authority, as Raz and certain of his critics would currently have it—a distinction that would deny the governing role of epistemic authority in the operation of reasons for action. Were that the right way to understand the world, the practical implications of the service conception of authority would clearly be significantly constrained, as would the possibilities for a government based on legitimate authority so understood. It would not follow, however, for the reasons Raz now gives, that there is any more comprehensive conception of legitimate authority available, let alone that it is to be discovered in the kind of constitutional genealogy that certain of Raz's critics

have favoured. What is perhaps even more worth noting than the implications for the service conception, however, and surely no less counter-intuitive, is that Dworkin's account of law, in which the explanation of legitimate authority involves nothing other than epistemic authority, would be fundamentally misconceived, and so would not even get off the ground, were it the case that epistemic authority had no power to guide our actions. If the role of the judiciary is simply to tell us what we could in principle discover for ourselves, then once the judiciary has told us what we need to know it would have no authoritative role to play in our practical lives. A legal judgment would be on a par with any other source of relevant information on the question of whether and how to act. With no possibility of any authoritative status, it could not provide any definitive collective practical guidance. That may ultimately be the right way to analyse the implications of Dworkin's account, as I have already suggested, but it seems much too quick a move to conclude that it is the right way to understand the preconditions of that account.

179. A potentially significant qualification needs to be entered here, however, which will return the discussion to the frontiers of reason and the role that can be played there by imagination in creating and sustaining a life in common. Exercises of supposed epistemic authority that lack legitimacy, just because they fail to satisfy the normal justification thesis and so live up to the service conception of authority, may, like their practical counterparts, have some potential for value as *de facto* authorities, though, to be precise, in the epistemic setting the authority would actually be spurious rather than *de facto*. I do not have in mind here what strikes me as the very limited potential for value in believing that information is true when it is in fact false. The authoritative promotion of illusion is almost always damaging and only very occasionally fulfilling. What I have in mind, rather, is the possibility that there may be value in regarding a supposed epistemic authority as authoritative, in the sense of being rationally determinative of one's actions, when in fact it is not (if Raz's more recent observations are correct). A belief in the sustaining value of epistemic authority, unfounded as it may be, has the potential to lend valuable strength to one's epistemic arm in one's actions, and in certain settings that kind of added strength in one's beliefs may be crucial to one's ability to act upon them successfully. It is possible that in this way *de facto* epistemic authority might offer a kind of mimicry of the role that I have maintained epistemic

authority plays in fact, and that such mimicry might in certain cases be sufficient to secure the value or values that its allegedly real counterpart is said to secure.

180. As has already been suggested, it is in these settings, where a greater warrant is claimed for the force of reason in support of a life in common than reason can support, that an appeal to the imagination may serve to bridge the gap between reason and action and so sustain the scope and force of the authority's claim, in any of the various ways previously set out. On a Razian view of the world, in which the reasons that tell in favour of a particular proposal for a life in common are those that can be identified in accordance with the normal justification thesis, the potential significance of the availability of an appeal to the imagination, and hence of the influence of imagination in the construction of a life in common, would be greatly augmented were it indeed the case that epistemic authority has no role to play in governing action that is taken on the strength of what it has recommended. A population might, in certain cases at least, need to be persuaded that the claims of an epistemic authority were rationally determinative of their actions (as in fact they would not be on the present assumption) and, given that the use of force is typically ineffective to that end, it would fall to the exercise of imagination to lend to the claims of the epistemic authority the appearance of rational weight and finality that is necessary to make the claims effective. More tellingly, on a Dworkinian view of the world, and once again assuming the absence of guidance from epistemic authority in the determination of action, the role of imagination would need to be a great deal more dramatic, for it would have to do the whole work of sustaining a claim to authority the only basis for which was epistemic, as that envisioned by Dworkin is.

B. The Criteria of Legitimacy and Their Value

181. There is a final question to be considered, a last perspective from which to assess the connection between the legitimate constitution of authority and the legitimate exercise of authority. For Raz, the latter consideration operates as a condition of the legitimacy of the practical implications of the former: the exercise of authority is

legitimate only if it is legitimate in the setting of its exercise, on grounds that are independent of (though they may include reference to) the legitimate constitution of authority. For his critics, however, the former consideration effectively pre-empts the operation of the latter: the exercise of authority is legitimate if and only if the authority in question has been legitimately constituted. How should this impasse be resolved? Is it possible, as Raz would have it, for a legitimately constituted authority to exercise authority illegitimately, let us assume as and when the normal justification thesis is not satisfied (all due regard having been accorded, in the application of that thesis, to the legitimacy of the constitution of the authority in question)? And if the answer to that is in the positive, what does that tell us about the nature of authority?

182. It is not entirely easy to answer this question without begging it in one direction or the other. On the face of it, there can be no denying the existence of wrongs done by legitimately constituted governments. The history of democratic regimes is replete with discouraging examples, and unsurprisingly so: given the frequency with which each one of us mistakes his or her own interests, or at least some portion of them, there is no reason to expect any less frequent error in the identification of our interests by those who represent us, even assuming that their concern for our interests is no less than their concern for their own interests, as so often it is not. Yet recognition of that fact merely raises the question rather than answers it. Is the proper response to such examples of the wrongs done by legitimately constituted governments—or more precisely, to those examples in which the wrongs can be reasonably regarded as significant because they have a real impact upon human well-being—to conclude that the operative conception of a legitimately constituted government needs to be revisited? If so, are the examples to be regarded as only *prima facie* evidence of the illegitimate exercise of authority (and thus to be vindicated if and only if the government is found, by analysis that is undertaken with reference to other considerations, to have been illegitimately constituted) or are they to be regarded as themselves constitutive of the illegitimate exercise of authority? The former position assumes that the legitimacy of the exercise of authority is a function of the legitimacy of the constitution of the authority; the latter assumes that the two are separate questions, in the Razian manner. Without further development, both positions beg the question.

183. Suppose, to take a well-worn example, that a democratic government has acted in ways that are oppressive of people of a particular kind, whether those people are members of religious or ethnic minorities and are singled out as such, either directly or indirectly, or whether they are constitutively committed to a distinctive social practice or a set of social practices that involves, whether as part of its aim or as the by-product of an aim, a degree of non-conformity, on whatever ground, with the social expectations that are embodied in law, protected by law, or endorsed by law, either implicitly or explicitly. In contemporary Western societies the standard response to such examples is to view them as violations of rights; to regard violations of such rights as illegitimate exercises of authority (on the basis that a proper respect for rights is a condition of legitimate authority); and, further and most crucially, to claim that the institutional protection of rights of the relevant kind is a condition of the legitimate constitution of authority. This standard response embodies a strong connection between the wrongs done by an authority and a lack of legitimacy in its constitution.

184. Yet, as the sequence of its description makes clear, in itself this is to risk assuming two crucial conclusions (that there are such rights, and that institutional protection of them is a condition of legitimate authority) by embracing what may well be too hopeful a view of the nature of legitimate authority, namely that a properly bounded government is conceptually incapable of the illegitimate exercise of authority. It is not that sound institutional arguments cannot be offered for rights and for their proper respect, and for a view of legitimacy that incorporates those facts. Such institutional arguments are as familiar as the wrongs that they seek to explain and redress. Rather it is that among the premises for such arguments may well be an unargued-for conclusion as to the nature of legitimate authority. That conclusion is vulnerable to an obvious Razian challenge, namely that the measure of proper bounding upon which it relies, including that which supports the basic commitment to democracy, ought to be determined with reference to the potential for wrongdoing of any given proposal for the legitimate design of institutional authority, which in turn ought to be assessed by reference to criteria that are tantamount to a straight-forward application of the normal justification thesis. Yet, at least as so framed, this challenge is no less vulnerable, in that it no less risks assuming its conclusion, by regarding institutional authority as ultimately answerable to

the demands of the normal justification thesis (or something like it). Thus the potential impasse of one conclusory position confronting another.

185. In matters such as this there is little prospect of settling the issue definitively. It seems to me, however, that there are at least two plausible ways in which the relationship between a legitimately constituted authority and the legitimate exercise of authority might be tested without begging the question in one direction or the other. The first is to push the examples of the wrongful exercise of authority to a regress, so as to determine whether there is an inescapable possibility of wrongdoing despite all constitutional refinement. The second, which is simply the obverse of the first, is to ask whether any of the examples of wrongdoing are intelligible as instances of illegitimate authority quite apart from their constitutional analysis (a positive answer to which would undermine assumptions of the exclusivity of the constitutional perspective), and, further and more tellingly, to ask whether any of the examples of wrongdoing have no tendency to call into question the soundness of the particular constitution of authority that gave rise to them.

186. Begin with the regress, working from the case of democratic action that is oppressive of a certain way of life. If the institutional response to any such example is to posit the existence of a right that will protect against the possibility of its arising, the test of the soundness of that response must be to push the limits of what can be posited as a right, whether in terms of scope or of depth. Is it possible to develop an understanding of rights against authority that is so encompassing, multifarious, and fine-grained as to preclude the wronging, in any significant degree, of any of the ways of life that authority shapes and governs? That seems doubtful. In terms of *scope*, it seems plausible to think that there may well be wrongs that do not give rise to such rights, either because the interests that they affect are not sufficient to ground a duty, or because the interests that they affect are not sufficient to ground a duty of the appropriate, institutional kind. If that is the case, then the wrongs in question can only be identified and guarded against by assessing the exercise of authority separately from any assessment of the constitution of authority. The limits to the depth of *detail* that can be achieved in the understanding of a right are rather more difficult to assess, because greater detail can always be filled in by adjudication, at least in principle. If that were the case in practice, no wrongdoing would be so

fine-grained as to avoid its barring through the articulation of rights. Yet that seems an overly hopeful conclusion, given the relatively coarse response to wrongdoing that is made necessary by the institutional constraints governing constitutional courts and the rights they adjudicate. Moreover, even were the conclusion correct, there is further reason to doubt that the detailing of rights could ever preclude the wrongful exercise of an authority that fully observed them.

187. It seems plausible to think that the details of the rights that we currently recognize and endorse, which arise from their application in particular cases and which it is normally the task of the courts to develop, need not be developed with only the limitation of authority in mind. Not every principle that the courts rely upon in reaching their conclusions seems analysable in terms of the proper constitution of authority. On the contrary, a judge might well be animated by the conviction that there are wider values at stake and greater goods to be achieved through the development and consequent exercise of rights than that of preventing the wrongful exercise of authority. If that is a legitimate conclusion for a judge to reach, then the fostering of such goods by the courts through the articulation of rights would itself have to be understood as part of the legitimate exercise of authority, and any purported instance of it would need to be assessed by reference to something like the normal justification thesis. However, if that is not a legitimate conclusion for a judge to reach, then the courts are not entitled to develop rights on other than structural grounds, and so are bound to confine themselves to the project of delimiting the constitution of authority. That conclusion can only be avoided by identifying rights governing the development of rights, and institutions capable of vindicating those rights-governing rights. That is not an impossible view of the political world, which is why argument is unlikely to settle the issue definitively, but it is a view that puts a significant degree of interpretive strain upon the understanding of some familiar judicial activity.

188. These observations can be more or less inverted, so as to provide a different perspective on the same conclusions. It seems entirely possible to reconcile unimpaired faith in the constitution of authority and proof of the wrongful exercise of that authority. In part this is because wrongdoing can be anomalous, as the issue of the detailing of rights against it implied, and so need not impugn a constitutional order just because it is not ordered itself and so does not in itself imply any possibility of better ordering. More profoundly, however,

the authorization of error may well be an attractive, although not a necessary, implication of the legitimate constitution of authority. It is entirely possible that it is better, other reasons aside, that the constitution of authority be designed in such a way as to permit rather than preclude error.

189. One way to perceive this is to remember that it is important not to lapse, without broader enquiry, into the position of determining the proper relationship between the legitimate constitution of authority and the legitimate exercise of authority exclusively by reference to questions of practical possibility and the claims of competing values, as I myself have done so far. To do so is, once again, to risk assuming one's conclusion, namely that a legitimately constituted authority is, *ipso facto*, one that does not exercise authority illegitimately. In order to avoid that assumption, it is necessary to confront, directly and in its own terms, the possibility that the capacity to exercise authority illegitimately may form a part of what makes the constitution of authority legitimate. Once that possibility has been confronted, it becomes difficult to see why it should not be the case, and correspondingly easy to recognize a familiar Millean argument as to why it should be. Is the opportunity for error not central to the capacity to live well, whether individually or collectively, and to the governance of one's thoughts and actions toward that end?

190. Yet that question, important as it is, is insufficiently probing. To know that the opportunity for error may be central to good government is not to know that the legitimacy of authority ought to be assessed in terms of the exercise of authority rather than in terms of its constitution, for the simple reason that both conceptions of legitimate authority are capable of embracing opportunities for error. On the face of it at least, without some degree of further reflection on error and value and the precise nature of the connections between the two, whatever value there may be in the opportunity for collective error is entirely capable of being captured in a sound understanding of the proper constitution of authority. That being the case, proof of the existence of the value of governmental error in itself has no power to push the question of the legitimacy of authority from the context of the constitution of authority to that of its exercise. It cannot establish on its own that recourse to the service conception of authority, and the attendant normal justification thesis, is necessary to the achievement of a successful life in common. In order to demonstrate that one must make a further move, from action to

reflection, and to the connections between the value of an action and the value of reflection on that action. One must establish a link between the value of the capacity to err and an awareness that one has erred, and further, must establish the dependency of that awareness, in certain settings at least, on the possibility of applying the normal justification thesis, or something like it, to assess whether the requirements of the service conception of authority have been met in those settings.

191. Consider the following argument along those lines. The significance of error for the good rather than the bad lies partly in the support that acceptance of the risk of error offers to creative ventures, but partly also, and just as significantly, in our subsequent reflection on and assessment of on the success or lack of it, in whatever degree and kind, of such creative ventures. We are in a position to profit from error only if and to the extent that we are able to recognize it as error, and we can recognize it as error only by calling upon some benchmark of value, however complex or multifaceted that benchmark may be, in terms of which to assess what we have done and may have erred in; by identifying an appropriate occasion on which to make such an assessment; and by exercising the rational capacity to make the assessment in question correctly. In the absence of any or all of these things our creative ventures would be as random and uninformative as the selection of numbers in a lottery—a lottery moreover in terms of whose outcome we would not even know whether our selection had yielded a winning or a losing ticket.

192. Where the errors in question are the errors of a law-maker, the relevant benchmark is necessarily that of legitimate authority, in whatever way or ways that idea ought to be understood. On the Razian account of authority, the benchmark is supplied by the service conception of authority and the normal justification thesis. Both the makers of law and the addressees of law are able to assess the value of what they have done and are being asked to do or not to do, piece by piece, act by act, in light of that benchmark. The role of the benchmark, as Raz describes it, is to assess authority by reference to its exercise, and that being the case, the distinctive value of the benchmark in identifying error is a function of its capacity to identify errors in the exercise of authority as and when they occur, in all their concreteness and particularity, for the good of those who have exercised authority in the contexts in question and of those who are being subjected to authority there. The benefits of that assessment,

and of the consequent identification of error, flow to the governors and to the governed in respect of governance as it takes place.

193. Where, however, the legitimacy of authority is a function of the constitution of authority, the relevant benchmark is the best available conception of the proper constitution of authority, so that the errors that are disclosed by the application of that benchmark are, consequently and necessarily, errors in the constitution of authority. What the process of assessment yields in this case, therefore, is a catalogue of errors that is identified by reference to constitutional principles for the benefit of constitutional actors. This makes a difference that can be of real practical importance. The possibility of error here, and the possibility of knowing it as such, enables a community (or such of its members as may be charged with that responsibility) to make a better constitution for itself. On the Razian account, by contrast, the possibility of error and its identification enables the members of a community to make better laws and to lead better lives, one by one and each by each, by drawing appropriately on the guidance of laws (or by refusing to do so), including the kind of guidance that a sound constitution makes possible. Each of these approaches yields value or, more accurately, a package of values, of a different kind. Which approach one prefers is ultimately a political question, the answer to which in any given community depends on the role that people there would have authority play in their lives, and the extent to which the value of those lives depends on the access of each one of them to the possibility of challenging any and all claims to authority over them, as and when those claims are made. Access of the community as a whole to the possibility of challenging the constitution of authority is available on either account, but only the Razian account permits fine-grained as well as constitutional challenges, while only the constitutional account yields authority of a kind that could plausibly defend the existence of a general obligation to obey it by reason of its very status as an authority, or more particularly as an authority that can claim to have been legitimately constituted.

194. It is this distinction between conflicting understandings of the value that community and citizenship can bring to our lives that I had in mind when I noted, at the outset of this section, that those who believe that the legitimacy of authority turns on the legitimacy of its constitution offer a critique of Raz's account that amounts to a

fundamental challenge to the service conception's tacit understanding of the proper relationship between power (imaginative as well as coercive) and reason. The value of authority that these commentators are seeking to elucidate is the value of power, ideally but not necessarily democratic power, while the value that Raz is interested in is the conformity of our lives to reason, including the reason to acknowledge a power, democratic or otherwise, in those who govern our lives through law—an acknowledgement that is sufficient to enable us to lead our lives in accordance with reason, but no greater. It is the appropriate scope of that acknowledgement, in any given setting, and of the reasons that sustain it that the normal justification thesis is designed to track and secure. It is the task of all of us in the conduct of our lives, whether as makers of law or as its addressees (or both), to assure ourselves of the presence of that justification, just as far as that assurance and the cost of securing it enable us to live well and no further, so securing the presence in our lives of a sound, albeit delicate, balance between effective scrutiny and debilitating second-guessing.

195. If all this is true then the limits to the service conception of authority are not to be discovered in reasons that it overlooks, or in exercises of institutional authority that it fails to capture, for the service conception has the scope and the flexibility necessary to avoid those shortcomings. Rather they are to be discovered in the fact that the service conception and the normal justification thesis do not have, and do not pretend to have, any capacity to dissolve the conflicts of values that arise, perhaps typically but certainly very often, in the various courses of action that confront us at any given moment in the project of constructing a successful life in common, and in the consequent lack of rational pre-eminence in the particular course of action that is directed or forbidden to us by law. That is why, as I suggested at the outset, the service conception is sound yet incomplete as an account of the role that law can play in the achievement of a life in common, as Raz himself implies. There is more to the story of the authority of law than the role played in it by reason, and that being the case there is a need to explore the roles played in the authority of law, for better and for worse, by will and by imagination. Raz's achievement, and it is a striking one, lies in his analysis of the rationality of authority, and in the ways in which that analysis dissolves the conflict between acknowledgement of authority and the exercise of reason. The inescapable limits to that achievement are

to be found not in rival accounts of rationality or of authority, but in an account of the necessary partnership between the rational and the irrational in any exercise of practical reasoning in every project of living well.

196. One should be careful not to overstate the point being made here. As Raz himself has observed, there is no inevitable conflict between the claims of the normal justification thesis (in favour, let us suppose, of a reason to pre-empt one's own judgement) and those of the independence thesis (in favour of thinking for oneself), for the simple reason that the value of thinking for oneself about the merits of a prospective course of action or inaction is a value that is capable of being captured in the application of the normal justification thesis.[7] Yet conflict is certainly possible and may in practice be close to endemic, on issues great and small. Just how frequently such conflicts actually arise in any given community, and thus just what limits there are to the prospect of a broad reconciliation of the claims of the normal justification thesis and of the independence thesis in that community—a reconciliation sufficient to ground a successful life in common—are a function of the degree of incommensurability in public affairs, both generally and in that community, as to which people differ, and of the particular social and political character of the community in question. Those are issues to which I will return presently. What needs to be borne in mind at this stage is that this kind of reconciliation is possible in an individual life just because and to the extent that the identification of goals in that particular life, goals designed to shape and direct the life over time, generates exclusionary reasons to attend to reasons that serve those goals and to disregard reasons that are incompatible with them. In the project of creating and pursuing a life in common, by contrast, the existence of such goals cannot be taken for granted, because it cannot be assumed that the goals of individual lives in that prospective community are consonant with one another; there are thus variations from culture to culture in the extent to which communal goals exist of their own motion, because they have arisen organically, and the extent to which they will need to be constructed for the community through the exercise of imagination and of will on the part of actors—usually legal but not necessarily so—who have the authority,

---

[7] See 'The Problem of Authority: Revisiting the Service Conception' in *Between Authority and Interpretation* (2009) 126, at 137ff.

de jure or *de facto,* to articulate such goals for the good of a life in common in that setting.

197. There is one further lesson that the critique of the normal justification thesis advanced by Darwall, Perry, and others has to teach us, in addition to the fact that the normal justification thesis does not tell us all that we need to know about the authority of law, or about the nature of the claim that law seeks to make upon us, or about the various modes of appeal that law and law-makers are bound to resort to in order to perfect in the minds of their addressees—and thereby lend an appearance of pre-eminence to—the course of action that the law prescribes or forbids, fosters or discourages, in its attempt to forge some kind of life in common. One branch of their critique, that just addressed, concerns the extent to which the normal justification thesis allegedly fails to sustain a sufficiently rich account of the role played in our lives by those institutions, such as legislatures, that we think we know have authority over us. The other branch of their critique concerns the extent to which the normal justification thesis appears to confer the status of an authority upon persons and institutions that we think we know have no authority over us. This second branch raises the question of the extent to which the true roles played by reason, imagination, and will in collective action, the action that describes and shapes a life in common, do not depend upon law, or upon those who are charged with making law for us. How far is law necessary to a life in common?

C. Alternative Authorities, Alternative Regulation

198. Underpinning the idea that the legitimacy of authority is a function of the legitimacy of its constitution is a familiar thought about the right nature of the relationship between a state and its subjects, between those who possess legal authority and those who are addressed by it. According to the service conception of authority and the particular values it is capable of giving rise to (those just described), that relationship is at heart a contingent one, dependent upon the satisfaction of the normal justification thesis in all that the state demands, and thus vulnerable to whatever rational challenges

may be offered by rival reasons and rival claims to authority (or autonomy) that are based on such reasons. Put shortly, our fealty is limited by, and so subject to the scrutiny of, our rationality. To many, that seems an insufficiently full-blooded, implausibly detached account of legal citizenship. It is true, of course, that some sort of fundamental bond between a state and its subjects is captured by the service conception, for the simple reason that among the reasons that apply to a subject are the reasons to have an overall relationship with the state that is intrinsically as well as instrumentally valuable, and what is more to have an overall relationship with the state that yields instrumental value indirectly (by drawing on the possibilities that arise from an intrinsically valuable relationship) as well as directly. But are those reasons enough? Do they capture the full scope of the exclusivity of our relationship, as it is or as it ought to be, to the state of which we are subjects, whether territorially or otherwise? Are a state's directives exclusionary merely in regard to other reasons, and thus in regard to other authorities only *pro tanto*, or are they, rather more fundamentally and more sweepingly, exclusionary in regard to other authorities *per se*?

199. Stephen Perry has pressed this point by developing his example of a law regulating the transportation of dangerous goods—in this case, as he imagines, a law of the state of Pennsylvania. As he presents it, that law imposes a categorical obligation upon its addressees, namely drivers in Pennsylvania who are engaged in the transportation of dangerous substances, to abide by its terms. It matters not to the law of Pennsylvania, or to the nature of the claim to authority that it makes, that the drivers in question might do better by following the law of California on the point. Pennsylvania expects its drivers to obey Pennsylvanian law, for better or for worse. Its claim to authority over them, and their duty to respect that claim, is unimpaired by the availability to them of better directives in other jurisdictions. Yet the normal justification thesis tells us that, on the contrary, in such a case the law of Pennsylvania, whatever it may claim, has no authority over such drivers, who are rationally bound to follow the law of California (assuming that co-ordination problems do not arise as a result) just because they would do better—that is, would transport dangerous substances more safely—by doing so. Perry concludes that in maintaining this, the normal justification thesis fails to account for the true nature of the claim to authority made by the state of Pennsylvania—a claim that is entirely characteristic of

legal authority wherever it is found—and, what is more, attributes to the law of California an authority that the law of California does not either possess or lay claim to. Pennsylvania law has an authority over Pennsylvania drivers that no other law is capable of enjoying, whatever the strength of its rational appeal may be.

200. It seems to me that there are different ideas of exclusivity at work here, some of which are captured by the normal justification thesis, some of which few democratic states today would lay any claim to, and some of which, if claimed, should be rejected as incompatible with rationality and autonomy, at least all other things being equal and with due regard to whatever sanctions the state in question may impose for breach. Begin with the most straight-forward case, with the idea in mind that the relatively straight-forward conclusions it yields may prove a helpful starting point for a more complex rendering of the contours of the problem. Where the value secured by the authority of law is the basic value of co-ordination (as in the case of most rules of the road), the state's claim to authority is typically exclusive, and is bound to be accepted as such, as indeed a sound application of the normal justification thesis would tend to confirm. There cannot normally be more than one co-ordinating authority in respect of the same matter for the same persons, for the simple reason that competition among co-ordinating authorities tends to undermine the very possibility of co-ordination, and in the world that we live in reasons of ready recognition, of convention, and of simplicity have in virtually all settings identified that one co-ordinating authority with the authority of the state.

201. Yet it is important not to read too much into this fact. All it shows is that claims to exclusivity of authority on the part of a state are not only made, but sometimes warranted, most obviously in typical cases of co-ordination. It does not show that all claims to such exclusivity are warranted. It does not even demonstrate, for example, what in fact would be plainly untrue, that there can only be one co-ordinating authority in any given jurisdiction; or that a co-ordinating authority must either be the state or operate by licence of the state; or that co-ordination need be backed by a sanction. Nor, and most fundamentally, does it show that it is impossible, in principle or in practice, for there to be two co-ordinating authorities on the same topic in the same jurisdiction. If no more can be shown, and if a state's authority need not be exclusive on even such an elemental legal project as that of co-ordination, where ready identification of

an authority might plausibly be thought to be essential to the success of the project, then all the more reason to question whether a state's authority need be exclusive in its other legal projects, where general public recognition plays a less central role. What makes reference to state authority typical in the straight-forward case of co-ordination, and is that feature necessary or contingent?

202. In point of fact we are all entirely familiar with the presence of a range of different regulatory authorities within a jurisdiction, some licensed by the state, some not; some competing, some enjoying a monopoly in their field; some with teeth, some without. Of course there can be little doubt, in any community governed by law, that the law is a prominent, indeed in most communities today the pre-eminent, vehicle for social co-ordination, and that much of its success in achieving that co-ordination depends on the fact that its addressees are by and large expected to treat its authority as exclusive. The question that remains, however, is the extent to which the exclusivity of legal authority necessarily goes beyond what is required to sustain this kind and degree of co-ordination. Is that authority comprehensive, as Perry suggests, or can the addressees of law be guided more broadly on any given matter—that is, on questions other than standard questions of co-ordination, by other sources of authority, including other sources of law? If so, is that guidance something that the state can accept as legally permissible, because broadly reconcilable with its own claim to authority? In particular, is there any reason for a person transporting dangerous goods across Pennsylvania not to be guided by the higher standards of California law, and if not, is there any reason for the state of Pennsylvania to object to such guidance?

203. The answer seems almost as straight-forward as in the typical case of co-ordination. Where a good depends upon the presence of a life in common, and where a life in common depends upon law, then the addressees of law are rationally committed to obedience to the law in question for the sake of the good that it secures, in just the ways and to the extent described earlier—which themselves depend, put broadly, on the law's rational pre-eminence, actual or apparent, the latter sometimes derived from and sometimes constitutive of whatever goals are embodied in the life of a community and of the persons who make up that community. In most cases the law in question will be the law of a place, Pennsylvania perhaps, simply because access to a good that the law secures by virtue of its authority is dependent upon

mutual recognition, by all potential participants in the good, of that law as the relevant source of the governing criteria of a life in common in a setting that is today almost always composed of strangers (that is, strangers to one another rather than to the setting in which they find themselves) as well as subscribers, and in the modern world the law of a place has long been accepted as the standard and hence as the conventional basis for such mutual recognition.[8] In that sense it is entirely true to say that the law of a territory is standardly exclusive of its rivals, and that the law of Pennsylvania is accordingly exclusive, for those in Pennsylvania, of the law of California in standard cases. In certain defined circumstances, of course, this kind of reliance upon the law of a place can be partially displaced by other considerations, in ways that have become embodied in the doctrines of private international law, but the doctrines of private international law are themselves in turn normally authorized and governed by the law of the place in which they are deployed (although the existence of successful claims to extraterritorial jurisdiction makes it clear that in practice there can be exceptions to this relationship, *de jure* as well as *de facto*). Nevertheless, it remains the case that the authority of law is normally exclusive within a particular territory. Recourse by persons there to other sources of authority is dependent upon the permission of that law, explicit or implicit.

204. When should such permission be granted, and what should a person do if it is not granted when it should be? The place of any authority in the construction of a life in common is dependent upon mutual recognition by its addressees of its status as the governing authority on the issue in question. Where the project of a life in common speaks to strangers (understood as previously described) as well as to subscribers, the various considerations sketched earlier combine to require that legal authority be regarded as exclusive by those to whom it is addressed in order to be effective, so yielding exclusive authority in the law of a place, such as Pennsylvania.[9] In

---

[8] This is not to suggest that there is any special let alone inevitable connection between life in common and the law of a place. See most famously Karl Llewellyn and E Adamson Hoebel, *The Cheyenne Way* (1941). In saying that the law of a place has long been accepted as the standard basis for mutual recognition I mean to say only that it has commonly been treated as such. For fuller consideration of the question, see Chapter 8, Law and Life in Common.

[9] As noted above, such authority is contingent upon the existence of a prevailing convention in Pennsylvania that the law of that place is to be recognized as the relevant

such cases there is no room for rival authorities, though there is usually a good deal of room for individual dissent from what the law of the place has required. However, a number of goods in common are accessible, either in whole or in part, to subscribers rather than to strangers, and indeed some such goods are often most fully realized only when access to them is restricted to subscribers. That kind of restriction may be predicated on either capacity or choice: some goods in common are accessible only to those who are committed to a particular form of life in common, and although many such commitments arise more or less naturally, without deliberation, so as to become part of a person's innate capacities, others arise by choice, and of course yet others by a mixture of the two. Whenever there is that kind of restriction of goods in common to subscribers, it is open to all those who would subscribe to authority by virtue of the restriction and for its sake to subscribe to whichever authority the requirements of which best enable them to build the particular life in common to which they are committed and the value of which they are seeking to realize, and in doing so to dissent, if need be and to that extent, from the requirements of the law of the place. That kind and degree of dissent, and of a corresponding attention to the requirements of some other authority rather than those of the law of the place, may be undertaken either individually or collectively. In some cases the dissent is characteristically individual, just because the good in question is constituted, in part at least, by the fact of individual subscription. In such cases the state may permit, even foster, the dissent in question (as in many settings it should do), or may prohibit the dissent, and the presence of the state's permission or its prohibition will bear upon the value of engaging in that dissent in particular settings, sometimes directly, sometimes indirectly or even perversely, in ways that are entirely familiar to denizens of liberal political cultures.

205. In a range of other, only marginally less familiar cases, however, dissent (or some other, less confrontational form of disregard)

---

source of the governing criteria of a life in common there, to the extent that such a life in common depends upon the mutual recognition of the authority of law. In other words, the law of a place possesses exclusive authority over those whom it addresses just if and to the extent that a convention exists attributing such authority to the law, as Hart explained, rather more precisely and elegantly, 50 years ago. What remains to be established is the extent to which the existence conditions of such conventions are sufficiently accommodating to permit rival sources of authority, and thus a range of possible reconciliations between the requirements of those authorities and those of the law.

may be undertaken collectively, through a common subscription to a rival authority on the matter or matters in question, and as such may be similarly permitted or prohibited by the state. The basis of such dissent may be conscientious or religious, ethnic or linguistic, social or economic. It may even lie in a view of the safest way to transport dangerous goods, as if, for example, a federation of transport drivers were to require its members to observe the different and, in its judgement, more effective safety requirements of California law rather than those of Pennsylvania law. Whether such dissent would be justified in any given case would depend, at a minimum, on the particular safety requirements in question and their effectiveness. Justification would also have to take into account the fact that Pennsylvania highway safety inspectors (who would almost certainly be strangers to the federation's scheme) would continue to treat the law of Pennsylvania as having exclusive authority on the issue of the transportation of dangerous goods in Pennsylvania and, what is more telling, might well be correct to do so from their perspective as Pennsylvania highway safety inspectors, a fact that among other things would be liable to result in the imposition of penalties on the drivers in question for their breach of Pennsylvania law, notwithstanding their observance of the requirements of a law that was better than the law of Pennsylvania in terms of the very goals that the Pennsylvania law was enacted to achieve (given that Pennsylvania would almost certainly have had the goal of safety in mind and so would not have enacted the law in question merely as a demonstration of the authority of the state of Pennsylvania).

206. Might a state claim greater authority than this, and further, might it be warranted in doing so—that is, might a state rightly insist upon obedience to a less compelling safety standard just because that standard was its own? Clearly the answer to both parts of the question must be in the affirmative. Pennsylvania would almost certainly claim that the requirements that it had imposed on the transportation of dangerous goods within its borders were no less safe than those of any other scheme, including the one embodied in the law of California. It would be likely to add that even if its requirements were, in certain respects at least, less safe than those laid down by the law of California, Pennsylvania drivers ought to obey Pennsylvania law by reason of the dependency of Pennsylvania law and the good that it is capable of giving rise to upon such obedience, not only in the particular domain of transportation but also more generally, so

giving rise to a general obligation upon all those present in Pennsylvania to abide by all requirements of Pennsylvania law. Any of these claims would be capable, in principle at least, of amounting to good reason to treat Pennsylvania law as what it in fact was not—namely, a sound authority on the matter of transporting dangerous goods within Pennsylvania—and if and when that proved to be the case (as many have doubted when extended to a general obligation to obey the law), the reason in question would by its very nature be recorded by the normal justification thesis.

207. Might a state such as Pennsylvania go further yet, to claim authority greater than any that could be grounded, immediately or remotely, in the reasons to comply with what it has required; that is, to claim authority for what its laws require solely by virtue of its constitutional existence as a state, as Perry maintains? The answer is that a state might well do just that, although the claim would in practice probably be difficult to establish clearly absent the presence of an explicit assertion of such overreaching authority in the language of the state constitution—an assertion that could not but be regarded as having been addressed to all who are *prima facie* subject to Pennsylvania law and as extending to cases of this kind. Assume, however, that such evidentiary difficulties could be overcome, and the existence of the claim could thus be established: could a state such as Pennsylvania ever be warranted in making such a claim? The answer is 'quite possibly', but the warrant for that answer would have to be looked for in the reasons that those who are *prima facie* subject to Pennsylvania law might conceivably have not to be autonomously rational—that is, the reasons they might have not to think for themselves about the true value of the government of the state of Pennsylvania and of the laws that the state had laid down (either in the particular case or in general): laws to which they were alleged to be subject even though compliance with them was in every other respect than that of constitutional fealty demonstrably less rational than an identifiable alternative that was open to them in the situation in question.

208. Such reasons certainly exist, and help to inform certain valuable relationships between governors and the governed, but they are reasons akin to the reasons to be a child before the age of reason, as it was once put, and so to be under the governance of one's parents just to the extent that one lacks the rationality of one's parents—or, more precisely, to the extent that one has not yet assumed the full

burden of the reasons that apply to one's condition and circumstances. In the context of government, they are the reasons for a dominion to be colonial in its relationship to what is, perceptively in this respect at least, commonly described as its mother country, and so to be under the governance of that mother country just to the extent that the dominion in question lacks the national maturity to be fully self-governing. These are reasons the absence of which in the fabric of our lives we often mourn yet cannot regret, for they cannot be reconciled with the condition of full responsibility for one's existence—whether as a person or as a nation—and so cannot be reconciled with the basic foundations of proper self-respect. For that reason they cannot be regarded as reasons of democracy or of citizenship, and so cannot be regarded as warrant for the status of a democratic society and the laws that it lays down. The democratic order is predicated upon a deeper and more universal expectation of rationality, one that calls upon all members of the *demos* to respect the claims to authority of those who seek to govern them only as and when the authority that is claimed is designed and exercised in a manner that is capable of satisfying the requirements of the normal justification thesis, or something very like it.

209. Yet that much having been said, it must be acknowledged that a supporter of Perry's position might quite plausibly suggest that the preceding discussion had rather missed the point that Perry was attempting to make, and might reasonably propose that all that the discussion had actually succeeded in showing is that claims to authority that do not satisfy the normal justification thesis do not satisfy the normal justification thesis. Of course, it would not follow from the soundness (such as it is) of this suggestion that the discussion had indeed entirely missed the point, for in showing just what it means to satisfy or not to satisfy the normal justification thesis it is possible to show just how little room there is for the development of claims to obligation that do not satisfy that thesis, and thus how little room there is for an exercise of authority that can rightly claim to be warranted on constitutional grounds alone. Yet even when qualified in that manner the suggestion proposed in Perry's defence continues to have real force, because it shows that the challenge that Perry has offered to the Razian account is in certain important respects being approached from the wrong direction here, by examining the normal justification thesis and what it is capable of sustaining rather than by examining the nature of properly constituted authority

and what it is capable of justifying. It might be rather more helpful, therefore, not to say more sympathetic, if I were to take up the suggestion frontally, by approaching the problem in just the way that Perry proposes—that is, by probing the exclusivity of constitutional authority that, as Perry rightly points out, is indisputably and consistently claimed by all governments, such that Pennsylvania claims an authority for its law-making that California recognizes, and in turn recognizes a like authority in what California claims (requirements of the US Constitution aside). Do such claims to authority transcend in a manner that one could recognize as characteristic, or at least as being consistent with what is characteristic, the boundaries of any claim that could be justified in terms of the normal justification thesis? Do they betoken a relationship between legitimate governments and those they govern that the normal justification thesis simply has no capacity to comprehend?

210. Comprehensive absences are notoriously difficult to establish, but their conceptual underpinnings need not be. Is it not implicit in the preceding examination of the normal justification thesis and the scope of authority it is capable of warranting that the exclusivity necessarily claimed by governments is exclusivity of sovereignty, not exclusivity of authority, whether the latter be understood in terms of the exclusion of other authorities or the exclusion of modes of reasoning that do not refer to authority? Surely the government of Pennsylvania is sovereign within its jurisdiction to the exclusion only of like claims to sovereignty, such as might otherwise be made by California or, more plausibly, by some neighbouring state (in domains other than that of highway safety, perhaps), and not to the exclusion of the presence of other authorities within its jurisdiction, even if the authority in question is that of another sovereign state, nor at the expense of the independent-mindedness of its citizens? Put another way, the exclusivity of authority that is claimed by Pennsylvania and by every other state is surely exclusivity of sovereign authority, not exclusivity of authority. Vindication of the former claim is plainly crucial to the very existence of Pennsylvania; by contrast, any attempt to vindicate the latter would be not only exhausting but largely self-defeating, for exclusivity of sovereignty is very often, indeed perhaps typically, bolstered in practice by the presence of other authorities within the jurisdiction of a state such as Pennsylvania, the successful functioning of which is in many cases crucial to the flourishing of Pennsylvania and its

citizens. What is true of sovereign authority is true of authority generally: authorities need to be exclusive within their domain in order to be authoritative, because the reasons that they set out to create are exclusionary in nature and that exclusion is the source of the value that acting upon those reasons is capable of giving rise to in the lives of their addressees, but the exclusivity of their authority runs only in the domain in which their authority is both distinctive and potentially valuable, which, in the case of Pennsylvania, is the domain of sovereign authority. If those who would transport dangerous goods in Pennsylvania are able to treat the law of California on the matter of highway safety as authoritative, it is just because the content of that law has been endorsed and adopted by some non-sovereign authority in Pennsylvania—such as a federation of transport drivers—in a manner that is not only effective but compatible with the functioning of Pennsylvania law (as previously outlined), despite the non-subscription of all those drivers who do not belong to the transport federation, in circumstances such that neither the existence of the transport federation nor its adoption of the content of California law on this particular issue is of a kind that would, by its nature or in its practice, threaten the sovereignty of Pennsylvania.

211. Yet even that much must be tempered if it is to be entirely truthful, for we are all familiar with the presence of competing claims to sovereignty within the same territory (and, more generally, with the presence of competing claims to authority within any particular domain of authority)—not just in some transitional moment of uncertainty and change, be that revolutionary or something less dramatic, a moment when one sovereign (or other) authority is challenged by a rival for its place, but as an everyday matter of regulatory competition, challenge, and negotiation, leading ultimately and most commonly to positions of tolerance, co-operation, and sometimes even collaboration on the part of the sovereign (or other authority) and its rival. Legal authorities, at least as we are familiar with them in settled societies, are indeed sovereign within their own domains, in ways that might in many cases appear to be more or less immutable, but their domains are always open to challenge in ways both great and small, and in terms of either scope or depth, on the part of other candidates for authority, whether those candidates are advancing similar or rival conceptions of sovereignty (or other authority), so that any particular instance of sovereignty can never

hope to be anything other than contingent—although the strength of the contingency, in the case of a successful authority, may be such that whole lives, indeed generations, are pursued successfully within its shadow and attendant cultures are consequently generated, thereby bringing to fruition a portion of whatever benefit the particular depth and contours of the contingency in question, and the authority that it sustains, are capable of giving rise to in that setting. Sometimes challenges to sovereign authority are mounted by state actors, sometimes by non-state actors; sometimes they are mounted against states, sometimes against the legislature of a state or even the judiciary there; sometimes the compromises that the challenges give rise to are embodied in politics, sometimes in law; sometimes those compromises (whether they be legal or political) are manifested in individual rights and freedoms, sometimes in collective rights and freedoms; sometimes compromises are manifested in federal structures and practices, sometimes in regional relationships among states or their courts; sometimes in international relations, sometimes in a recognition of extraterritorial jurisdiction.

212. To illustrate briefly, there are at least two very familiar arenas in which legal sovereignty is subject to on-going negotiation with rivals for its reach. The first is the setting of a federal state, the setting in which Pennsylvania and the United States negotiate, legally and politically, with one another as sovereigns in the articulation of their constitutional relationship, for the advancement of political ends that both are committed to, but that each seeks to achieve in the service of its own goals and by its own means. Such negotiations are of course relatively structured, and their scope is correspondingly limited, by the terms of the US Constitution and by the well entrenched political practices that have arisen in response to those terms, yet that structure is contingent upon the stability and permanence of the existing constitutional arrangement—which is undoubtedly very great indeed as matters currently stand, but need not and will not always be so. Less structured negotiations take place in the setting of newer and/or more fluid sovereign relationships, such as that which characterizes the European Union at present (in terms not only of legislatures but also of courts), or that which characterizes international relations, whether those be among states in general or between states in particular (some of which have arrived at well established patterns of mutual recognition and consequent respect, others of which have not).

213. The second familiar arena in which legal sovereignty is subject to on-going negotiation with its rivals, of course, is that which describes the sovereignty of the courts, which depend for their authority entirely on their on-going endorsement by all those who are nominally subject to that authority, from citizens to state actors, as courts themselves are all too keenly aware, and as they are just as careful not to draw special attention to. The authority of the courts in any given society is a function of the respect in which the courts are held there, which itself depends, at least in part, on approval of their record, institutionally and over time, by all of those who are subject to the jurisdiction of the courts—an approval that courts cultivate obliquely through the successful exercise of the judicial politics sketched earlier. Nor is that all: in settings in which the jurisdiction of a particular court is still in the process of articulation, the authority of that court is something to be negotiated not only with legislatures and citizens but also with rival courts, as we know from the history of clashes between statutory courts, between statutory courts and common law courts, between courts of law and of equity, between courts and tribunals, and between courts and arbitrators.

214. In practice, the authority of any sovereign is frequently contested, in just the sort of manner that the normal justification thesis seeks to capture, and as frequently reshaped and renewed, surviving as a continued authority, whether comprehensively or in any particular respect, only through the strength of on-going social acceptance (be that active or passive) on the part of the subjects of authority, and on the embodiment of that acceptance in social practices and conventions. As was emphasized at the beginning of this section, the status of a state, and the exclusivity of sovereignty that is central to that status, is in practice highly contingent, in ways that are usually entirely recognizable to the addressees of law—as indeed the preceding discussion of authority should have led us to expect. To establish the present exclusivity of a claim to authority, in whatever respect, is to show only that the claim has succeeded, to some particular extent and for the time being at least, not that it was bound to do so. The kind of full-blooded relationship between citizen and state that certain commentators invoke, whatever its other attractions may be and whatever special values it may be capable of giving rise to in the lives of those who are party to it, is neither a relationship of

maturity nor one that typifies constitutional functioning in the modern world.

215. It need hardly be said, of course, that there are necessary limits to the scale and frequency of such challenges if the authority is to remain an authority, and those limits are set by the capacity of the authority to remain generally recognizable as an authority by its addressees, to a degree that enables it to function as a practical authority in their lives and thereby to maintain the potential that authority possesses to bring value to those lives in and through acknowledgement of it and reliance upon it, in the various different ways considered earlier and others more or less like them. When those limits are exceeded, authority is lost, and so gives way to rival authority or to anarchy. This need not be a bad thing. Many human possibilities are lost thereby, but other possibilities are correspondingly gained. The authority of law is not essential to human life, though it may be something close to essential in the lives that we lead today—for the simple reason that those lives have been formed and described in the shadow of law, so as to become in many ways constituted by practices that depend on law and, more specifically, on laws of particular kinds, so that without the presence of law they would lack an aspect of their very constitution, leaving a structural rent in their fabric. This dependency can be and indeed usually is overstated, either on behalf of law in general or on behalf of laws in particular; in any event, the passing of the lives in question is liable to erase it, leaving only its echoes in successor lives.

7

Ideas of Easy Virtue: Descriptions and Evaluation

216. The normal justification of authority, according to Raz, is to be found in the capacity of authority to enable those who follow its directives to do better than they would do were they to exercise their own judgement, where the alternatives of heeding the authority's direction and reasoning for oneself are evaluated according to the same standard. In other words, authority, when properly exercised and properly attended to, can help us to comply more fully with reasons that otherwise apply to us. When an authority functions in this way it is justified; otherwise it is not. As we have just seen, for those who understand the justification of authority in terms of the constitution of authority, Raz's account looks for the justification of authority in the wrong place, and so offers, even when fully satisfied and hence at its most robust, an account of justified authority that is narrow, insubstantial, and at odds with the everyday experience of law and the workings of a legal system. For yet others, however, of whom John Finnis is the most notable, Raz's account and those of his constitutional critics, despite their differences, are in fact united by a common, yet utterly profound misapprehension of law, and as a consequence miscarry for the same basic reason, namely that they both fundamentally misunderstand the very essence of the relationship between law and its justification. Justification, according to Finnis, is not some kind of exercise that one performs upon law, whether successfully or unsuccessfully, or whether in the setting of the constitution or of the application of legal authority; rather it is an all-but-essential aspect of the very fabric of law itself, so as to make

it ultimately impossible to comprehend law, in any substantial sense, other than in terms of what might justify its existence and place in our lives. One could say, put rather briefly, that law is intricately constituted by its own justification, in the sense that justification is the life force of law, in all its richness, complexity, and perhaps even mystery. Without justification there would certainly still be law, as Finnis is quick to make clear (so distancing himself from views such as that of Dworkin), and that fact matters greatly to the good that law can do, but a law that fails to discover the justification that law exists to live up to is law that miscarries in terms of its very reason for being, and so is law in name only, an artefact stripped of its life purpose.

217. Finnis's claim is set out persuasively, with admirable clarity and succinctness, in the justifiably famous opening chapter of his *Natural Law and Natural Rights*.[1] He relies upon Aristotle, albeit tempered by Max Weber, for the basic thought. In attempting to contemplate an object or practice, such as the social institution of the law, one is bound to isolate the practice from its conceptual neighbours, first by attending to its point, and second by distinguishing central cases of the practice from those that are peripheral. Indeed, it might be said (though Finnis himself does not put it this way) that it is this that makes something such as a practice an *object* of our reflection: we look to it (the object) with a purpose in mind. Given that we have many reasons to contemplate a practice such as the law, and so may have as many purposes possibly in mind, a person who wishes to describe the practice without endorsing any purpose in particular (a person such as a legal theorist) is able to establish a stable picture of the practice only by identifying central cases of the purposes we might possibly have in mind and, through them and by extension, central cases of the practice itself. According to Finnis, this is to be done by identifying not the most common, but the most reasonable cases of self-interpretation on the part of those who are engaged in the practice. In doing so, one identifies the point of the practice. In the setting of the law, he suggests, the central point of view is that of practical reasonableness, and the most reasonable case of that point of view is the view that is in fact practically reasonable, and that is as a consequence free (or at least as free as we can make it) of contingency, misunderstanding,

---

[1] 1980, second edition 2011. The claim is renewed in the Postscript to the second edition, at 426–36, and in the Introduction to *Philosophy of Law: Collected Essays of John Finnis, Volume IV* (2011).

and myth. It follows that we can only understand law by understanding what would make law practically reasonable, that is, what would make it both good and effective as a design for living. In short, justification is an intrinsic aspect of our understanding of law.

218. One prominent feature of this way of thinking of the law is to give new life to the old proposition that an unjust law is not a law. Finnis offers a delicate reinterpretation of this idea: as he sees it, an unjust law is recognizable as law but barely so, like a paring knife that cannot pare, or a friend who is constitutively prepared to betray one's friendship. Set out like that, Finnis's position clearly courts, without quite falling into, an equivocation as to the meaning of law, because it embraces the apparent paradox of laws that are not laws, or (to pursue my own illustrations) paring knives that are not paring knives and friends who are not friends, while distancing itself from the possibility that such laws are laws in one sense but not in another, and so on for paring knives and for friends. Yet striking though the proposition is on its face, it is rather less clear what might be interesting about it, even in its reinterpreted form. After all, both Finnis and those, such as Raz, whom he seeks to take issue with on this point agree that a person is justified in not attending to such a law. How much does it matter then, and for what purposes, whether what a person rightly rejects the claims of in such a setting remains fully law or only formally so, whether legal obligation in that setting is non-existent or entirely hollow? Is there anything more at stake here than the rationality of regret?

219. It seems to me that the interest and significance of Finnis's position become a good deal clearer when viewed from the opposite perspective. If an object or a practice is indeed tied to a point or purpose (presumably a human purpose that other creatures might have access to, since purposes must find their origins and direction in the mind of some agent, and Finnis clearly has human agency in view), closely enough to make that purpose all but an essential element of the identity of the object or practice in question (although not quite essential, given that Finnis makes clear that something of the object will survive even in the face of complete failure to fulfil this purpose), then the connection between goods (objects or practices) and what they are good for is not only necessary, as he alleges, but also unified, stable, and closed.[2] Law

---

[2] When Finnis maintains that a practice cannot be understood apart from its point, he cannot be taken to be maintaining that the practice cannot be understood apart from its value, or he would be assuming his conclusion.

exists to serve practical reasonableness and no other, as paring knives exist for paring, and friendship exists for whatever the point of friendship is taken to be. It is not open to human beings to invent, or, to put it from the opposite perspective, objects and practices are not open to acceptance of, not susceptible to finding themselves the bearers of, fresh points, fresh purposes, new values and disvalues, or unfamiliar admixtures of various values, disvalues, or values and disvalues wrapped up together. This is not to say that such inventions and attributions do not take place. Rather, it is to say that, on the logic of Finnis's account, when they take place they must be peripheral rather than central cases of the practice, or they must be once peripheral but now central cases that have come to displace some formerly central case of the practice, or that their intervention in the practice must be sufficiently alien and of sufficiently long standing as to have given rise over time to new objects and practices, which have thereby become descendants of and neighbours to the objects and practices in which those new points were first deployed. Unity, relative stability, and closure are fundamental to the concept of point as Finnis deploys it.

220. Are these several variations in fact exhaustive of the ways that practices and values interact in our lives? Is it not possible to believe that the relationship between practices and values is multiple, fluid, transitory, and open-ended, so that it would be misleading or conclusory to speak of a central case, or a point (singular), other than from a sociological perspective perhaps—a perspective that Finnis specifically sets aside, precisely because it would bind practices to perceptions of their point and correspondingly detach them from their true potential for value (or lack thereof)? Is it not further possible that the point of certain practices may be, or at least may include, a bad one, so that the relationship of certain practices to practical reasonableness is just to that extent negative? In particular, might law not have or, more precisely, be capable of having many points, including bad ones; might it not even be the case that law is on the whole more of a bad thing than a good thing, more the enemy of practical reasonableness than its friend? To return to the general perspective once more, could the significance of description in the project of human understanding be thought to lie in anything other than the fact of its evaluative promiscuity? Are descriptions not, at their core, ideas of easy virtue, placeholders for the various values and disvalues with which their objects may be from time to time infused, in the course of manifold engagements with those objects by agents from different

backgrounds with different purposes in mind? Is it not their relative distance from evaluation that makes them valuable in themselves, as descriptions, what makes them something more, in other words, than mere placeholders, makes them vital resources in the realization of value by agents through the exercise of their reason, imagination and will?

221. Begin with what strikes me as helpful and true in what Finnis has to say. Underlying the broad claim that Finnis is seeking to make about the relationship between social practices and what is said by him to be their point, or in particular between the phenomenon of law and the pursuit of practical reasonableness in circumstances of moral and human diversity, is an entirely sound observation, and indeed a worthy reminder of an Aristotelian insight, as to the basic elements of the rational quest both for value and for the understanding needed to attain it and the role that social practices, and our comprehension of them, may have to play in that quest and in its success or failure, whether the latter be in whole or in part.[3] Our encounters with the world, and the various concepts that we call upon to organize, direct, and reflect upon those encounters, are all undertaken with some species of evaluation in mind. Our interest in the features of the world, including its purely moral features—our very capacity to identify them as features—is always and only ever with what ought to be in mind (or, more precisely, with our perception of what ought to be); in that sense every ought is an is, all values are facts, and all facts are evaluatively inspired. It is simply not possible to comprehend the world rationally apart from a sense of the value or disvalue that comprehension might be thought to yield, directly or indirectly. Where neither value nor disvalue is at stake, actually or potentially, one can identify features of the world only by extension and with an accompanying attitude of something close to bafflement: what, one might ask, could one possibly make of such a feature, and why, assuming that one could possibly make something of it, would one have any interest in it? Comprehension is nothing more or less than comprehension of the possibility of value and its

---

[3] This is not to suggest that Finnis would for a moment endorse the interpretation of his achievement set out in this paragraph. Indeed he makes entirely clear in the course of his 'Reflections and Responses', in *Reason, Morality, and Law: The Philosophy of John Finnis*, ed John Keown and Robert P George (2012) 459 at 540, that he does nothing of the kind. It remains a question, of course, whether he has identified his achievement correctly.

place in our lives: just as our eyes register light waves, and our ears register sound waves, our cognitive faculties register value (and disvalue), sometimes entirely by dint of their own internal operations and sometimes, perhaps more often, by their interaction with what our external, sensory perceptions have registered, separately or in combination; that is to say, with what we have seen, heard, smelled, touched, or tasted.[4]

222. So, for example, when we come across an unfamiliar object we seek to grasp, and are bound so to seek, just what the object might be good for, as it is often put colloquially—or more precisely, since the thought that the object might be good *for* something focuses on instrumental value, potentially to the exclusion of intrinsic value, just what to make of the object in question in terms of its value or disvalue. Adept as we normally are in navigating our particular circumstances, and conventional and controlled as most of those circumstances are in relatively stable cultures, the experience of seeking to grasp the value of an object or practice is somewhat unusual in the course of adult life in one's native culture, all the more so the older, more practised, and more settled one becomes there. Yet, as we have all had occasion to observe, the experience is entirely familiar to children, and by the same token as familiar an aspect of adult engagements with children. Objects the value of which is entirely obvious to an adult are often turned over uncomprehendingly in a child's hand, then perhaps put in the mouth to taste and feel, then dropped as apparently meaningless or, in a more dramatic response, firmly rejected, apparently on the basis that they either are or might soon become a source of disvalue in the child's present scheme of activity. While less common, a similar incomprehension invades adult life as and when one strays into a culture, or some aspect of a culture, the objects and practices of which are foreign to one's experience in some way: according to many narratives of voyages of exploration, aboriginal peoples have frequently been baffled by certain aspects of their engagement with the objects and practices of non-aboriginal peoples, and vice versa; according to stereotype, and not always falsely so, the old are often baffled by the ways of the young, and vice versa; artists are often baffled by the

---

[4] This is to assume that comprehension is sound when in fact, of course, it is often not so. I will return to the issue of misperceptions of value later.

views and practices of scientists, non-technophiles are often baffled by technophiles, and so on.

223. In all these settings people find themselves baffled just because the value that is latent in and accessible through certain objects or practices, objects and practices that are in the salient respect alien to the people in question, is quite literally imperceptible to them, thereby rendering the objects or practices themselves incomprehensible. Those objects and practices, and the values that underpin them, are such that they can only be grasped by those among us who are cognoscenti, of the appropriate kind and in the appropriate degree. This does not, it should be emphasized, make such objects and practices in any sense unusual as objects or practices. On the contrary, the value or disvalue of any object or practice is only ever intelligible to those who are cognoscenti. Comprehension is always and only ever comprehension of the possibility of value or disvalue, so that in any setting where one is, for whatever reason, not in a position to be cognizant of the possibility of value or disvalue, one is consequently in no position to comprehend the object or practice in question, be the object or practice valuable in itself or be it partially constitutive of a value; be it a vehicle for the realization of value or be it a component of such a vehicle. The experience of incomprehension is unfamiliar in adult life only because and to the extent that we normally operate in domains in which we are cognizant of most of the objects and practices that we are liable to encounter and of at least some of the values and disvalues that they are capable of giving rise to. Yet that normalcy is for the most part the product of learning and habituation: the intellectual passage from childhood to adulthood, from a relatively limited, visceral, native response to the presence or possibility of value and disvalue to a much more sophisticated, reflective, wide-ranging, and contemplative grasp of the range and depth of what the world has and might have to offer, is in large part a transition to the position of a cognoscente.

224. All this simply goes to confirm much of the moral instinct and conceptual insight that Finnis is seeking to vindicate in the opening chapter of *Natural Law and Natural Rights*. Broadly speaking, and so setting aside for the moment the admittedly vital nuances of what has just been said, there is no essential divide between description and evaluation, no fundamental separation between law and morals, as long, of course, as one remembers to speak, or at least to think, of the latter in the plural. Yet that last rider is crucial, for its

presence breaks the connection between the evaluative underpinning of description and the identification that Finnis is seeking to make, of description with evaluative purpose. It is that fact, that the realm of what ought to be, the realm of evaluation and of morals, is multifaceted and fundamentally so, that makes description (as a qualitative rather than a quantitative exercise) possible and indeed necessary, and so distinguishes the project of description from its indispensable companion, the project of evaluation. It is the further fact that the objects and practices that description captures are typically susceptible to the on-going direction of imagination and will, be it human or otherwise, a direction that makes them the bearers of different values and disvalues in different hands and at different times (and also susceptible to misdirection), that makes it highly unusual to be able to bind description to evaluation with regard to any given object or practice, the more so when the object or practice in question is, like law, multifaceted and complex, even when evaluation is understood compendiously, as it is in Finnis's rendering of law.

225. Consider some everyday cases. A saw, so it would seem, is a tool that was originally designed, however long ago, as a way of cutting wood. It is, of course, far from being the only way of cutting wood (axes and adzes are older and in some ways superior means of performing many of the same tasks that a saw is called upon to perform), so something of its original purpose is shared with other tools. What is more, wood is not the only material that a saw can cut (there are hacksaws for metal and there are water-cooled saws for stone and concrete), which is to say that a saw has acquired purposes other than the one for which it was originally designed. More strikingly, and perhaps more surprisingly, a saw is also, at least in its form as a handsaw, a musical instrument. In serving this purpose it is not in any sense reconfigured; on the contrary, it is simply repurposed, and that only temporarily, for something of the significance of a musical saw lies in the fact that its musicality is compatible with its original and more familiar purpose of cutting wood. When people seek to make music, yet lack either conventional instruments or the skill to draw music from them, they often explore the percussive and melodic possibilities of what surrounds them. If the exploration is successful, and if the lack that inspired it is a common one, then the consequent musical exploitation of the everyday may become conventional, as in the case of a saw, a washboard, or a steel drum. Each of these musical instruments is a straight-forward instance of finding a new purpose

for an article that was designed with an entirely different purpose in mind.

226. If one moves from the setting of an artefact to that of a social practice a similar pattern emerges. Marriage, whatever its antediluvian origins, by the nineteenth century came to acquire in English law the purpose of voluntarily uniting a man and a woman for life, to the exclusion of all others.[5] That was, one might have been tempted to say, its point. Yet each and every aspect of that familiar purpose (or point, to speak that way for the moment) even as enshrined in English law, has subsequently come under pressure, most interestingly, in ways that qualify but do not displace the original purpose as embodied in law: marriage today may be arranged, and so be something less than fully voluntary; it may, in many though not all of the jurisdictions that have inherited English law, unite members of the same sex; it need not last for life (though for the time being it must be intended to do so); it need not be to the exclusion of all others (polygamy aside, in many jurisdictions descending from English law adultery is not recognized as a ground for divorce unless it amounts, on separate considerations, to the ground of marriage breakdown). In short, the on-going development and extension of the possible purposes of marriage, and of the many values and disvalues that the institution of marriage can consequently give rise to, is almost as straight-forward a case as that of the on-going development and extension of the purposes and possibilities of a handsaw, once again amounting to the development of, in this case, a social practice, along lines that invest that practice with new purposes, without thereby turning it into a different practice (other than *pro tanto*). In fact, quite to the contrary.

227. What is most noticeable about such developments of purpose, and most controversial in the case of the currently broadening palette of the possible purposes of marriage, is that each new purpose depends for a significant portion of its meaning and value on the continuity of the contemporary, multi-purposed practice with its more narrowly purposed forebears, and indeed on the compatibility of the contemporary practice with the purpose or purposes that those forebears expressed and facilitated and that the contemporary practice continues to express and facilitate. As with the musical saw, something of the significance of same sex marriage lies in the fact

---

[5] *Hyde v Hyde and Woodmansee*, LR 1 P & D 130 (1866).

of its compatibility with marriage's older and more familiar purpose of uniting heterosexual couples for life. Indeed, it is precisely that fact, of concomitance and compatibility, that makes the investment of marriage with new purposes as controversial as it is. In respecting the social practice that they elect to engage in for its traditional and most familiar purpose, husbands and wives today are bound to respect the other (valuable) purposes for which that practice may also be engaged in now, for the simple reason that those other purposes are every bit as at home in the practice as is the one that they have chosen to embrace, and for that reason must to some extent necessarily be engaged with by any and all of those who engage with the practice, albeit that they do so for other reasons, with other purposes in mind.[6] Were that not the case, and were concepts actually tied to particular purposes (or points) in the way that Finnis contends they are, nobody would or could be arguing, in either one direction or the other, about the proper purposes of marriage, for such a thought could not be the basis for an argument that anyone could rationally pursue. Marriage between members of the same sex would be logically impossible, rather than morally desirable or undesirable (as in fact all participants in the current argument of necessity take it to be).

228. Underpinning these observations is a more profound point, which can be brought out by a final example. In certain settings evaluative promiscuity runs rather deeper than the previous two instances would suggest, to the extent that openness of purpose becomes partially constitutive of the practice itself (or, less commonly, of an artefact). To put it more precisely, in the setting of certain social practices, and of our concepts of them, the development of new purposes is not simply a possibility, something that may happen to the practices in question given the energy of human beings, the richness of human imagination, and the plasticity of the practices, but rather constitutes

---

[6] It is worth noting, though perhaps it need hardly be said, that the practice of respect is necessarily reciprocal in this setting, so that in respecting the social practice that they elect to engage in for its new and still relatively unfamiliar purpose (or, more precisely, their purpose, bearing in mind the claims made at para 234ff), same sex couples are bound to respect the other (valuable) purposes for which that practice may be engaged in, including that for which it has traditionally been engaged in and still continues to be engaged in. It follows that such couples are as rationally committed to belief in the value of traditional marriage as is any traditionalist, and by the same token are as bound not to believe in the special (that is, the enhanced) status of marriage as they themselves know and experience it in and through their relationship.

a significant, perhaps definitive aspect of the practices as we know and pursue them. Consider, as a relatively familiar case in this regard, the theatre, by which I mean the set of interrelated practices of writing, performing, and participating in drama, whether as an author, actor, or member of a theatrical audience—in the last instance whether it be in a physical theatre, before a screen, or as the reader of a script. What can possibly count as drama is frequently the question, and the challenge, that animates not only particular dramas but the broader social practice of the theatre of which they are a part, certain presently prevailing conceptions of which it is the purpose of those particular dramas to develop, extend, and on occasion even confound by advancing a dramatic agenda that self-avowedly presents itself as having no less a degree of theatrical value, and no more remote a connection to the realm of theatrical practice, than the prevailing conceptions that their agenda challenges. We engage in theatre, in part at least, just to discover what theatre might be capable of.

229. In this respect, it is worth noticing that the practice of theatre is conceptually more capacious than are some of its offshoots, be those offshoots performance-oriented, such as opera and ballet, or text-based, such as the novel and the short story, each of which either is, or is a descendant of—a reification of—what was once a historically and evaluatively distinctive exploration of theatrical possibility. Various answers to the fundamental question of what theatre might be capable of—some persuasive, others not—have been offered over the ages by authors, audiences, and more broadly distinct cultures of theatre that have existed in certain times and places, some of them still flourishing among us, others now a matter of historical record. Some of those answers have been only fleeting because they have failed to take root in a social practice; for that reason they remain suggestive and their value is to be looked for in that fact. Other answers have become established in practice to such an extent that they have become characteristic of their time and place, even if only temporarily and locally, without any broader legacy. Every such rooted answer establishes possibilities of a certain kind by closing off other possibilities, while leaving the general, overarching, expansive project of the theatre unaltered. That is what it means for those answers to have been reified, and so to have become art forms in their own right. It is their relative closure that makes them distinctive, just as it is the correspondingly relative openness of the theatre to on-going possibility that makes it what it is.

230. Each of these examples can certainly be reconciled with the terms of Finnis's account, simply by identifying one of the many possible purposes to which the practice in question might be put as central to the practice, and thus as the point of the practice. Yet the crucial question is, of course, just how is one able to do this and, even granted the ability, at what price? Finnis would, it seems to me at least, almost certainly take the purpose of a handsaw to be that of cutting wood; the purpose of marriage to be the union of a man and a woman for life, to the exclusion of all others; and the purpose of theatre (I am on more speculative ground here) perhaps to be the oral presentation of imagined experience, by one or more actors in a public setting, in a manner that is both entertaining and instructive to its audience. But just what is it that might be thought to make these or any other purpose *central* in the sense that Finnis has in mind, the sense in which it becomes possible to describe a particular purpose as the *point* of an object or practice and by that means to identify whatever value may be yielded by the realization of that purpose with the very meaning of the object or practice in question? Finnis rightly discounts the possibility that such centrality is to be discovered by an empirical canvas of the purposes that people actually have in mind when engaging in the practice, so as to discover the purpose for which the practice is in fact most commonly engaged in, for that would simply be to identify the value of a practice with the most common perception of that value and thereby render the meaning of the practice vulnerable to whatever is the most common misperception of its value.

231. Finnis suggests instead that centrality is to be discovered by identifying the most reasonable cases of self-interpretation on the part of those who are engaged in the practice. Yet it is clear that this suggestion requires a degree of refinement if it is to be at all plausible, given that a great many—perhaps most—practices are characterized by, or at least are susceptible to, a wide range of competing cases of self-interpretation on the part of those who are engaged in them, not all of which can be discounted as unreasonable. Might one seek to identify the central case of such self-interpretations by weighing the various reasonable purposes for which they are undertaken against one another, so as to determine which of them is the most reasonable? Finnis clearly does not think so, for that kind of approach would be dependent for its success upon the commensurability of value—something that Finnis not only rightly denies, but

that the essence of his account of law is dependent on the denial of. Might one identify the central case of a practice with the original, or foundational, purpose for which the practice was first engaged in? Surely not, for that would be to return to the empirical canvas and so once again would be to identify the value of a practice with a perception of that value, in this case an historical rather than a contemporary perception. It is true, of course, that certain long-standing practices have come to be closely associated with their originating purpose, in a way that has made them relatively resistant to attributions of any different purpose, but that fact in itself tells us only of the strength of cultural convention in certain settings, of the limitations of human imagination and will in the face of such conventions, and of the brute character of certain practices. It does not yield any general insight about the relationship of purposes to practices, let alone an insight that would explain what criterion makes a purpose central.

232. Might one say, then, as Finnis actually does with respect to the social practice of law, that the central point of view is that of practical reasonableness? On its face that would seem simultaneously in part to assume one's conclusion (that the point of a practice must be practically reasonable rather than practically unreasonable) and in part to beg the question, which after all is just which aspect of practical reasonableness, as manifested in the various purposes for which people engage in the practice, is to be regarded as central to the practice, in a manner and to an extent that makes it sensible to regard that aspect of practical reasonableness as the very point of the practice. Reference to practical reasonableness will not help us to distinguish cutting wood and making music, or traditional marriage and same sex marriage, all of which are practically reasonable as purposes and yet only one of which can be regarded as central in each case if the practice in question is to have a point (singular).

233. Yet underlying these several difficulties, it seems to me, is a much more fundamental question: namely, how might a point of *any* kind, be it central or otherwise, come to be connected to a practice? Granted that the meaning of a practice is intrinsically connected to its value and disvalue, what basis is there for believing that the same is also true of point? On the face of it, purposes proceed from people, or more precisely from agents,[7] and practices have a point, therefore,

---

[7] I am here bracketing the possibility of passive practices.

just to the extent that they are invested with a sense of purpose by those who engage in them. This is certainly what Finnis assumes. If that is the case, however, then it would be a mistake to attribute point to a practice other than as one aspect of the record of a particular engagement with the practice by an agent with a certain purpose in mind, a purpose that to the extent of the engagement had become the point of the practice or, at least, of a particular instance of it. To think otherwise would be to connect value and its perception (which necessarily underpins and informs purposes) in precisely the way that Finnis is at pains to reject, as he does in rejecting the identification of point with the most common cases of self-understanding on the part of participants in the practice. If that much is true, then it would further seem that it is a mistake to allow oneself to think that there is, other than in certain highly specialized cases, a special bond between a social practice and any value in particular—a bond that could be captured by the idea of a central case and its associated point, other than the aptitude of the practice for the realization of the value in question, in the setting of a particular project that is pursued by an agent or agents with a particular purpose in mind, just the sort of connection the rational basis of which is discoverable through the application of the normal justification thesis (where authority is at stake) and the other bases of which are to be found in the exercise of imagination and will, in the manner certain elements of which have been traced earlier.

234. It is important to be rather careful here, however, lest one run purpose and point together in a way that may be encouraged by certain terms of Finnis's account, yet is not required by them. There must be a significant conceptual distance between purpose and point or it would not make sense to think of them separately, other than as something approaching synonyms. What is more, the significance of the distinction aside, there would be no need for those who engage in a practice with a certain purpose in mind to invest the practice with a corresponding sense of point, the sense that roots, however transiently and contingently, the purpose that they have in mind, or at least certain crucial aspects of it, in the practice. It seems to me that the explanation of these phenomena is along the following lines. The distinction between purpose and point is real and important, but its significance is to be discovered in the equivocal character of point, lying as it does between the realms of purpose and of value, while partaking opportunistically of both. It is the investment

of practice with purpose that gives practice its alleged point, and in return (here reversing the direction of influence) it is the identification of point with the meaning and value of practice that allegedly imbues a purpose (which drives the attribution of point) with some portion of what has been independently recognized as the meaning and value of the practice. This process of identification and attribution lends practices—in the form of what is taken, from time to time and agent to agent, to be their point—an appearance of singularity of point, call it centrality, that they in fact derive from the capacity of purpose, in the hands of certain agents on certain occasions, to be singular and focused;[8] thereby obscuring the multiple possibilities for meaning and value that exist for virtually all practices while simultaneously imbuing purposes with value, or purporting to do so; thereby diminishing or even concealing the role played by perception in the identification of purpose and correspondingly diminishing the consequent prospects for error that are embodied in any purpose that proceeds from an agent capable of error, and that are accordingly and consequently translated into point. In short, the attribution of point is a way of colonizing a practice and its value, so as to align the practice with the purpose that the agent has in mind, and in doing so to invest the agent's purpose with some portion of the value that the practice is capable of giving rise to.

235. Yet it is also important not to overstate this qualification. The idea of point may occupy a place, equivocally and opportunistically, between the realms of purpose and of value, but it does so because its role is to associate purpose (in the case of law, human purpose) with the value or values, real or perceived, that animate purpose. That being the case, it exists as a byproduct of purpose, a companion in the same endeavour, and for that reason is subject to all the possibilities and all the frailties that purpose is subject to. Objects and practices that are engaged in with a purpose or purposes in mind may be successfully invested with a wide range of points, as wide in fact as the range of purposes that inspire those points, for good and for ill. They may correctly be said to have many points, and not all of those are good ones.

---

[8] Purposes can of course be multiple and shifting, and often are, and so can be much like the value of a practice in that respect; what I am emphasizing here is that they can also be fastened upon, and that it is when they are fastened upon in the course of engagement with a practice that it becomes possible to speak of the point of the practice in terms of them.

236. If this much is true then the difficulty in the story that Finnis sets out to tell about the point of law as a social practice, and more generally about the relationship between the meaning of social practices and their value, stems from his dual commitment to the idea of a central case and its identification as the point of a practice. The image of a central case is but a metaphor, which only has purchase in terms of a purpose, and indeed and more precisely in terms of certain kinds of purposes. It is in terms of purposes of those kinds that a point may be rightly regarded as central. Yet the identification of such a purpose necessarily takes place against the background of the variety of values that are to be discovered in a practice, the variety of purposes for which the practice may be engaged in that are discernible through the exercise of reason and imagination, the capacity to fasten upon one purpose rather than another through the exercise of reason and will, and the vulnerability of the whole enterprise to rational error on the part of agents, however that error may be engendered. To extend the metaphor of the central case any further than this, in the way that Finnis seeks to do, is to suppress the roles of imagination and of will in the identification of purpose, as well as to suppress the governing role of reason in supervising, however imperfectly, the exercise of those capacities.

237. What does this imply for the project of description, be it of the practice of law or of anything else? What criteria should a person call upon in order to describe a social practice correctly? Clearly descriptions are necessary not only to reflection upon engagement with practice but also to engagement itself, where that engagement is self-conscious. Yet if a practice lacks a central case, how can a theorist ever establish a stable picture of the practice in order to meet the challenge that Finnis sets himself, that of describing a practice and so determining its point, without endorsing any purpose in particular? The short answer is that a theorist can only do so with a particular purpose in mind, a purpose that the theorist must be prepared to account for in such a way as to warrant the presence and absence of the features that the description so favoured by the theorist includes and excludes. It is simply not possible to arrive at a description neutrally, in a way that does not have evaluative implications, foreclosing certain prospects for value and fostering others. Nor is it possible to arrive at a description neutrally in a different sense, namely in a way that shields the purposes that inform the description from evaluative contention, whether by calling those purposes central or otherwise. In short, convention aside,

there is no such thing as a central, stable, correct description. Rather, there are many possible such descriptions, of which many are in turn central to one purpose or another, so that a standard description can only be established by convention and even then will always remain both tied to the context in which the convention exists and vulnerable to the wide range of challenges that can be offered to conventions. Yet it is also important to recognize that there is nothing in any of this to be particularly dismayed by. On the contrary, it is precisely these features that lend descriptions their value.

238. The underlying point of descriptions is to identify an object or practice without thereby identifying it with any value in particular.[9] The consequent and converse point of much of descriptive practice is to speak of an object or practice in such a way as to trade upon the open and uncommitted features of description while simultaneously offering a particular rendering of the object or practice, the effect of which is to close and commit its description in such a way as to serve better a certain evaluative purpose. Descriptions, as a project, exist at least in part in recognition of this evaluative permissiveness. That being the case, they can be couched in a host of different ways, with as many different implications for the values to be realized from what is described. Certain forms of couching will by their nature make certain evaluative pursuits more central to a description than do others. When those forms of couching claim such centrality for themselves, they enter the realm of persuasive definition. Other forms of couching trade upon their evaluative plasticity, and of course between those two poles there is a rich continuum of actual and possible descriptions, each with its own evaluative potential.

239. In analytic philosophy, the conventional approach has been to be as minimal as possible in terms of the elements of description so as to be as catholic as possible about the potential for value and disvalue of engagement in the social practice as so described. It is in that spirit that one might propose philosophically that law, for example, is constituted by the union of primary and secondary rules, or must claim authority for what it requires, or must seek to create

---

[9] This is to put the claim idiomatically. Lest I contradict myself in doing so I should perhaps say, more precisely, that one of the chief (that is, both characteristic and successful) functions of descriptions is to identify an object or practice without thereby identifying it with any value in particular. Of course the promiscuity (or catholicity) runs in more than one direction: descriptions also identify values without thereby identifying them with their instantiation in any particular object or practice.

a life in common. Doing so minimizes the degree to which one's philosophical conclusions are assumed as part of one's premises for analysis and discussion. Yet such an approach is nothing more than a familiar tradition in philosophy, one that makes certain insights possible at the expense of others. What is important to recognize as a more general matter is that even when descriptions are tightly tied to a particular evaluative point the distance between the two is not a fiction, for the simple reason that while descriptions exist to aid evaluations, they are neither evaluations themselves nor constituents of evaluation.[10]

240. What then of paradigmatic descriptions? How are they to be understood? The answer follows reasonably straightforwardly from what has already been said. Descriptions become paradigmatic for a certain community when the sharing of those descriptions, and of the concepts that they embody, yields or is believed to yield a value or access to values that would be inaccessible, or at least less accessible, in the absence of that shared access. Paradigmatic descriptions enjoy no greater status than this, no greater bond to the social practices that they seek to capture, no greater immunity from the possibility of repurposing or from losing their status as paradigmatic.

241. Where does this leave the idea that an unjust law is not a law, even in the delicately nuanced form in which Finnis presents that idea? In what circumstances might moral error be thought to threaten description? It is tempting to think never—that evaluative failures depend on conceptual success, and so have no capacity to threaten description. A knife that cuts well or badly is a good or bad knife only because it is indisputably a knife—that is, because it has already succeeded in falling under that description. Other articles that cut well (such as scissors) or badly (such as chopsticks) do not for that reason become or cease to be knives; it is only when *knives* cut well or badly that they either live up to or fail to live up to their descriptive status as knives. If that were the end of the matter, and if the enabling of practical reasonableness were the point of law, the failure of law to be practically reasonable would be something that

---

[10] The account offered here is in accord with what is proposed by Julie Dickson in *Evaluation and Legal Theory* (2001), other than in its denial of any special status to the species of evaluation that she describes as meta-theoretical. That species of evaluation is distinctive in all the ways that she describes, but it is not, in my view, in any other sense an evaluation of a special kind, with an evaluative status that differs from the status of other evaluations.

one could identify only in and through the identification of a certain social practice as law, and thus as burdened with the project of practical reasonableness in terms of which it had been found to have failed. If that were true then an unjust law would necessarily be a law, albeit a deviant instance of law, given its failure of point. In recent writing Finnis himself has offered a view along these lines, although in doing so he does not explore in any detail the idea of deviance, and so does not explain the sense in which an unjust law is both fully a law (so as to be in a position to be adjudged to have failed as a law) and yet barely a law (because of its profound evaluative failings).[11] Yet it seems to me that the thought that connects evaluative failures to conceptual success is rather too neat, rather too quick. In most settings evaluative failures do not in fact trade on conceptual descriptions, and so do not in any sense depend on the success of those descriptions. In certain settings, however, evaluative judgements do indeed trade on conceptual descriptions, with the result that evaluative failure may threaten those descriptions, just as evaluative success may confirm them. That is the case when evaluative success in a particular respect is taken to be a necessary, albeit not a sufficient, condition of falling under the description.

242. When a knife is dull one normally notices that fact alone—the fact of a failure to realize a particular value—and so reaches for another knife, or perhaps a pair of scissors, with which to perform the task at hand, without thereby reflecting or needing to reflect upon the impact of dullness on the knife's description as a knife. Suppose, however, that the blade of a spreading knife snaps just as one is in the course of using it, leaving one with but a stub of the blade. It seems to me that once again one would normally continue to treat the article as a spreading knife—perhaps to be thrown away as unfit for further use, perhaps as a candidate for repair by fastening a new handle to the shortened blade (indeed, I have undertaken such a repair and still have the knife in my drawer)—so addressing the specific inability of the knife to spread effectively without reflecting on its status as a knife, or, more precisely, taking its continued status as a knife for granted. But suppose that one is on an airplane, or at a picnic, and is presented with a plastic knife with which to cut rather than to spread one's food. As most of us have discovered to our frustration, cutting is a task that is often difficult to perform satisfactorily

---

[11] Finnis, *Philosophy of Law, Collected Essays IV* (2011) at 7.

with a plastic knife, and it seems to me that when confronted with the failure of a plastic knife to cut satisfactorily one's reaction to the inadequacy of the article for its appointed task might well be to question its status as a knife, despite its physical profile and suggested use. The question is why and in what circumstances that should be so, or more precisely, why that reaction should be regarded as a sound one.

243. The answer, it seems to me, is that because descriptions of articles and social practices are typically couched in such a way as to encompass and accommodate the aptitude of those articles and practices for the realization of a wide range of values, and because the relationship of descriptions to the values that are capable of being realized through the articles or practices to which those descriptions refer is both malleable (in all the ways set out earlier) and evolving, descriptions are typically not in any way threatened by the failure of a given article or practice to realize a value in particular. On the contrary, descriptions are threatened by failures of value only as and when those failures are either comprehensive or critical in character. Failures of value are *comprehensive* in character when it is impossible to imagine a value that might be realized through the article or practice in its failed state, or more precisely, when it is impossible to imagine the realization of a value that could fall anywhere within a description of the article or practice either as it stands or as it might be amended (it is possible that the broken knife is now just junk, but it is also possible that it could become a pick or a scraper of some kind). Such comprehensive failures of value threaten description comprehensively, because they threaten to make the object or practice in question unintelligible. Failures of value are *critical* in character in all those settings in which achievement of some value in particular through the article or practice is a condition precedent of recognizing the article or practice as falling under the description in question. That might possibly be true of the failure of what is presented as a knife to cut one's airplane meal satisfactorily, not because cutting is central to knives but because what is presented to one as a knife on one's airplane tray is a knife for that purpose alone (I am here consciously bracketing its alternative function of spreading butter on one's airplane bread roll), so that a failure to satisfy that purpose is also failure to satisfy its definition as a knife. Such critical failures of value threaten particular descriptions, because they make an object such as a knife unintelligible under that particular description, while leaving open the possibility that what can

no longer be recognized as a knife may be captured under some other description.

244. All this is but to say that failures of value and of definition are cross-cutting and cannot be mapped onto one another. Their connection is a contingent one, so that it would be a mistake to suggest either that an unjust law is never a law or that an unjust law never fails to be a law by reason of its injustice: as much of a mistake, and for connected reasons, as it would be to suggest that there is a central case of law and that it is to be looked for in the purpose for which law is most reasonably engaged in. This is a conclusion, needless to say, that on its face is at odds with the terms of Finnis's account, yet, paradoxically, it is not entirely clear how far Finnis himself is in fact committed to rejecting the conclusion by embracing anything like a mistake of either kind, for he is deeply equivocal about the extent to which he is committed to the idea that laws are laws without regard to the question of their justice and, to the opposite effect, that unjust laws fail to be law by reason of their injustice. In particular, as he has subsequently emphasized in the Postscript to its second edition, the opening chapter of *Natural Law and Natural Rights*, pungent as it may be, is not strictly necessary to the extremely illuminating account that follows of the various contributions that law is capable of making to the pursuit of practical reasonableness in circumstances of human frailty, moral abstraction, and value pluralism.

245. Herbert Hart was famously criticized by Joseph Raz for advancing what Raz called a practice theory of norms—that is, for believing that norms are constituted by practices. One could make a like observation, albeit to the opposite effect, about the work of John Finnis, Hart's pupil, for Finnis advances what might be called a norm-based theory of practices—that is to say, he believes that practices are inherently constituted by morally valid norms, thus making any practices not so constituted deviant by definition (and thus, strictly speaking, not practices at all, but rather purported instances or applications of a practice). The implications of this position run very much deeper than the question of whether unjust laws are or are not laws, for Finnis thinks of the social practice of law in this way just because he thinks of any and all social practices in this way. That is a real shame, for just as Hart was led by his practice theory of norms to neglect the significance of morality in any account of law, so Finnis is led by his norm-based theory of practice to neglect the like significance of social practice, however normatively soundly, or

unsoundly, or soundly and unsoundly, the social practice in question may be inspired and directed. It is true that this neglect is only partial, which is why Finnis is free to suggest that the first chapter of *Natural Law and Natural Rights* is not strictly necessary to what follows. Yet the neglect is also central, for it runs like a thread through the book—in particular in Finnis's reluctance to follow through on the logic of the book's rich central observations on the value that law, as a social practice, is capable of bringing to the project of practical reasonableness. The significance of social practice is something that Finnis is comprehensively committed to capturing in regard to particular laws—at least when speaking positively of the ways in which the moral project of a good life, collectively and individually, can be furthered by law—but is equally set against acknowledging with regard to the broad social practice of law itself.

246. As I have said, that is a real shame, because it amounts to a failure to recognize the full significance of instantiation in human endeavour: a failure to recognize the full implications, for good and for ill, in artefacts and otherwise, of the surviving cultural record of a distinctive and telling series of interplays among the human faculties of reason, imagination and will—interplays that have yielded, in a way that is fundamental to our political and social orders, the legacy not only of particular laws but of the very idea of law itself. It is a shame, finally, because *Natural Law and Natural Rights* does so much to transcend the pseudo-conflict between those who think of law as a natural phenomenon and those who think of it as a human artefact, so much to show that the connections between law and morality or, put more broadly, between law and other forms of reasoning about value and how to realize it in one's life, individually and collectively, are central to the idea of law.

247. That said, there is a good deal more than regret to take fair notice of here, a good deal more that one should pay tribute to. In fact, it seems to me that there are at least a couple of helpful lessons to be learned. The first of these is the broad lesson to be drawn about the limits of what can usefully be said in general terms about the relationship between law and morality, or, to be less parochial about it, about the relationship between law and the challenge of a rational life. The limits in question are structural in character, flowing as they do from the minimalist, structural character of the accounts of law that philosophers tend to offer. From such premises only certain conclusions can be derived, and the limit to those conclusions is to

be discovered in the extent to which the substantive features of law are established by the very idea of law and the correlative extent to which that same idea of law entails that the features of law be established interstitially, so as to constitute the fabric of law in all its richness and variety, as it exists and has existed, from place to place and from time to time. Between those two poles there is, of course, a good deal of territory that is disputable, and that territory is the ground of the moral challenges that are as much raised by the idea of law as resolved by it.

248. The other lesson to be learned here has to do with the extent to which law is or may be engaged in the project of redressing its own moral failings, a project that is of course only conceivable if and to the extent that one is prepared to acknowledge the possibility of such failings—something that Finnis is only partly willing to do. Broadly speaking, there are three ways in which law is susceptible to moral failure and so is correspondingly morally bound to offer mechanisms that are capable of redressing, or at least of minimizing, that failure. The first and most obvious of those susceptibilities to failure is the tendency of law-makers either to fail to identify correctly the good at which they are aiming or, having identified a good correctly, to fail to design laws in such a way as to promote the realization of that good effectively. Those kinds of failure give rise to a need for legal and political schemes by means of which to challenge and revise the content of law, substantively and procedurally—schemes that are a standard and well understood feature of all legal systems. A second category of failure arises from the ways in which laws, even when soundly aimed and soundly designed to further those aims, exact costs that are, for one reason or another in contravention of the fundamental political commitments of the culture in which the laws in question have been enacted, although no greater than the benefits yielded by the laws in question, so as to outweigh them morally in the manner of the first kind of failure (perhaps because they are incommensurable with those benefits). In contemporary Western settings, this second category of failure has given rise to widespread and expanding schemes for the protection of rights and liberties, schemes that, in Dworkin's famous idiom, function as trumps against laws that contravene them. Again, this is a well understood and much analysed feature of legal systems.

249. However the final, least acknowledged, yet in some ways most significant category of moral failure arises from the inescapable

costs of the very existence of a legal system, and in addition the costs of the prevailing legal system rather than some other that might have existed in its stead—costs that are felt most keenly by those who are at once most aware of other possible worlds and most sensitive to the anarchic value of intelligent minds, be those minds their own or the minds of others; minds concerned to pursue rational possibility in a manner that not only is independent of prevailing mores (as those mores are embodied in the existing legal system, and so embodied in what it fosters and what it permits) but also does not fit within the established conventions of dissent as laid down by the legal system's scheme of rights and liberties, either as that scheme exists or as it might be amended. It is that category of failure that the law cannot redress yet is bound to take account of, by coupling its moral appeal to strategies of imagination and of will so as to secure at least a measure of acceptance from those whom it cannot expect to persuade.

250. So much for the structural moral failings that law is bound to remedy in itself. What of law's achievements? In what directions might they be looked for? If law and morality are not independent of one another, then how exactly are they intertwined, so as to help people to reason practically rather better than they would without law's assistance, in ways that a broad structural account of law is capable of registering? Given that every such account is coloured by the purposes that animate it, the answer will need to be looked for from the perspective of the particular structural account in question. From the point of view of an account of law that is concerned to highlight the implications of the project of a life in common to which any legal system is necessarily committed, there are three domains in which the law can intervene successfully: the domain of that which is both morally compulsory and legally compulsory (the domain in which law serves to promote compliance in the face of *akrasia* or irrationality of judgement, by creating moral considerations other than those that of their own force tell directly against the conduct in question); the domain of that which is both morally permissible and legally permissible (the domain embraced by those aspects of law that create or extend liberties, through power-conferring rules, and those aspects of law that acknowledge and respect liberties, through rights and freedoms—both of which aspects also help to protect against law's failings); and finally, and perhaps most distinctively, the domain of that which is morally permissible but legally either

impermissible or compulsory (the domain in which imagination and will are needed in order to supplement and so make effective the rational claims embodied in law). Within and through these domains a legal system that attains any degree of moral achievement enforces, respects, and enlarges—but also constrains—the moral world that its subjects inhabit. To observe this much is simply to extend rather than to overlook the point that John Finnis develops so persuasively, that law refines the imperfectly guiding character of morality in those settings in which the directions of morality are overly abstract or are in conflict with one another. Each of us could do those things for ourselves, but a life in common requires a device like law. Yet this gives rise to a significant question, which can be looked at from either of two perspectives. Is the law necessary to all lives in common? Are there any other devices that might take its place, perhaps rather more satisfactorily in certain settings?

8

Law and Life in Common

A. Life Without Law

251. At one level, law is clearly not necessary to the existence and successful functioning of all lives in common, for the reasons given at the outset. Circumstances of congeniality, co-operation, and community not only can but normally do arise organically, through those on-going patterns of interaction and negotiation that virtually all human beings undertake with one another, in and by virtue of their condition as social creatures who are bent, by their basic rational commitment to the achievement of a life well lived, on engaging with a range of goods and values most of which are as much collective as individual in their character and in their aptitude for realization. People are capable of interacting with one another only as and when they discover or forge some common ground for understanding and engagement. Even the differences that we perceive or foster in ourselves and others, and the conflicts that they can give rise to, exist and have meaning for us against the backdrop of some deeper ground in common. That ground constitutes the fabric of our daily lives, and only limited aspects of its outlines derive, let alone need be derived, from law. What is more, it is only upon a foundation of organic and naturally arising versions of grounds in common that it is possible to build the logically consequent superstructures of the kinds of life in common in which law might claim to have a part to play.

252. Nor is the social practice of law the only, let alone the best, way of developing a life in common consciously and deliberately

rather than naturally and organically. We are all familiar, in the course of our everyday lives, with sets of rules and conventions that are proposed and subscribed to by small groups of people, as ways of regulating their interactions with one another, as and when organic, unconsciously arrived at structures of community either break down or come to seem inadequate. These rules are usually informally arrived at and often intermittently observed. Yet they exist not because those people who subscribe to them have failed to develop some more deliberate, more sophisticated scheme of interaction, such as that laid down by a legal system, but because their very informality, and the consequently tentative, unpresumptuous nature of their claim upon us, is part of the value they have to offer us, and part of the relationship, and sense of community, that they help to constitute.

253. This is true in the setting not only of small groups of people but also of large groups, not only in relatively simple social structures but also in complex ones. The movement to law as a social practice is not a movement from lesser to greater sophistication, though it may be a move to modernity as we know and understand it. Societies that lack law are in that sense and to that extent recognizably pre-modern, but they are not consequently unsophisticated. It is true, of course, that the intricacies of legal order, perhaps because and to the extent that they are recorded in writing, can be arcane and technical in a way that can claim to be distinctively sophisticated, but it is also true that many non-legal orders are rich, baroque, and haunting in ways which law has yet to show itself to be capable of, ways indeed that it is quite plausible to think that law is unsuited to. Law, in short, constitutes only one species of possible progress in the ordering of human affairs, a species that even at its best and least qualified is not, all things considered, better than its alternatives, whatever its particular virtues may be.

254. So as human beings we come together in all sorts of places and in all sorts of ways that lack the governance of law yet are successfully regulated nonetheless, and are often all the better for that. We come together actually and virtually, comprehensively and fragmentarily, continuously and intermittently, as friends, neighbours, families, colleagues, peers, and strangers; as kindred spirits in art, activity, and association; or, in less positive terms, as adversaries and wary disputants in practices of negotiation and exchange and, when all breaks down, as opponents in schemes of conflict. When we do

these things the structure of our exchanges is largely laid down by our culture and self-understanding, as individuals and as denizens of communities of all sorts of kinds, many of them overlapping, none of them with an exclusive hold upon us, so that we come to know and govern ourselves—and to expect like governance in those with whom we have dealings—in part (but only in part) as people who can be expected to act in recognizable ways in a range of recognized settings, settings that are themselves defined by the very practices that help to define us. Activities as straight-forward as having coffee with a friend are often deeply ritualized, and rituals such as these are extended and replicated in a host of further settings, of increasing scope and complexity, so as to come to constitute, however transiently and fluidly, entire social orders. All this is possible without law and may in fact be frustrated by law, in certain settings at least.

255. One must be quite careful about speaking of such non-legal forms of social ordering as if they were a legal system, as if they were bound to do the same things as a legal system albeit in a somewhat different way, so as to make their social role modally but not functionally, superficially but not fundamentally, distinct from that of the project of law. On the contrary, a large (though not the only) part of the point of organic forms of regulation—one of the ways in which they are distinct from law, and one of the reasons to engage in them (to the extent that such engagement is optional)—is their connection to practices of spontaneity and improvisation and the values that those can give rise to, and indeed to other kindred practices. It is this distinction from law that drives the sense in which one might say, or might be tempted to say if one were a lawyer (as admittedly I am), that these forms of ordering are not regulation, or are not regulation as we know it. In fact they are clearly regulation, but the values that they are capable of giving rise to stem from the flexibility, creativity, and sense of personal investment that attend them at their best; the sense in which they are our own and deeply so, so as to help to constitute us as the people and the society that we are; the sense in which it is open to us to make them more so by an on-going, incremental, and naturally arising process of improvisation in which value is discovered by a process of trial and error. As much can be said, of course, of the corresponding disvalue of such forms of ordering, the sense in which there is a case to be made against them and in favour of law and legal system.

256. The distinction between legal and non-legal approaches to social ordering goes further. Organic and naturally arising forms of social ordering are not only spontaneously arrived at, at least for the most part, but also and by the same token largely tacit, opaque, and unselfconscious in their origins and implementation. Revisions to their content can take place almost invisibly, as by-products of actions and undertakings that may never have been intended to have that effect yet did so, and as a consequence the revisions in question may remain subterranean and unrecognized until they become salient, at some later date and in some different context. In this regard, naturally arising changes to a social order are to be contrasted with changes to the content of a legal system, whether those be interstitial or foundational, which are characteristically deliberate, overt, and transparent, and for that reason are correspondingly detached from the daily, vernacular, organically revisable fabric of individual and collective life.

257. One must be careful finally, however, not to make the opposite mistake, of speaking of these different and in some ways rival forms of ordering as if they were in fact incompatible—kinds of waters that do not mix, like those of the Bosphorus on their way to and from the Black Sea. Indeed, quite the opposite is true, for every social order that possesses a legal system also, simultaneously and interdependently, possesses organic and naturally arising forms of regulation, so that what typically distinguishes social orders in this respect is for the most part the particular character of the balance that each society has struck between the two forms of ordering. In any given society, and in any given setting there, the relationship between the two forms of ordering is constituted by a scheme of compromise, itself arrived at organically in part and deliberately in part. The presence of such a scheme is close to inevitable. In fact there is reason to believe that there is a degree of social peril, born of self-delusion and its costs, attached to the very idea that such compromise can ever be escaped, whether that idea is fostered by the forces of modernity or of pre-modernity.

258. This is not to say that large distinctions of emphasis are not discernible in the relationship between legal and non-legal forms of ordering in different societies. On the contrary, such distinctions are not only evident but often profound. Many societies are deeply marked by their commitment to one form of ordering in preference to the other, and a number are close to committed to the position

that one form of ordering ought to prevail over the other to the point of virtually eclipsing it, although it is perhaps more common for a society to be mildly confused or in conflict with itself over the feasibility and the desirability of such transcendence of the legal over the non-legal, or vice versa. In truth, although there can clearly be social orders without law, there is no possibility of a legal order without attendant organic and naturally arising forms of social ordering.

B. Law, Social Change, and Modernity

259. How do these various distinctions play out in practice, and in the kind of contributions that law can and cannot make to the achievement of a life in common in the world we know? Many of the features previously described are relatively familiar aspects of contemporary legal and social orders, functioning there in ways that have come to characterize those orders and the relationship between them, and by extension have come to characterize the political cultures of particular societies, making them more or less distinctive by virtue of the role and place they have assigned to law. Most obviously, it is broadly characteristic of a fluid society (of which a liberal society is but one example), or a new society, to rely on legal order as and when that society seeks some sort of conscious break with the past—whether comprehensively, as in a revolutionary moment, or in certain definitive respects, as in a modernist, reforming moment. Rival social forms and practices, those formed by custom and tradition in circumstances of stability or of gradual evolution, are simply not available in such a setting, or for such a project.

260. In such contexts the presence of a legal system is crucial to the achievement of a social and political order that embodies and inspires the possibility of change, be that change momentary or continuous, a transformation from one state to another, or a state of transformation, be it for good or for ill or, more plausibly, for both. Without a legal system that is capable of capturing change, or change of a kind that is capable of securing a fresh legal order (which in itself would require the endorsement of the prevailing scheme of social ordering, be that legal or non-legal), any change to the structure of society that is rapid or profound will give rise to anarchy in the strict sense, for better or for worse, depending on one's views of anarchy.

The vital role of legal system in such cases is to channel change, so as to secure it for ends and in ways that remain within recognizable bounds of order, and it is this role that has been played more or less successfully by many legal systems and their patterns of succession in the post-traditional, post-imperial contemporary world.

261. Of course, for critics of law, what has occurred in these settings has been the blunting of the possibilities of change by protection of the interests of those who are committed to order, who are assumed to be those who have a stake in order in its present form, and so have a stake in limiting and controlling the nature and scale of departures from that form. There is a measure of truth in this charge, but in its suspicion of the commitment to order it overlooks the widespread costs of change experienced by people in all walks of life, and the dependency of every change, however radical, on some order that can sustain it—an order that cannot arise naturally in the short term and so must be supplied by law. Even tyrannical force requires some enduring structure if it is to sustain itself, a structure that cannot be entirely supplied by the accumulated record of the tyrant's improvised responses to the exigencies and fluctuations that flow from the raw challenge of enforcing his or her will. Fluid societies, as much as those that endure, owe their existence and their survival to the stabilizing presence of law and the structure it offers to them.

262. It follows that there is an irony in the role currently played by law in securing the broad outlines of a social order that is otherwise fluid, otherwise predicated on renewal and change, which is that even in societies where law is called upon to be stabilizing and foundational in this way, law today very often has a broadly liberal, facilitative, and permissive agenda, with a correspondingly weak sense of overall direction or commitment to an enduring social vision. The consequence of this is that the substance of law undermines or at least threatens, even as it upholds, the social practices that legal order in such a setting is called upon to foster and inspire, thereby threatening the social cohesion in circumstances of diversity that is a central aspect of its endeavour and its possible achievement. This is a problem born of a species of liberal culture and liberal practice that has an insufficiently developed connection to what Joseph Raz has described as the morality of freedom—the idea that the value of liberty stems not from the bare exercise of liberty but from the value that liberty, when suitably directed, makes it possible (be it

instrumentally or constitutively) to realize, value that we are bound to attend to if liberty is to be properly valuable in our hands. Indiscriminately liberal agendas raise few such concerns, have little need to attend to the problem of their containment, when they are pursued in the face of illiberal orders, be those legal or non-legal—for what needs to be challenged in those settings can also be looked to for support, in the familiar, quasi-pathological interdependency of stability and critique, culture and counter-culture. Perhaps that is why newly liberal orders often neglect the challenge of ensuring their stability, or regard it as contrary to their nature. Yet without this the pursuit of liberal agendas in liberal orders can often be self-defeating.

263. If significant change, be it broad-ranging or circumscribed, requires the intervention of legal order to support and sustain it, it is also the case that legal order, not only in that setting but in any other, depends for its efficacy and practical existence on the support and sustenance of non-legal order. Those who inhabit cultures, such as that of the United States, in which the legal system—and particularly its constitution—is regarded as the ultimate authority are often sceptical of the idea that tradition can be relied upon to be forceful and effective, as it is relied upon to be, albeit to a diminishing degree, in a culture such as that of the United Kingdom. What kind of protection, some such ask—only partly rhetorically—could tradition possibly be thought to offer; how could anyone regard it as an appropriately robust alternative to the protection of the law, at least when that law is fundamental, as is the law of the Constitution? And yet, quite obviously, this is to overlook the extent to which legal order, including that which is embodied in a constitution, depends on tradition for the respect in which it is held, and for the attention that people can consequently be expected to pay to what it requires.

264. This is not to suggest that there is no fundamental difference between the two ways of ordering, just because both ultimately turn on respect for tradition. On the contrary, of course, there is a very real difference between them, stemming from the difference in what tradition is being asked to sustain in each case. A tradition of respect for a legal system and what it requires, however fragmented and intermittent that respect may be in a particular population, tends to be less difficult to establish than respect for other traditions, for there is a strong incentive to secure order when the alternative is not simply disorder but, more tellingly perhaps, failure of all those goals

that depend on order: the very goals that originally inspired a challenge to the existing order and what it stood for, and so gave rise to the need for a new order in its place. There need be no like incentive to establish other traditions in a manner and to a degree that commands respect. On the contrary, one of the distinctive features of such traditions, as already indicated, is that they arise organically and often imperceptibly, rather than through deliberation and decision. Their origins are typically accidental, though their maintenance is as typically self-conscious; in the case of law, something like the reverse is true. In sum, then, the tradition of deference to law is rather easier to establish, though perhaps more difficult to maintain, than the traditions that law supports and stands in for.

265. However, this fact tends to give rise, in the minds of both those who make law and those who are addressed by law (a fair number of the latter of whom can be expected to encourage and support its making), to the illusion that law is rather more effective than it really is; that it is capable of delivering change locally, in respect of specific issues, in the same way that it is globally, in respect of its very status as a scheme of ordering. For those who think this way, whatever may be the case of law in general, particular laws are free-standing and self-sufficient, though they may well require a degree of enforcement, itself provided for by law. In some cases this appears to be true. Where the change that law seeks to bring about is of a kind that is or can be expected to be accepted by participants in the practice that law is aiming to amend, and where the change that law calls for is consonant with existing features of that practice, there may be good reason to believe that the law in question will be effective on the basis of its terms alone. It is with an eye to the existence of conditions such as these that the contemporary state routinely amends its regulatory schemes in the full and reasonable expectation that the amendments will be more or less automatically effective. In this way tax laws, customs codes, health and safety regulations are all routinely revised, and the revisions thereafter seamlessly incorporated in the practice of existing social orderings, so as to enjoy all the effectiveness of the rules they have replaced, without any thought of consonant social structures or need for such a thought.

266. In other, just as familiar and important settings, however, law can do little to change the world unless a climate of support for what it requires either already exists (in which case the law in question functions at its strongest as a catalyst for the further development

and increased sophistication of that climate, and otherwise as expression, confirmation, and official emblem of the social achievement that preceded it) or is apt to come into being thereafter, more or less in tandem with the making of the law, perhaps as a result of the social impact of the law in question and the political circumstances of its enactment (in which case the law functions as a catalyst for the initial construction of a climate of support), or perhaps because of the independent development of a consensus that the law anticipated or simply hazarded upon. When and to the extent that law-makers neglect this fact, that is, neglect the dependency of their political projects on the presence of climates of support, and so neglect the role that they and others may well have to play in fostering and developing those climates, their projects are liable to miscarry. Politicians, at least in the early or otherwise vulnerable stages of their careers, are by the terms of their profession unlikely to make this mistake, but over-confident politicians, and politically competent but legally naïve pressure groups that seek to influence politicians and judges—particularly the lawyers among them—are all too apt to do so. We are all familiar with laws, and even legal regimes, for which there is little respect, little sympathy or understanding, and in certain cases broad contempt. We are just as familiar with laws to which the public to whom they are addressed are more or less indifferent, acknowledging their existence intermittently, observing their requirements sporadically if at all. These laws may well be good ones, but they lack the resources to carry their audience.

267. The story is a weary one, of the absence of shared ideals. So various prohibitions on the consumption of a series of intoxicating substances, from alcohol to drugs, have foundered because of a lack of broad public support for the prohibitions, either because the public did not agree on the danger or because it thought that the danger was of a kind that one should be entitled to court in a free society. Something similar is happening today in relation to copyright law, where the issue is not danger but exploitation of the copyright holder or, more precisely, the author whose work has given rise to the copyright, whoever may hold it thereafter. When people share electronic files with one another, and so share the music, let us suppose, that is embedded in those files, they no more believe that they are engaging in improper exploitation of the musician than they would if they were to lend one another the original recordings in question. As far as they are concerned, the moral character of the exchange is not

altered just because it takes place electronically rather than materially, by the transmission of data rather than by the transmission of the physical bearers of that data. One cannot escape the contrast between these and other at least superficially aligned legal prohibitions, such as that on smoking in certain places or that which protects design (be that embodied in software or hardware) for which respect is still widespread, though now showing signs of ebbing. Such laws are supported, and even extended, by social practices that have grown and developed in tandem with them and on lines that are consonant with them. Between these two poles lies the broad terrain of the kind of laws considered above, in relation to which attitudes are as important as actions. Anti-discrimination laws are not only likely to be ineffective in the absence of a public culture that is committed to the same or similar ends, but may actually have perverse effects, such as the protection of men, the able-bodied, and racial and ethnic majorities. One is never sure quite how the partnership between attitudes and actions works, but one knows, or at least ought to know, that it is necessary, and that it involves rather more in terms of a supportive public culture than the various practices of consciousness-raising.

268. As many disappointed politicians approaching retirement or electoral defeat, and many tired civil servants contemplating the ineffectual character of much of their careers, are all too painfully aware, a government can pass laws until it is blue in the face while the world to which those laws are addressed remains much as it was, or, more often, changes in ways that were not engendered by those laws, and indeed may be so out of sympathy with them as to make them appear quaint and irrelevant. In part this stems from the presence of rational alternatives to what the law has required, and in liberal societies to the structures of freedom that law has designed, established, and encouraged people to engage in (for not only may people want freedom of a different kind, but they may well want absence of freedom, or as they would think of it, they may well seek a sense of order and direction that the law does not provide them with, so substituting new ties for those that the law has set out to release them from, and so generating absence of possibilities in place of those that the law has set out to multiply). It is circumstances like these that give rise to a need for law and its makers to draw upon the resources of imagination and will to enhance the rational case that law is able to make for itself on the strength of its terms alone, and so to lend law the appearance of rational priority. But it is also a

matter of being persuasive in a different domain—one that lies outside the reach of its terms, so as to harness imagination and will not simply in the political moment of enactment and those that follow shortly thereafter, in the life of the enacting government, say. It is a matter of embedding the requirements and possibilities of the law in sustaining, naturally developed social forms and practices, a matter of recognizing that responsibility for social change does not lie with law-makers alone, nor with law-makers before others whom law-makers inspire and direct, but rather lies with us all, both in those settings where change is necessary and thus a duty and in those settings where it is permissible, and thus one implication of the successful use of those freedoms that law confirms and creates.

C. Law, Regulatory Sophistication, and Ambition

269. So much for the challenges of social innovation, their dependency on the support of law, and the correlative dependency of law on consonant non-legal orderings. Less obviously, perhaps, it is characteristic of societies that tend or aspire to a high degree of complexity of regulation, be that regulation social or economic, to rely on legal ordering. It is of course entirely possible to establish and maintain complex social orders without the presence of a legal system. As I have already noted, non-legal orders can be complex, rich, and baroque. Complexity of social and economic *regulation*, however, where the idea of regulation is understood in terms of authority, raises particular challenges that tend to be responded to through legal ordering. First, as the exercise of authority gradually takes on complexity, participation in its direction correspondingly multiplies, so making the structure of authority itself increasingly complex—a complexity that mirrors and is mirrored in the catalogue of what authority requires. Law provides a ready vehicle by means of which to prescribe and capture such a complex architecture of authority, in a manner that is both accessible and enduring, and to record the exercise of authority in terms that do not, at least in principle and on the face of it, require the development of sustaining social forms and practices. The tendency to have recourse to the resources of law and a legal system in such settings is reinforced in a number of societies by the scale and

pace of change that attend many schemes of regulation, or at least that have attended them in the modern era in which the particular forms of complexity with which we are now familiar have arisen.

270. To these reasons for legal ordering must be added ambition, the aim of extending a regulatory ambit so as to embrace people who are not members of the particular organic, naturally arising community that is immediately relevant to the regulatory goal in question—whether that community is one of another place or, as Hart drew attention to in considering the deficiencies of Austin's account of the sovereign, one of another, later time.[1] I have already noted the practical limits of such ambitions, and the extent of their dependency on non-legal orderings. Yet it is also true that impatience can have its own rewards, and that the very dynamic of legislative ambition (for it is an ambition rarely possessed by the judiciary, as rarely as the judiciary is institutionally dynamic) can carry a good deal with and before it, so engendering structure in response to its very momentum and thereby building the foundations on which its achievement rests, at least in part. A truly modernizing regime is exciting to many people, in ways that make those people want not only to be part of the excitement, as the regime has defined it, but to make the project of modernity and reform their own, and in doing so to carry it forward into

---

[1] A similar point has been made persuasively by Dori Kimel in *From Promise to Contract: Towards a Liberal Theory of Contract* (2005), with regard to the particular social practice of entering into binding legal contracts, and the distinction between that practice and the non-legal social practice of promising. At a more general level, Hart's observations on the limitations of Austin's explanation of law in terms of a sovereign are distinct from his observations on the deficiencies of pre-legal orders, yet it must follow that if what Austin describes fails to capture the concept of law what it captures (if anything at all) is a non-legal form of order, in which it is impossible, according to Hart, to establish and maintain continuity of a certain kind. Non-legal orders clearly secure continuity, by their very nature, but they also have a special relationship to continuity. On the one hand, traditions are not dependent on particular human lives, be those of individuals or generations, but rather survive to shape the lives of those newly in being and yet to be. This enduring quality of tradition may be reinforced by a prevailing and governing tradition of conservatism about traditions. On the other hand, traditions of every kind belong to those who inhabit them from time to time, and so are subject to continuous shaping by those inhabitants, deliberately or accidentally. Law, by contrast—particularly that of a constitution, such as that which structures sovereignty—seeks to project the convictions of a present community beyond the life of its present members, so as to bind future people to those particular convictions, and thereby make those people part of the present community, or of some extension of it, by creating legal impediments to their power and tendency to do otherwise than what is permissible within what the law has laid down as a guiding structure, foundationally or otherwise.

domains to which they have access and the regime does not (at least directly).

271. I have spoken so far as if these distinctions were basic and as if their components were mutually exclusive, so as to characterize legal orders at the level of their very constitution. In fact, of course, and as already suggested, they are not anything of the kind. We all inhabit legal and social worlds that embody mixtures of the qualities and commitments previously described and that shift regularly in the particular balance of their engagement with legal and non-legal orderings, both in general, as legal systems, and in particular, in relation to specific domains of law and of social ordering. So old worlds and new worlds alike rely both upon traditions and upon laws as means of advancing and developing their social, economic, and other human agendas, and the patterns of their reliance, while distinctive and consistent enough to mark out an old world from a new in this as in other, more marginal respects, are fluid and relatively unpredictable. What is more, the prospects for change in any particular world, be it old or new, are often counter-intuitive, so that traditional orderings on occasion are revealed as being rather more accommodating of change of certain kinds than are formal legal orderings (recent reform of the British House of Lords is one prominent example), while in new world settings legal orderings can rapidly calcify so as to become the greatest practical obstacle to the very kinds of changes that they were originally designed to facilitate and to house (one thinks here of certain aspects of the United States Constitution, and indeed of the capacity of that document as a whole to structure the kind of self-directed, forward-looking, practical, imaginative, and hopeful political venture that its authors appear to have had in mind for the nation that they had set out to construct).

D. Law and Community, Past, Present, and Future

272. Where does this leave law in the project of a life in common, the project that any government must have in mind when it calls upon law to serve its goals? The conclusion must be that law's role in building society is relatively modest and dependent, expressive and catalytic, contingent rather than assured. This should not be terribly

surprising, let alone disappointing. Most people are aware that the terms of their life, individual and social, are for the most part for them to shape, individually and socially, independent of governance by the state (or other legal authority). We do not expect, or even accept, direction in most such matters. By and large it is only when we too casually contemplate our role, as citizens, in directing the lives of others—so that they do what we expect of them and cease to do that which we find objectionable—without proper regard to the very real limits to direction that we would accept in our own lives, and further, when we seek to attribute responsibility for the occurrence of collective misfortune—which we too often misguidedly take it to be the duty of government to succeed in wholly preventing—that we are apt to lose sight of this fact. These tendencies are rather more fully developed, and take on somewhat different contours, in the minds of certain lawyers, and more broadly and perhaps more prominently in the minds of those who would idealize law (whether directly or as part of the idealization of certain political structures), and in doing so take law to be a necessary and largely sufficient means of securing an enlightened social order. The general tendency to overrate the power of law in ways such as these, and to exaggerate its capacities: it is this that constitutes law's (virtual) empire, the romantic extension of its actual realm, the pretence that not only the content of law but its form has rational priority over other forms of social ordering, other forms of co-operation. It is an empire of dream, and while dreams have their value they are also dangerous, for they can lead one to attempt the impossible in ways that go beyond the expressive value of gesture and that in doing so may well exact a very significant price in terms of what might otherwise genuinely have been achieved.

273. And yet one should also be careful not to go too far in the opposite direction here, lest one fall into the trap of being overly dramatic, self-consciously iconoclastic, excessively demystifying and non-idealizing. It is important not to give up too quickly on the place of ambition in the operation of law and on its supporting and attendant Enlightenment dream, important not to be too knowing about law's limitations. The practice of law too often descends into thuggishness, the practice of politics too often descends into deceit, just because lawyers and politicians allow themselves to become too knowing about the law, too sceptical of its rational pull and consequent power to motivate, too insensitive to the ways in which law

has the power it does just because of the aptitude it possesses for fruitful partnership among reason, will, and imagination; too neglectful, in short, of the bonds between realism and romance. Thuggishness and deceit are the destinations that will and imagination are liable to lead us to when they are insufficiently tempered by respect for reason and belief in its power, and also by constructive imaginings of what might be achieved in the pursuit of particular rational paths, and the exercise of courage in the pursuit of those imaginings. The fact is that the enterprise of law can civilize in ways and for ends that we cannot arrive at without its assistance. It has a crucial role to play in building life in common: in that lies much of the value of the rule of law. This is a terrain that we have reason to defend and to enlarge, to be hopeful about the possibilities of, while remaining alive to its vulnerability and its limitations, and how they might best be managed.

274. Societies and cultures that underrate law, and thus underestimate what can be achieved with its assistance, thereby deny themselves access to basic goods without which it is very difficult—perhaps impossible in most settings today—to build a decent community of any kind. Exceptional cases aside, the rule of law is not an optional extra in our public life. On the contrary, it provides the indispensable structure for any significant social achievement by bodies of people who are committed to negotiating some species of life in common, within and across all the many differences that unite some people and divide them from others both in general and on particular matters—differences not so much of personal character or conviction, but in the kinds of goodness to which people of different kinds are rationally bound to attempt to commit themselves. It is largely in light of law that people in complex societies act and interact, spontaneously or deliberately, in the various moments of their lives and in the narratives that those moments gradually and cumulatively give rise to, by bringing the exercise of their reason, their imagination, and their will to bear upon the manifold activities in which they seek to engage, with all the flickering yet striking energy and power of their brief and fragile existences, both as individuals and as communities.

275. And yet something in the order of a qualification should perhaps be added here, by way of a contemporary afterthought. There may be lessons in all this for the increasingly global world that more and more of us find ourselves inhabiting today, whether consciously

or unconsciously, willingly or unwillingly, enthusiastically or reluctantly. I have spoken so far of societies, and of the legal and non-legal ways in which societies have come to be structured. Yet that way of thinking embodies an assumption—namely, that we actually inhabit a world that is more or less entirely made up of societies: of various kinds, of course; overlapping, of course; but ever-present, ever-available, and above all ever-governing. Put differently, the way of thinking that I have engaged in so far is a story about law and society, and what it has to tell us is significant to us to the extent that we actually inhabit a world that is made up of societies. Yet do we still? And if we do not, to what extent is the practice of law tied to societies as we know them? What other schemes of authority might it serve or instantiate? Just how contingent are the connections between law and the project of government as we currently understand it?

276. I will end this book in something of the same spirit as that in which I prefaced it, a bit speculatively and suggestively, and my comments here should be read in that spirit, for whatever it is worth. As a general proposition, what we know as societies arise organically, so as to be constituted, in whole or in part, by what we usually refer to as their cultures—namely, their ordinary, everyday social forms and practices (to which more conscious constructs may be appended), enduring yet evolving, commonly though not inevitably tied to a territory; and further, by the subsequent and super-imposing operation of law and legal systems and the distinctive social orderings that those are capable of giving rise to, via what I have sought to describe in terms of a distinctive interplay of the forces of reason, imagination, and will; and of course, most typically in the modern era, through various forms of complex, fluid collaboration between those two, related modes of social ordering. As I have already noted, there is a view of social history according to which we have progressed from non-legal to legal forms of ordering, from the supposedly primitive rule of mere culture to a more sophisticated rule of bodies politic and the laws that bodies politic give rise to. That view of social history has rightly been questioned by those who would challenge its notion of progress, yet the questioning has assumed that progress or no progress, we now live in a world that is largely governed, or at least that is largely governable, by law.

277. Yet the global world that most of us inhabit today might be thought to look rather more like that which Matthew Arnold

contemplated from Dover Beach: unstructured, unshaped, unguided either by law or by the everyday cultures that law is supposed to have supplanted, or at least supplemented and extended. There is no developed global political order, of the kind that was dreamed of by idealists in the middle of the twentieth century. Our present predicament is one that in key respects seems to be defined by a near absence of any mechanisms of governance, transparency, or accountability, and worse by little prospect of the emergence of a global culture, or of a global legal system, or of some other social practice or set of practices that might be capable of performing similar functions of guidance. In these respects the modern world has come to wear something of a medieval aspect, as the modern achievements of politics and nationhood have been steadily and inexorably eroded and diminished, together with the significance of the bodies politic on which they depended. We find ourselves in states of crisis; or, less dramatically, in circumstances of difficulty; or, at the very least, in awareness of a need for planning and direction, without access to any of the levers that have become familiar to us from domestic politics and government—levers that might, if globalized, have enabled us to navigate our present circumstances more or less successfully. The most important global challenges of our time, most prominently that of reconciling the project of developing and distributing, as ecumenically as possible, the resources and circumstances of human well being with the commitment to do so in a way that is environmentally sustainable, appear to be quite beyond our grasp. At the same time, and as a consequence of many of the same forces, we seem to be losing our grip on challenges in the domestic political environment that we once believed ourselves, wisely or unwisely, to be entirely capable of overcoming. Hence our present angst and frustration, and our tendency to attribute responsibility and blame to those, such as bankers or the bond markets, who seem to have achieved what we have found ourselves unable to achieve, by establishing—gallingly (but not surprisingly) very largely in their interests and contrary to ours, or more precisely in their interests as identified by them rather than by us—a self-governing, mutually understood, global community.

278. Sound as it may be, once again the point should not be pressed too far. Difficult as they are, the circumstances in which we find ourselves at present are not the circumstances of melodrama. Some sort of ordering is likely to emerge. Nevertheless, it is unlikely

to be a legal ordering, at least in the foreseeable let alone immediate future, for the simple reason that no legal ordering could emerge without the prior, or at least the simultaneously arising, existence of some non-legal ordering on the forms and practices of which that legal ordering could rely for its respect. Law is a social practice, and legal order is derivative of non-legal social order. It need hardly be said that there is no such non-legal global social ordering available at present; matters would be very much easier for us than they actually are if there were. It follows that the challenge that we currently face is the challenge of establishing global community, in all its variety and complexity: a community (or set of communities) that is constituted by global social forms and practices, to some extent unself-consciously and inarticulately and to some extent consciously and explicitly (through existing national and international institutions, and the laws and social practices that sustain them), and of ascertaining, and indeed to some extent creating, the values that ought to inform that community (or set of communities). It is a challenge that can be met by law and regulation only locally, as and where non-legal orders already exist, and at a global level, derivatively and interstitially.[2]

279. That suggests yet one more reason to be properly modest about law's possibilities and prospects, for the time being at least. The fact of globalization, whatever that fact may actually turn out to be, should not be allowed to tempt us into thinking that all we need is a stronger dose of international law as we know and understand it, or the extension of a particular legal empire—ideas that are often gestured at under the label of global governance. Those ideas are not only mutually dependent but are also (or at least may turn out to be) by-products of law and society as we now understand and live through them, and it is a real question how far and how readily they can be adapted to accommodate the fact of globalization and, more to the present point,

---

[2] I am assuming here that the problem of globalization as I have described it exceeds the reach of international law as it currently stands. I am further assuming that the social forms and practices upon which international law relies, and the communities that those forms and practices constitute, are by and large local rather than global in character—that is, not international themselves. To the extent that this is untrue, the comments on globalization that follow need to be correspondingly tempered. Yet the assumption that really needs to be guarded against, or at least bracketed in this discussion, it seems to me, is the assumption that international law as it currently stands is founded upon a set of social forms and practices, be they local or global in character, that is capable of underpinning the kind of legal response that globalization might be thought to make necessary. If that assumption were sound, globalization would be a concern of a rather different, lesser character than most of us take it to be.

on just what they will need to rely. Law is by its nature incapable of doing on its own the kind of work that so clearly needs to be done at the moment. It requires the support of will and of imagination, in this case global will and global imagination. What we need to discover and establish, therefore, in order to meet the global challenges we now face, is a new and much stronger sense of global community (or set of such communities) that would help to constitute some degree of global life in common, together with a greater global awareness and sensitivity in the practices of law and behaviour of our existing national and regional communities, of the kind that is sometimes, and not always helpfully, labelled transnational.[3]

280. In itself, of course, that project embodies a nascent paradox, of the kind earlier considered: that which stems from the apparent superfluity of law in all those cases in which law depends for its effectiveness, indeed for its purpose, on social underpinnings that already embody the very goals that law is seeking to realize. If we were in possession of a sense of global community in relation to the issues in question, the presence of law might well be largely unnecessary. Indeed, something of the kind already exists in reaction to international trading practices, which, while sometimes gathered under the title of *lex mercatoria*, amount to the practice of lawyers that neither constitutes law nor is determined by law. That might be thought to be a prominent case of having community and not needing law.

281. What is more, and perhaps more important, to speak of global community without some further specification of the idea of community in that setting is in many ways to beg the question of what it might mean to constitute a global community. After all, it is plausible to believe that the kinds of community that may come to exist at a global level are no more likely to resemble regional and national communities, and that the forms of global governance and the reach of global laws are no more likely to resemble regional and national governance and laws, than the nation-states with which we

---

[3] I have already said, near the beginning of this book, that there is no such thing as a collective will, and so do not mean to suggest here, in linking global will and global imagination to global community, that the former are artefacts of the latter so as to give rise, mysteriously, to global collective will. Rather what I have in mind is the idea of global community as a setting in which the forces of will and imagination could be played out, just as they are now played out in the setting of the nation state, so as to acquire a global function without becoming global phenomena in their own right.

have become familiar in the modern era resemble the forms of governance, bases of community, and regulatory ambitions of the social orders that preceded them. For that reason, it would almost certainly be a large error to believe that the world as we now know it in these respects is likely to be, or even capable of being, projected more or less recognizably onto a global canvas. The odds are that the world that we are moving into will be a new and relatively unfamiliar one (indeed, if it were not to some degree unfamiliar, it would not make sense to speak of it as a world that we are moving into), a world that instantiates a new and relatively unfamiliar approach to social ordering rather than a global extension of the forms of social ordering that we know and understand in the world we now inhabit. Among other things, it seems plausible that the facts of diversity and contingency will run very deep there, so as to be the rule rather than its exception. It seems further plausible that legal authority, as and when it arises, will be derivative of and dependent upon not only political authority as we know it (be that authority democratic or undemocratic), but also forms of authority other than the political as we know it—as of course law once did derive from and depend upon very commonly, and as it still does in certain special settings.

282. Community is constituted by a shared sense of problem, by common concerns and common ambitions. One should not expect such sharings as may come to arise in the international arena to map on to, or to be embodied in, social practices that resemble the legal and non-legal practices, and associated institutions, with which we have been familiar in the modern and pre-modern worlds. The challenge that confronts us in our present quest for order, structure, and stability in what is an increasingly global social environment is that of discerning potential global communities, of problem, concern, and ambition, and of then constituting, at a global level, legal or quasi-legal forms of authority that could be reasonably expected to be capable of addressing the interests of those global communities more or less successfully. What global actors are seeking to identify at the moment, and to give legal substance to, is global community of interest (which may well take the form of a series of such communities), where the interest in question is possibly but by no means inevitably derived from the sharing of territory, or sense of neighbourhood, or of convictions (be they religious or secular) that in themselves transcend the territorial or sense of neighbourhood, and yet have in common with those forms of connectedness comprehensiveness of

concern (however topically limited) and an inclusiveness of approach to those who fall within that concern. As I queried early in this section, what we do not yet know is the extent to which these interests need be vested in something we would recognize as a society. In claiming authority over people in any particular respect law must of course claim some form of exclusivity for its authority, for it is in the very nature of authority to claim exclusivity for itself. Yet the communities of interest within which law may claim exclusivity of authority are in many respects contingent, and so may turn out to be polychromatic or monochromatic, and in either case to co-exist within the same territory or within the same realms of social practice as other overlapping and competing claims to such exclusivity. Endemic conflict between legal regimes would then become avoidable only by reference either to the terms of an overarching constitution that provided for their reconciliation or to some practice of conflicts of laws, itself quasi-constitutional in character.

283. To put it slightly differently, communities of interest are as apt to be defined by the matters that identify the particular interest in question as they are to be defined by their constituent subjects, those who populate the community and then subsequently define its interests by reason of their stake in the particular interests in question. That is to say, the order of influence in the constitution of a community and its concerns may be from matters to people rather than from people to matters. Instead of looking to the lives of certain people (people who share a territory, for example) and asking what interests they have in common, one can look to a particular interest and ask which people are picked out by it, without otherwise undertaking responsibility for the well-being of those people in the standard manner of government as we know it.[4] As and when that is the case, the authority upon which a claim to legal authority rests will be something other than the kinds of political authority with which we are familiar, and with which we have come to associate

---

[4] I do not mean to suggest here that the order of influence in the constitution of a community is a matter of choice. On the contrary it might be thought that the circumstances of influence, such as they are, predetermine the fact and character of the chooser and the rationality of the choice, if and to the extent that choice, be it direct or indirect, is an issue at all. If, for example, for whatever reasons of circumstance, we find ourselves, as in many ways we now seem to, in what is commonly characterized as a world of horizontal relationships, multiple identities, and myriad belongings, we by extension find ourselves in a world that has already committed itself to a condition in which the order of influence in the constitution of community is from matters to people.

legal systems in the modern era. That being so, the pattern of the global future may turn out to be one in which legal communities are increasingly topical and sectoral, in ways that are neither derivative of nor dependent upon the fact of political community, such as that which is embodied in the state, so as to focus their concern on certain human interests in particular rather than upon the interests of certain human beings. The question that such a possibility prompts is whether the rules of such communities would be laws or whether they would simply be law-like, in something like the manner of *lex mercatoria*. It seems possible, for example, to imagine global trading organizations whose monopoly and hence ground on which their claim to authority rested was not state-derived. Of course the existence of such organizations would be contrary to present rules of trade and competition, but that surely would be the point. The issues that the possibility of such organizations, and the communities that they would constitute, raise are: first, that of their viability, which can be left to speculation; second, that of their legal status, as to which I will offer some brief thoughts.

284. It seems plausible that the legal rules of such communities might well come to look more like the rules of a game or of a social club than they currently look in the political communities with which we are familiar. In such settings, whichever actors were able to constitute authority over the matters in question might (depending on one's understanding of the concept of law) in doing so become the constituting legal officials responsible for the identification of the legal rule(s) of recognition, to adopt and adapt slightly the picture that Hart offers. Legal systems (to call them that for the moment) that emerged in that way would be more likely to be

---

We may simply accept that condition, whether out of pragmatism or out of despair. If we do so, we thereby abandon the possibility of choice (without necessarily choosing to do so, bearing in mind that acceptance need not involve choice). If we do not accept the condition, we may either embrace it or seek ways to alter it; we thereby actively engage with the condition through the exercise of our moral and political convictions. Yet in acting in either of those ways whatever effect we may have on the presence and shape of community is not a function of our decision, for while such decision may sometimes be necessary to effect it is rarely if ever sufficient. Fresh ways of life cannot simply be willed, although their forms may be (in some respects at least). Even willed forms of life must be inhabited in order to become ways of life (for ways of life are by definition living things, such that the particular character of any one of them is a function of the distinctive manner in which it is lived), and the fact and particular character of their habitation is by and large unpredictable and self-generating, and so for that reason and to that extent not susceptible to direction.

plutocracies, or technocracies, than to be developments of the various forms of democracy and autocracy that underpin legal systems as we know them today. As and when that were to occur there would be an unfamiliar distance between law and politics—and hence, in what would in that setting be in other respects democratic societies, between law and the *demos*—such that the *demos* would be but one actor among many, and law would be the expression of the authority not only of the *polis* but of many other rival communities of interest and influence. That would give rise to a new and relatively unfamiliar challenge to the authority of the *polis*, and to the various forms of democratic (and undemocratic) legal order that the authority of the *polis* has made possible, on the part of rival communities of interest and the supporting legal orders that those communities would in this way have created (or would claim to have created)—a challenge that would be just as democratic or as undemocratic as was the membership of those rival communities of interest (which by definition would not be seeking to replicate the *polis* in its reliance on universal suffrage, and which would in practice typically be constituted by those relatively few actors with access to the resources needed to operate on a global basis, namely, in today's world, corporate actors). It would also give rise to a worry, albeit one that proper consideration of is beyond the scope of a project such as this book: what possibilities are there for the achievement of democracy on a broad and complex scale beyond the idea and practice of the nation-state (and the smaller, more local governmental entities that the nation-state arose out of and that it from time to time devolves to), on the existence of which the experience of modern democracy has been built?

285. Bracketing that worry for a moment so as to address yet another, the function of communities of the latter, nominally non-political kind would be to speak for certain human interests rather than for all of them, to capture and to be responsible for some portion of human well-being rather than the whole of it. The claim of those communities to our fealty would thus be based on the constituent claim that, in certain settings at least, our interests are better served (or may be so) by acknowledgment of another's authority over them one by one, rather than comprehensively. This would be interest-group politics without the politics, on the face of it at least, for the interest groups in question would be stepping out of the political theatre as we know it, at least in part, so as to define and to commit themselves to rival settings for the vindication of their concerns—settings that might

be designed to co-exist and collaborate with the practice of politics as we know it or that might seek to displace it, in whatever degree. This is one of the implications, for better and for worse, of the possibility of transnational law: such law (if it is indeed law) would empower, to the extent that law confers power, and legitimize, to the extent that law confers moral and political legitimacy, the special interests of transnational actors (for example, in making certain powers available to themselves, or imposing certain duties on themselves, the powers and duties that they take to suit them, and thereby displacing or avoiding rival schemes of empowerment and responsibility, together with their different, less welcome attendant powers and duties)—actors who would otherwise be remitted either to present political order (both national and international), with all its attendant costs to them in terms of transparency and accountability, or to global anarchy, with its special attendant costs in terms of loss of whatever order and legitimacy flow, distinctively and exclusively, from national and international authority (depending, of course, on the proper view of the implications of anarchy in these respects, as to which transnational actors, like many academics, disagree). This may be on the face of it, as I have said, interest-group politics without the politics, but in fact it is non-political only because and to the extent that the politics that would otherwise apply to the governance of the interests in question has been displaced to a new setting, that of the constitution of a transnational, interest-specific set of social orders, and of parallel legal systems in their service. It is no doubt true that some such displacement may be inevitable in the circumstances in which we now find ourselves, but that does not make the displacement any the less political, any the less a matter of moral concern.

286. Such a development would mark an end, or at least the beginning of an end, to the species of collective responsibility that is often described, pejoratively, as paternalism, but that more fundamentally embodies many of the most laudable ambitions of the modern state and the broad scheme of social protection by means of which those laudable ambitions have been brought to life in the paradigmatic commitments of a contemporary welfare system—to health, to education, to protection of the vulnerable, and to the various other dimensions of what we currently take to be proper communal concern, the general terms of which the modern state inherited from its pre-modern predecessors, but then set out to do a rather better, more comprehensive, more transparent, more accountable job of living up

to. Devolution of responsibility to an interest-specific set of social orders and to the legal systems in their service would amount, to put it somewhat dramatically, to a dehumanizing of responsibility, to a move from a concern for people as people (and derivatively for the various interests that, taken together, compose the well-being of those people) to a concern for specific human interests (with no derivative concern for human well-being), from a concern for the whole person to a suite of concerns for aspects of a person, impersonally perceived.

287. Were it to take place, such an end to our present scheme of collective responsibility would also be an end to corresponding recourse on the part of those whose interests were at stake, from demands for accountability to revolution. Such demands would be misplaced because there would be no institutions against which they could sensibly be brought, none having assumed, or having been in a position in which it could be expected to assume, the responsibility that was said to have been neglected. Against whom might such demands be lodged in the absence of our present conception of collective responsibility and its associated institutions and rules? Is not the internet, the global networks that echo it, the schemes of exchange and the character of the communities that it constitutes, designed so as to be proof against not only such forms of challenge but also the underlying sense of responsibility from which they proceed? In insulating itself against the challenge of nuclear missiles, as it was created to do, the internet insulated itself, in principle as well as in practice, against the political challenges that, however unwisely, might have inspired the launch of such missiles.

288. The consequence with which we now have to live is that the various actors and activities that contemporary global networks distinctively sustain and empower, and the communities that they give rise to—which seem to be growing in number and significance daily—are everywhere and nowhere at once, responsive to everyone, and yet answerable to no one.[5] These social practices, and those who are responsible for them, speak not to a people or peoples, but rather

---

[5] To put it more precisely, bearing in mind the existence and impact of new forms of social media and the collective action that they enable and embody, these actors and activities are politically answerable in the conventional sense, the sense with which we are familiar and that we have come to expect of our governments, only in the ways and to the extent that commercial responsiveness, and the pressures that prompt it, are tantamount to a scheme of political accountability—which no doubt from time to time

to aspects of people and peoples, who are neither people nor peoples to them. In such a world the issue of collective responsibility would survive, of course, but there would be no door at which failures in that regard could be laid. They would be general failures of the age, rather than of any one or more of its actors in particular. We can see this failure of collective responsibility manifested, albeit somewhat dimly and fragmentarily, in the currently popular wave of protest at the fact that certain corporations pay little or no tax to any political jurisdiction. Tax is but one, particularly annoying, aspect of the political responsibility that the contemporary global environment enables avoidance of, of the irresponsibility that it licenses.

289. Law, depending on the correct understanding of it, may be an idea and a social practice that is flexible enough to be capable of serving either of those ends—that is, those of the *polis* or those of the rival communities of interest that appear to be emerging at the moment. Certain of what we have taken to be necessary aspects of law, just because they have been close to universal in the world we are familiar with, are bound to be exposed to scrutiny, challenge, and pragmatic assessment in the world we are moving into. That scrutiny may show that they are not in fact necessary to law. The enduring and perhaps deepening democratic deficit in the European Union (which is a deficit not merely in terms of democracy but also in terms of the bodies politic from which the European Union historically derived, and to which it remains in principle accountable), the installation of technocratic leaders that has taken place in the face of financial crisis in Italy and Greece, the commingling of political, technological, financial, and commercial leadership and planning that now occurs in a growing number of significant global summits, may become typical rather than exceptional. Should they become typical, the authority that such communities of interest would have over any given non-participants (be they state or non-state actors) would be just

---

they are, in terms of some at least of their consequences, but which more fundamentally they are not, for commercial pressure and the reaction to it, if and to the extent that they can be in any sense regarded as politics broadly speaking, are politics of a different, more focused, more interest-specific kind, with a quite different meaning and import from the political accountability with which we are familiar and that we believe ourselves to be entitled to. A potential for commercial embarrassment is ultimately a function of the kinds of commercial shaming that cannot be commercially weathered, so that its modes of operation and nodes of significance are very different from those of political accountability as we know it. In particular, the application of commercial pressure cannot be predicated on a failure of concern for human well-being as a whole, for no such concern was ever promised or could be thought to have been owed in this setting.

that which derives from the interest of those non-participants in gaining access to the benefits that such communities of interest make possible (in much the same way that one has always had to accept the authority of certain religious communities if one wants to enjoy the benefits of membership in them). The other possibility, of course, is that whatever regulatory schemes might be laid down by the institutions and practices of such communities would not be law, with the consequence that the role of law in such a world would be even more modest than I have suggested it is in the world today, together with the further and correlative consequence that the social orders of the communities in question would to that extent lack access to the values and disvalues that flow from the rule of law, for good and for ill.[6]

---

[6] Some, such as my colleague Roger Brownsword, are of the view that new and emerging forms of regulation require us to reconsider the concept of law, and to reshape it so as to capture the fresh ways in which government action has in recent years come, both by accident and by design, to influence our lives: ways, it is said, that cannot be captured by, say, Hart's rule(s) of recognition. This is not to maintain that Hart's picture is wrong; rather it is to maintain that the picture is outdated. Law has become something other than it was. I find myself troubled by this approach. It will be clear from all I have said that in my view it risks analytic confusion on two fronts (albeit a confusion that I trust Roger will avoid). First, it risks conflating the distinct phenomena of the project of government (which necessarily operates in more ways than through the enactment of law, and what is more, the laws of which for the most part could not function successfully, as I have tried to show, unless it did so) and of the practice of law-making (which is a function of the exercise of authority toward a life in common, in whatever plane, and so is a function of the project of governance broadly speaking, rather than merely that of government in the conventionally political sense). Indeed, one potential reward of a suitably nuanced understanding of the relation between government and law is that it enables one to grasp the degree to which law is a distinctive vehicle for influence of a particular kind by institutions of a particular kind, a vehicle that is paradigmatic of the project of governance by governments in our era, but which is not more generally definitive of either governance or governments. To identify law with regulation at large (rather than seeing law as a distinctive species of regulation) is to risk trading on an ambiguity in the term regulation between the ideas of law and influence. The other risk of analytic confusion to be concerned about in this approach to the concept of law, it seems to me, is that it obscures the fact that, strictly speaking, the concept of law is not susceptible to fundamental change: rather it is bound to remain the idea that it is. One can of course learn more about the idea, so that one's operative understanding of it deepens, whether for better or for worse. One can also notice changes in the social practices that have been traditionally covered by the idea and are still nominally so, as well as in practices allied to those social practices, so that bit by bit one begins to notice things that are law-like, rather than law, and then to correspondingly adjust one's application of the concept of law and allied concepts to the practices in question. Finally there are inevitable grey areas, both conceptually (when is something the same idea and when does it become a different idea?) and practically (when is it right to conclude that a practice has fundamentally altered, so as no longer to be law, even if it continues to bear the same name?). None of these things call for a change in the concept of law, or could do so.

290. All of this may sound rather bleak. And yet there is surely reason for a degree of guarded optimism[7] as well as pessimism in the face of the global possibilities that confront us, some reason to see our future in terms of its prospects as well as its problems. In human affairs the fact of change (to the extent that change is a matter of choice, in terms of either its moment or its direction) is often—perhaps typically inspired by the presence of challenge, and of fairly deep challenge at that—the kind that looks rather bleak. Otherwise the transaction costs of change would not be worth paying (though sometimes, of course, some human beings pay the price of change for change's sake when it is not worth paying, just as other human beings with different dispositions sometimes pay the price of forestalling change when that is not worth paying). Yet once change of whatever kind has taken place, its circumstances inevitably suggest possibilities that significantly exceed those that constitute anything that could be claimed to be an effective response to the challenge or challenges that inspired the change. We know this to be so from experience in many ordinary everyday settings, but the closest and most pertinent example in the present case, of course, is the set of changes that attended and defined the emergence of the modern nation-state.

291. The creation of the modern state, and of its attendant legal orders, did not merely enable human beings to address more effectively the many challenges that inspired that creation. On the contrary, once created, the nation-state enabled human beings to come together in valuable practices and through valuable institutions that did not exist and that could not have been invented before then, simply because those practices and institutions were not and could not have been made available in the circumstances of the pre-modern era. We today inhabit circumstances that came into being just because of and in company with the rise of the nation-state, and so experience forms of flourishing (as well as forms of decline) that would not have existed without it. The creation of the modern world, in fundamental outline and in the details of its institutions and practices, made possible much of goodness and badness as we know it, or, more precisely, as we now experience it.

---

[7] Thanks to Keith Hoggart (who was, at the time of writing, vice-principal, international, King's College London) for reminding me of this.

292. There is surely reason to believe that something like the same pattern will repeat itself in the world beyond the nation-state, as and when such a world comes to pass, partially or comprehensively. It is entirely possible, of course, that we will find ourselves unable to move beyond the dark circumstances of struggle and flight, to return to Arnold's language. Yet it is also possible (and so something to be striven for) that an emerging global order will not merely enable us to address at least some, hopefully the more pressing, of the many challenges that, as matters stand, seem to be quite beyond the effective grasp of our existing social, political, and legal institutions, but will also create opportunities for and so help give rise to new forms of human flourishing, albeit at the price of loss of local understanding and accountability—perhaps to kinds of flourishing that will be, in the global setting, rather richer, more complex, and more inclusive than those we know and pursue today, so as to extend the full achievement of human possibility to more people in more places than is now the case and thereby make our grasp of that possibility to that degree at least a little less self-centred, a little less selfish than it is among the globally privileged today (as well as the locally insular): those who at present most profit from the condition of law as we now know and experience it.

Index

All references are to paragraph numbers. Many thanks to Mikolaj Barczentewicz for undertaking the lion's share of the work of compiling this index.

action
   attitudes and actions, regulation of 97–99, 109
   collective 24–25
   epistemic basis for 169–70, 173–75
adjudication 113–23
   adjudicative reasons 113–15, 130, 138
   and authority 213; *see also* authority
   and imagination 113, 134–35
   arational considerations 116–22, 131
   bias in 131
   constitutional adjudication 119–20
   decisions by fiat 115
   in Dworkin's account *see* Dworkin, Ronald
   politics of 123–33, 213
   restricted rationality 138
   will of judges in establishing the law 32–34, 37–38, 45
arationality iv, vii, viii, xviii, xxiv, xxvii, 20, 56, 60, 64, 116, 119, 130–37
   and rational eligibility 145
   in adjudication 116
   in law-making 134
Austin, John iv, 24, 39, 73, 89, 270
   jurisprudence, method of 73
   on will 34
authority 1, 6–7
   alternative 198–215
   as perfecting reason 80–84, 87
   as supported by imagination 93–107
   as supported by will 9, 85–90
   claims of 205–11, 214

   complex 269–71
   constitutional conception of 166, 181–98, 209
   co-ordination 200–03
   de facto 179, 196
   desirability of opportunity for error 188–93
   epistemic 42–45, 166–80
   exclusivity of 200–10, 214
   legitimate 181–97
   legitimate constitution versus legitimate exercise 181–90, 192–94, 198
   normal justification of *see* Raz, Joseph
   obligation to obey 166, 193, 206
   of a court's decision 42–47
   parental 208
   practical 169–72, 176, 178, 215
   right to rule 166
   service conception of *see* Raz, Joseph
   sovereign 210–14
   state 200–02, 209–12, 214
   territorial 203, 206

beguilement viii, 48, 49, 56, 146
   cultural narrative 49
   political 54–56, 58, 146
   strategies of 53
Brownsword, Roger 289

Cardozo, Benjamin 119
Chang, Ruth 13
coercion xxiv, 24, 27, 70, 99, 100, 149; *see also* force, law

common law
    adjudication 127–30
    judicial law-making 127–30
concepts 68, 221–40
    of law 289
    multivocal 74–76
    univocal 72–73, 75
critical theories of law
    on the judiciary 32–33
    on will 24, 32–37
    versus Dworkin 9
    versus Hart and his
        followers 35–36

Darwall, Stephen 161, 168, 197
decision 10–23
    collective and individual 42
    judicial 32–35, 40
description
    and evaluation 216–40
    and point 231–36
    evaluative promiscuity of 220, 228
democracy v
    authority of 164–65, 182–83, 186,
        200, 208; see also authority
    rights 182–83, 186–87
Denning, Lord 118–19, 132
Derrida, Jacques 9
Dickson, Julie 239
disappointment
    addressees of law 136–39, 146
    conflicting ambitions 144
    with politics 134–50
dissent
    accommodation of 151, 204
    collective 205
    internal and external 143–44
    rationality of 145
diversity
    diverse society see pluralism
    of opinion 143, 194
    of responses to law 106
Dworkin, Ronald i, iv, xiv, xv, xxvi,
        7–9, 36, 39, 40–60, 113, 121,
        178, 180, 216, 248
    and imagination 48–50
    and value pluralism 36, 59
    and will 36

theory of law 40–49, 58–60, 73, 121
versus Raz on authority 7–9, 178

Finnis, John 20, 36, 119, 216–50
    central cases 217, 219, 230–33,
        237, 244
    comprehension through
        value 221–36, 245–46
    justification of law 216–17
    law and morality 247–50
    norm-based theory of
        practices 245–46
    practical reasonableness 217,
        219–21, 232
    purpose and point of a social
        practice 233–36
    unjust law 218, 241, 244
    versus Raz on authority 216
force 24; see also coercion
    and imagination 57, 96
    cannot compel belief 97, 99
    crucial for rational pull of some
        laws 89
    enforcement of law see law
    limits of 90
    not a necessary feature of
        law 28–29

Galston, William 102
Gardner, John xxx, 139, 142,
        164, 165
globalization 275–92
government
    authority see authority
    legitimate and illegitimate 163, 182
    point of 1
    tyranny 31

Hart, HLA iv, xii, 26, 32, 72, 89,
        106, 113, 245, 270
    on command theory of law 34–35
    on will 34–35
Hershovitz, Scott 161
Hoggart, Keith 290

imagination 20, 48–56, 60–64,
        91–92, 93–95
    action, gap between 51

and force 96–99
and reason 100–07
authoritarian 154
compliance with law 154
deceit 146
force, compared to 57
in Dworkin's account *see*
    Dworkin, Ronald
inspired by the law 94
judicial decision-making 113,
    129, 135
language 62
law-making 134–35
literary 54, 61–62
political 54–56, 58, 91–92
price of 134–50
proper use of 20
purposeful narrative 63
rational 51, 53–54, 60–64, 60
role of in life in common 23
role of in practical
    reasoning 20–23, 180
social change *see* society
used by tyrants 31
incommensurability 13–15; *see also*
    reasons
irrationality 64
    of discrimination 100–02

jurisprudence
    deep thinking xviii–xx
    methodology of x–xi
    usefulness of xiv–xvi
justice, through rationality vi

Keaton, Buster 54
Kimel, Dori 106, 270
Kottke, Leo xix

law
    see also authority
    and coercion 27
    and diversity *see* diversity
    and life in common 3–5,
        77–150, 251–92
    and literature 54, 59
    and social change 259–68; *see also*
        society

as fundamentally various 74–79
as practical reason 77
concept of 68–76
conformity and non-conformity 25,
    27, 57, 71, 91–92, 154
contracts 106
criminal law 85–93
enforcement of 25–30, 46,
    91–92, 97, 99
expressive approach in
    law-making 94–95
functions of 111
human rights law 94–97
identification of 5, 32–38
in general xviii, xxii–xxiii
inspiring imagination 94
kinds xviii, xxii–xxiii
making of 25, 32, 110, 125, 134–35
modesty about ix, 111, 272,
    279, 289
moral failure of 248–49
moral obligation to
    obey 159–60, 203
reasons for existence of 128–29
rules of the road 80–84, 87
sanction 85, 89–90
scope of, constitutional limits
    on 94, 96, 100, 150
superfluity of 107, 110 11
territory of 203, 206
transnational 275–92
unjust laws as 218, 241–44; *see also*
    Finnis, John
Leiter, Brian i, 161
legislation
    compared with adjudication 125–33
legitimacy *see* authority, law
lex mercatoria 280, 283
life in common
    and authority 2, 9, 204; *see also*
        authority
    and change 259–68
    and enforcement of law 27–30
    and global community 277–89
    and imagination 23, 52–53, 58
    and justification 216–40
    and societies 275–87; *see also*
        society

life in common (*Cont.*)
  and will 23, 24–25, 30, 34
  connection with law, role of
    law 3–5, 108–09, 149–50, 203
  meaning of 2–3, 152
  planes of commonality 153–55
  promise of 54
  rational appeal of the law not
    enough for 29
  variety of lives in
    common 151–52, 157
  without law 251–58
Llewellyn, Karl & Hoebel,
  E. Adamson 204

Macklem, Timothy 13, 102, 103, 139, 164
multiculturalism *see* pluralism
morality
  moral error 42, 47
  nature of 16
  no collective moral judgment 42
  provisionality of moral
    judgment 41
  role of in practical reasoning 16–18

Perry, Stephen 43, 161, 167, 197,
  199, 209
philosophy and close
  engagement x–xxi
pluralism
  pluralistic society 101–05
politics
  disappointment in v, 134–50;
    see also disappointment
  political ambition in
    law-making 93, 96–98, 107,
    110, 150
  political vision 54–58, 64, 91, 98, 112,
    120–22, 130, 137–38, 145, 149
positivism, legal 36, 57
  as incomplete 57

rationality
  and imagination 60
  insufficiency of 11, 17, 19, 93,
    104, 158–59
  legal rationality 132, 135, 138

  of discrimination 101–04
  rational ineligibility of alternatives
    to compliance to law 83–88
  rational pull (claims) of laws vii,
    xxvii, 89, 151
Raz, Joseph 1, 6–7, 9, 25, 43–45,
  65–66, 80, 101, 159, 161–62,
  166, 168–69, 171, 178–80, 181,
  192–96, 216, 218, 245, 262
  normal justification of authority 6,
    25, 65, 164–215
  service conception of authority 6–9,
    43–45, 65–67, 80, 158–215, 216
reasoning
  practical *see* reasons for action
  equal weight of alternatives
    in 11–13
reason vi
  and decision 10–23
  coercion 24
  exclusionary 66, 80, 210
  for action 5–6, 10–23, 28, 51–52,
    65–67, 77, 158, 169–70, 172–74;
    see also authority, action,
    Raz, Joseph
  for belief 5, 172, 174; *see also* authority
  inconclusive 11–13
  incommensurability of 13–19, 90
  instrumental 27
  legal 114, 135, 138
  moral 27
  pre-emptive 27, 30, 43, 45, 116,
    118, 172
  prudential 27, 30
  undefeated 5, 14, 142, 147–49
  versus conscience 22
rule of law 274
  as judicial reason 114

separation of powers xxvii, 124–33
  role of the judiciary 124–33
society 272–92
  community values 155–56
  global 275–92
  social change 140, 259–69
  social forms and practices 140–43,
    147, 149

Thorson, Gail 20
Twining, William xii
tyranny 31, 261; *see also* government, imagination, will

Unger, Roberto Mangabeira 9, 36, 37, 39

value
  as fact 221
  assessment of 69
  conflicts of 195–96
  failure of 243
  perception of 221–23; *see* also Finnis, John
  right attitude necessary 99
  way of life 143, 149

value monism 5, 13, 19, 59
value pluralism xxiv, 5, 7, 13–15, 36, 43, 47, 50, 57, 59, 102, 105, 244

will 21, 24–39
  and authority 9
  and life in common 23, 24–25, 30, 33
  and practical reasoning 20–23
  connecting reasons to action 37
  in conforming to law 25–57
  in establishing the law 32–38
  individual and collective 24, 42, 52
  proper use of 21
  of a tyrant 31
  of the judiciary 32, 34, 37–38
Williams, Bernard 10, 38, 51

Printed and bound by CPI Group (UK) Ltd, Croydon, CR0 4YY